K-12 CAREER DEVELOPMENT

K-12 CAREER DEVELOPMENT

AN INTEGRATIVE SOCIAL JUSTICE APPROACH

DAVID JAMES BRIGHT

State University of New York at New Paltz

SAN DIEGO

Bassim Hamadeh, CEO and Publisher
Amy Smith, Senior Project Editor
Abbey Hastings, Production Editor
Emely Villavicencio, Senior Graphic Designer
Alexa Lucido, Licensing Manager
Natalie Piccotti, Director of Marketing
Kassie Graves, Senior Vice President of Editorial
Jamie Giganti, Director of Academic Publishing

Cover image: Copyright © 2016 iStockphoto LP/baona.

Printed in the United States of America.

3970 Sorrento Valley Blvd., Ste. 500, San Diego, CA 92121

BRIEF CONTENTS

DETAILED CONTENTS

PREFACE

The intent of this book is to develop a clear and comprehensive text theoretical model for integrated, social-justice-driven career development practices. While many textbooks focus on career development, they are often too overly theoretical and dense, making the true principles inaccessible for counselors-in-training. As an instructor in a Counselor Education program who has taught career development courses and regularly teaches school counseling curriculum, I find that my students learn best from clear, practical examples and applications of material in everyday language. Social justice is not simply an academic philosophy but rather a guiding principle at the core of counseling and career development work. Social justice is not simply beliefs—it is action—and it is my hope that the accessible writing style of this textbook provides the guidance necessary to take steps in building a comprehensive K–12 career development program. While there are many valuable texts addressing career development and social justice practices, few offer a holistic focus on social justice principles as applied to K–12 career development. It is my hope that this book fills a necessary gap in the research and training literature and provides meaningful guidelines for how to conceptualize and address K–12 career development moving forward.

This text fills a necessary gap in the literature. Social-justice-inspired career development work is typically limited to a single chapter or research paper. Social justice is at the core of all school counseling work, and career development is a major focus of the school counselor. By giving social-justice-inspired K–12 career development practices the attention they deserve, this text will help empower the next generation of school counselors to provide quality services to all of the students they serve. History and theory serve as the beginning foundation of the book before it transitions into the steps, actions, and programming at the K–2, 3–5, 6–8, and 9–12 levels. This design allows students and counselors to emphasize particular grade levels while also reaping the benefits of witnessing intentional programmatic strategy and progression across all grade levels and buildings.

This book features specific career development philosophy and interventions across the K–2, 3–5, 6–8, and 9–12 grade levels, demonstrating a clear step-by-step progression with an intentional strategy. Each chapter ends with reflection questions designed to make the content of the chapter real and personally meaningful to the reader. The end of each chapter also comes with a case study intended to apply the principles discussed in the text to real-world-inspired situations. The book also features five examples of career development programming with associated resources. These five examples were contributed by master's level school counseling students researching the best ways to provide integrated and social-justice-inspired career development programming. These work examples provide templates for how school counselors can directly turn the content of this book into transformative action across the K–12 levels.

I'd like to acknowledge the assistance of Julia Cerrito, Laura Wentworth, Rob Carroll, Suneetha de Silva, and William Partham, who served as partial manuscript reviewers. Their thoughtful comments helped guide this text and allowed it to become what it is today. I'd also like to acknowledge Angelo Carpenter, Arthur Nelson, Caitlin Pastore, and Lindsay Weber, who each contributed practical resource additions to the book. You all have been wonderful students and will serve as magnificent school counselors. I'd like to acknowledge my students, both during my time as a school counselor and now, in my role as an assistant professor. This work is truly for you—thank you for how you've inspired me with your strength, courage, and wisdom. Finally, I must acknowledge my wife, Caroline Conners Bright. You keep me pushing forward even when work and writing seem overwhelming. Thank you for being my rock; I love you dearly.

PART I

Theoretical Foundations

CHAPTER 1

Career Development

A Systems Perspective

T ake yourself back in time to the third grade. Imagine sitting in the class you dislike the most. Maybe the subject isn't interesting to you; perhaps it is incredibly difficult, or maybe you just don't get along with the teacher. Let's pretend your teacher is demanding that you do the work in the class. She requires you to participate in the class assignments and activities despite your resistance. Take a pause and reflect upon this.

How does your third-grade self feel?

Frustrated? Angry? Dejected? Distracted? Sad? Hopeless? Are there any other words that put the feelings in perspective? Keep these thoughts in mind as we imagine that the lesson you are learning has no relevance to your interests and everyday life. Passion is as far away as possible within this particular classroom. When you finally speak up to ask the teacher why you are learning this subject, you are met with one of these classic teacher responses:

"Because it's what we're learning today."

"Because you won't always have a calculator on you to do your math."

"Because you need this knowledge when you grow up."

But at the time, I imagine you questioned if you really did need that knowledge. You probably didn't notice your parents using it in their day-to-day lives. And as you reflect back on that class you couldn't stand, how often are you really using those concepts in your present life? How is this subject related to the person you have become and the work you do daily? How clear was the linkage between academics and a lifelong career journey?

You're probably not feeling great about this third-grade class experience, but it may get even worse. Imagine that this teacher working with you doesn't know anything about you. She makes assumptions about your behavior and abilities. She is unaware of the challenges you face at home, within the school, and in the community. She knows nothing of your experience facing racism, classism, ableism, sexism, or any other form of oppression ingrained into your lived experience. The person who is supposed to support you in growing as a person is instead forcing you to do something you don't enjoy which seems to have no connection to your life, all while refusing to understand and honor you for who you truly are.

How do you feel about this experience?

Take a moment to jot down some of the words and ideas. These are worthy impressions to share in class. For some of us, this activity was likely all too easy, rooted deeply within our educational experiences. It's critical to keep these perspectives in mind and reflect upon them as you progress forward in this book and into your career.

Career development is "the total constellation of psychological, sociological, educational, physical, economic, and chance factors that combine to influence the nature and significance of work in the total lifespan of any given individual" (National Career Development Association, 2003, p. 2). This definition has major bearing on identity within American society. What is one of the first questions people tend to ask one another when they meet? When asking, "What do you do for a living?" we aren't only inquiring about a series of tasks a person accomplishes on a daily basis but also about the very nature of their identity. How one perceives themself and is perceived by others is often linked to what type of work they do within society. So much of our childhood and early lives are geared towards answering the question of what we will be when we grow up. Another way to ask this introductory question would be: "What has been the culmination of your educational and life experiences to this point?"

What does it mean for you to be on the route to becoming a professional school counselor? What would it mean to you to be able to introduce yourself in this manner? How does it feel to take the lessons and skills you've learned throughout your life and apply them to this role in society? How do you feel about the opportunity to become an empathic advocate for students of all backgrounds?

Reflection upon one's own sociocultural frame and life experiences is necessary to develop multicultural competence and awareness as a school counselor (Ratts et al., 2016). Your own lived experience has taken you through educational and career development systems. In theory, education should provide the guidance, skills, and abilities necessary to open doors for an individual to pursue their chosen career journey. In practice, however, we may find that educational systems accomplish the opposite.

Students who drop out of high school have emotionally disengaged from school as early as the third grade (McWhirter et al., 1994). If a system is not offering children a way to develop meaningful skills, relevant knowledge, academic passion, and pathways towards desired careers, all while marginalizing them, is it any surprise that many students lack motivation to complete school and continue their education? Students of color, women, low-income students, and students of minoritized identity backgrounds report reduced aspirations for college due to experiences of educational barriers such as sexism, racism, and homophobia (Irvin et al., 2012; Jang, 2020; Li et al., 2021). Due to negative educational experiences and a lack of representation, students may avoid applying to college because they perceive college to primarily be a vehicle reserved for White communities and their success (Ali & Saunders, 2009; Harper & Davis, 2012; Murphy & Zirkel, 2015). Feelings of being othered by educational systems due to a lack of representation in teachers, lack of cultural relevance in curriculum, and experiences of racism fuel minority student disengagement with academics as early as elementary school (Harper & Davis, 2012; Kunjufu, 1990).

School counselors act as social justice advocates by "reducing the effects of oppression on students and improving equity and access to educational services" (Holcomb-McCoy, 2007, p. 18).

According to the American School Counselor Association (ASCA), school counselors recognize individual and group differences within school settings and strive toward equitable treatment of all students through academic, personal-social, and career programming (ASCA, 2018). While more students are accessing higher education than ever, students of low-income, first-generation college, or minoritized backgrounds may have less access to family and community career development support. The school counselor is in a prime position to evaluate barriers students face, develop systemic programming to remove these barriers, and honor the identities of all students (ASCA, 2018).

Given this professional responsibility, the functioning of school systems and career development programming must be analyzed. It is imperative for a school counselor to ask, when working in a school: whose needs are being met and why? Is the school serving the holistic needs of the students and community? Are the services offered culturally appropriate and designed to allow the advancement of students through education and careers? Are we integrating a combination of self-awareness, social-emotional learning, career exploration, and academic enrichment for the sake of the students? If the answer to these questions is "no," then a school counselor must analyze what cultural and historical barriers exist within the school that are preventing this ideal function. The next step is tearing down those barriers through integrated career development, intentional partnerships, and work with students and families.

These questions and key philosophical tenets inspired the focus of this text. Rather than being added on as an afterthought in education, career development and social justice should be embedded as central cogs in the mission and function of all educational systems. To begin this process, school counselors must first understand the historical roots of educational and career development systems within the United States.

Career Development: A Historical Perspective

Have you ever met anyone with the last name Baker? What about Carpenter? Smith? Have you ever wondered where these last names came from? Throughout the world, but especially within Europe, family surnames were developed linked to one's profession (Clark, 2015). Back hundreds and hundreds of years ago, the world changed at a much slower pace, and access to job opportunities and different towns was limited. Therefore, many families were generationally employed, with each male child born into the family learning the trade. Class, education, and social status were passed on due to family lineage, keeping wealth and opportunity limited to those family lines that already had power (Clark, 2015). Individuals of low socioeconomic status could not afford to explore additional possibilities. Countless Africans had their freedom removed completely through the transatlantic slave trade. Women were not afforded the opportunity to have careers, nor were individuals with physical or developmental disabilities. Discrimination prevented individuals of color, certain religions, gender identities, and sexual orientations from publicly being themselves and pursuing their life passions. While the world has changed a great deal in these subsequent hundreds of years, the roots of these social norms are still prevalent to this day, not only in common surnames but also embedded within education and society (Liu et al., 2004).

Have you ever attended a school that utilized the bell system for changing courses? Can you recall the ringing or clanging of the bell, signifying it was time for you to gather your things and hurry down the hall to your next subject? The reason why the bell system was integrated into school in the United States is a surprising, yet pragmatic one. Can you think of a work setting one hundred or so years ago that utilized bell systems for work purposes?

After the Industrial Revolution, the United States had a boom in the availability of factory jobs, with many towns and entire neighborhoods of cities working jobs within textile mills, steel mills, production factories, logging operations, and many more. School was established to prepare children to be workers in the local factory, where they'd adhere to the structured bell schedule for work shifts (Arum et al., 2015). Choice in career development was a rarity in an age with limited interstate travel capabilities and entire towns relying upon single industries (Biddle & Azano, 2016). These working-class school districts often had children attend only until the eighth grade, when students would join the work force in support of their families. While working-class schools were structured to demand memorization, timeliness, and obedience, schools in upper-class sections of society were entirely different. These schools had students engage in creative thinking, problem solving, and self-directed activities (Bowles & Gintis, 2011). The very structure of education was linked to intended destinations in society. While individuals of lower socioeconomic status were viewed as destined to work in factories and other forms of manual and service labor, children of the upper class were given an education aligned with the skills necessary to succeed in college and navigate through society as leaders (Arum et al, 2015; Bowles & Gintis, 2011). Thus, while many of us may view education and career development as vehicles for children to find their passion and achieve their life goals in pursuit of upward mobility, it is important to recognize that education in this nation began as a system designed to replicate the existing class structure (Bowles & Gintis, 2011). The historical composition of these foundations embedded systemic processes, cultural perspectives, and biases which persist to this day, inhibiting all American children from accessing the benefits of education and career development.

Even when higher education is achievable for those who have not historically had access to it, multiple studies have found that, even after controlling for levels of education and skill, the highest predictor of class status in America is the class that one is born into (Carnevale et al., 2019). In fact, students from low-income or minority backgrounds with higher levels of skill or intelligence often access less career and financial success than only moderately performing students from wealthy White families (Carnevale et al., 2019). Those in the higher class often have access not only to the financial capital which opens doors for education and training, but also to the cultural and human capital which allow for successful navigation through educational and career development processes.

Consider a practical example. If one student grows up in a low-income rural area where there are few jobs available and a small percentage of college graduates, and their parents did not attend college, how likely are they to understand how to navigate the college process and how academics and skills link to the world of work? Let us consider another student, who is raised in an affluent suburb in which most residents are college educated and work in business and governmental jobs. How likely is this student to have access to quality information about how to navigate the college and career search process? How likely is this student to have resources and influences to help them find their path? How likely is their school to have a curriculum and resources positively aligned with these aspects? If both students attend college, and both have to switch majors with a significant financial cost associated, who is more likely to be able to finish college and find a job afterwards? Career development and success are not simply academic concepts—there are considerable social realities that must be considered within both counseling and education if gaps in opportunity are truly to be addressed.

If a community lacks the infrastructure to link education to career, and systemic realities make the pathways to attaining career significantly more difficult for some students than others, it would be a major mistake to remove privilege and social justice lenses from career development initiatives in every school district. While school counselors have a professional obligation to be social justice advocates for all students across the domains of academic, personal/social, and career success, it's important to realize that the role of the school counselor was not always intended to benefit all students. In examining the historical roots of school counseling, we can further analyze the roots of inequity that have shaped career development practices in our country to this day.

The History of School Counseling

The earliest origin of school counseling can be tracked to Frank Parsons, known as the father of vocational guidance (Jones, 1994). Originally trained as an engineer and lawyer in Boston, he witnessed the challenges facing immigrants coming to the United States of America. While trying to navigate cultural and economic barriers, these immigrants were unsure of how to find work best suited to their abilities. The immigrants were not tracked into professions based on their family background like many Americans were because they came to this nation on their own, disconnected from family trades in their native countries. Parsons believed that this was a problem not only for the immigrant population, but also for society as a whole, which could benefit from having people work in fields suited to their abilities (Jones, 1994).

Parsons took time to counsel the immigrant population to help link their skills and interests to available jobs in the city. Parsons (1909) also authored *Choosing a Vocation.* work, among the first of its kind, influenced the field of career development for decades. After working on his own as a vocational counselor, providing suggestions, guidance, and resources related to finding employment, Parsons went a step further and founded the Vocations Bureau of the Civic Services in 1908. He served as the inaugural director and a counselor within the organization; unfortunately, he passed only a few months after opening the service. His impact on career development remained, however, and many became open to the idea that individual interest and talent could be linked to employment for the benefit of all (Jones, 1994).

Vocational counseling further developed throughout the 1930s and 1940s. College deans, traditionally accustomed to solely dealing with matters of academics and discipline, increasingly found themselves addressing a greater array of needs, such as student social-emotional and career concerns. Many deans found themselves acting as advisors and mentors to students, helping them navigate the stress of college and consider what type of employment and life they desired after college. While not widespread, this practice was a radical departure from previous models within higher education, where achievement and career options were viewed as endeavors solely handled by an individual and their family. During the same time period, public school systems in cities began hiring school social workers to help assist with student and family needs beyond the classroom. This cultural shift in services rendered by educational intuitions began to lay the foundation for guidance counselors, who would eventually take on the role of school counseling as it's practiced today (Gysbers, 2012).

Schools saw the increasing value of having a professional who could address some social-emotional concerns as well as provide academic guidance. These guidance counselors primarily focused on academic issues such as scheduling and college applications; however, they also often spoke to students about associated ideas and stress related to these concepts. In the late 40s, the role of the guidance counselor grew so much that the ASCA was founded in 1952 (Gysbers, 2012). After the events of the Second World War, where mathematics and science were seen as integral in producing the technology necessary to win wars, the United States Federal Government set out to identify individuals with academic talent in these fields. The Guidance and Personnel Branch was therefore founded within the United States Office of Education. In 1958 the National Defense Education Act (NDEA) was passed, requiring states to submit plans on how they would identify academically talented students in the fields of mathematics and science. This push to require stats to track these students and push them towards higher education in these fields led to the proliferation of guidance counselors throughout the United States (Gysbers, 2012).

When evaluating the original roots of school counseling, it is important to consider whose needs were being met and why. While school counselors are now social justice advocates serving the holistic needs of all students, this clearly was not the case during the profession's inception. The push to identify students talented in science, technology, engineering, and math (STEM) fields came from governmental fears of falling technologically behind other nations, especially the Soviet Union. Government officials sought to pipeline those academically talented in STEM fields into government service work in order to keep pace with the Soviet Union during the Cold War and the Space Race. While linking those with STEM abilities may provide benefit to society through technological advancement, it is important to note that this goal is different from honoring the perspectives, needs, and dreams of all students. This educational pipeline was designed for certain students of certain abilities for the primary benefit of the military. The initial role of guidance counselors, therefore, was not to provide extended access to education and success for all students, but instead to pipeline the human capital of certain students for societal purposes. Thus, the profession lacked a holistic examination of student, school, and community needs. The intended role was more that of academic tracking, leaving out important social-emotional dimensions of students' lives which may have greatly influenced their educational outcomes.

The problems of this role became more apparent as school districts became racially integrated in the 1970s. Guidance counselors would stigmatize non-White students, often tracking them to lower-level classes and pathologizing disruptive behavior as the result of emotional disorders. These primarily White guidance counselors were not trained in multicultural competence or awareness. Their own limited social-cultural experiences created a framework in which they placed their biases upon the students they were supposed to be assisting (Vontress, 1970). Natural feelings of frustration due to the lack of support from school, and to racism inherent in the system, were instead categorized as defiant behaviors or even disabilities. The modern school counselor acts as a social justice advocate, reforming systems to provide equitable opportunities for success across the academic, personal-social, and career domains; however, the historical guidance counselor often accomplished the opposite by reinforcing the system, limiting the opportunities presented to students of color.

Throughout the 1980s and 90s, it became more apparent that for school counselors to address the needs of students, a more comprehensive and holistic viewpoint was necessary. This led to the rise in prominence of ASCA and the transition from the paradigm of an academically focused guidance counselor to the new transformed school counselor. In the early 1990s, it became more common for school counseling research and training to focus on multicultural awareness, competence, and systemic reform. This holistic view of students, schools, and communities was built into the ASCA National Model, published in 2003. This new vision was instrumental in transforming school counselors from responsive agents perpetuating inequitable educational systems to proactive social justice advocates transforming systems to provide equitable opportunities for all.

The Multicultural and Social Justice Counseling Competencies

The Multicultural Counseling Competencies (MCCs) were developed in 1992 by Sue, Arrendondo, and McDavis. These competencies served to provide professional standards for counselors to develop the skills and perspectives necessary to provide quality counseling service for all client populations. Multicultural competence requires counselors to reflect upon their own cultural background while increasing their knowledge of the client's cultural background in order to facilitate culturally appropriate interventions (Sue, et al., 1992). While multicultural competence is a major necessity for practicing counselors, it primarily focused on individual counseling relationships at that time. Therefore, a commission founded in 2015 examined how to expand and rework these professional standards to address the influence of systemic inequities on client well-being (Ratts & Greenleaf, 2017).

Many revisions were added to the original competencies. Perhaps most major was the inclusion of the dimension of social justice. Social justice competence requires counselors to evaluate the client within their social-ecological system. This entails considering how oppressive systems and attitudes within society influence the client's presenting challenges, identity, and actions moving forward. Clients, therefore, should not be considered solely as independent entities, but as people interacting within a series of complex systems. If counselors are not prepared to consider how societal systems favor some based upon their identity (privilege) while disenfranchising others (oppression), they are not prepared to truly work within the client's lived experience and address the true nature of their concerns. The Multicultural and Social Justice Counseling Competencies (MSJCC) required counselors to be competent in addressing concerns of power, privilege, and oppression, both within systems and in the counseling room (Ratts et al., 2016).

The four quadrants of the MSJCC provide guidance on how to approach concerns of inequity in counseling. Quadrant 1 covers the privileged counselor-marginalized client situation. Examples of this include a White counselor working with an individual of color, a straight cisgender counselor working with an individual who identifies as LGBTQ+, or a wealthy counselor working with an individual from a low-income socioeconomic background. Quadrant 2 covers the privileged

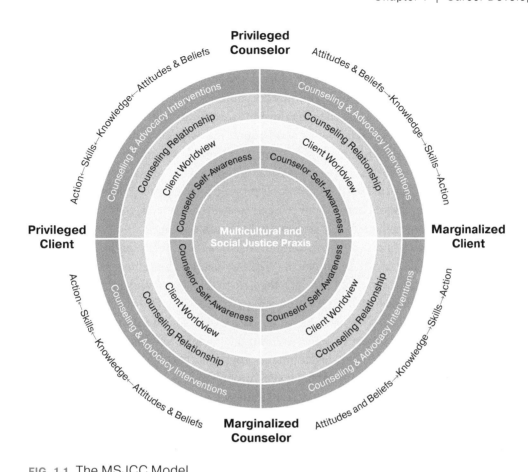

FIG. 1.1 The MSJCC Model

counselor-privileged client situation. In this situation, the counselor and client have social power inherent in their identity, such as coming from the dominant culture or from a high-income socio-economic background. Quadrant 3 details the marginalized counselor-privileged client dynamic, where social power lies in the hands of the client rather than the counselor: for example, a counselor of color counseling a White individual. Quadrant 4 conceptualizes a marginalized counselor working with a marginalized client, such as a transgender counselor providing services to a transgender client.

It's important to consider how counselor and client worldview come together within this frame-work due to differing lived experiences linked to power and privilege. These dynamics undoubtedly influence the counseling relationship due to perceived levels of safety, comfort, trust, and being heard. Counselor conceptualization must be considered within these lenses to critically analyze if the client is being heard and understood in the pursuit of developing appropriate interventions. Finally, it is imperative to consider that identity and privilege are multidimensional. A counselor or client may have some facets of their identity that are privileged (for example, being White) while other facets of their identity are oppressed (for example, being a lesbian from a low-income background). These elements of identity must be considered within both the counselor and the client to understand the relationship, the dynamics in the room, and helpful approaches with the client moving forward.

Social Justice and the School Counselor

The school counselor is well-positioned to address systemic inequities preventing students from accessing comprehensive, holistic, and culturally appropriate career development. As a social justice advocate, the school counselor is tasked with reforming schools through individual counseling, group counseling, classroom lessons, schoolwide and community-wide programming, the reworking of schoolwide systems, and the utilization of data analysis to guide school initiatives. This allows the school counselor to create partnerships and programs designed to promote social justice and equity within schools (Ratts & Greenleaf, 2017). If schools proceed forward giving the same standard model of career guidance to every student without critically considering social justice, they are replicating the oppressive class system historically present in American education.

While social justice is a central tenet to modern school counseling philosophy, social justice lenses are rarely applied to career development. While academic achievement and college admission receive significant attention in school districts, the holistic process of understanding self, passions, abilities, and the ever-shifting pathways of career are often left out of the discussion in schools. For the school counselor to fulfill their role as a social justice advocate and pave the way for the future success for all students, they must be leaders within their school buildings who help to create and deliver comprehensive K–12 career development programs. The school counselor must further advocate for all students at the professional levels through membership in organizations and lobbying for policies to reduce inequities in society (Ratts & Greenleaf, 2017). The following chapters detail how social justice and intentional career development should be integrated into schoolwide curriculum and programming. It is my hope that this is the beginning of a powerful and meaningful journey for you, in which you will be empowered to make a difference in the lives of your students, their families, and your school community.

CHAPTER SUMMARY

This chapter detailed how the historical foundation of education in the United States was related to the conditions of the local economy, jobs, culture, and economic status. Historically, education in the United States served to reproduce class status through preparing students for the work and tasks expected of those with their social standing. Frank Parsons, the father of vocational counseling, introduced the concept of aligning skills and interests to careers in the early 1900s. This vocational counseling approach eventually inspired the guidance counseling movement, which came into prominence in the 1950s as the United States Federal Government attempted to identify academically talented students to pipeline into STEM fields to allow the nation to remain competitive with the USSR in the Space Race and military growth. The original model of guidance counseling was reactive and academic, focused on pipelining students as human capital toward fields beneficial to the government. Over the last several decades, guidance counseling evolved into school counseling, which takes a multiculturally competent and social-justice-focused approach in order to evaluate inequities in education and society and provide quality academic, personal-social, and career-focused counseling to students of all backgrounds.

TABLE OF KEY TERMS

Term	Definition
Career Development	"The total constellation of psychological, sociological, educational, physical, economic, and chance factors that combine to influence the nature and significance of work in the total lifespan of any given individual" (National Career Development Association, 2003, p. 2).
ASCA	The American School Counselor Association. Founded in 1952, it is the leading professional organization establishing the standards and practice of school counselors.
NDEA	The National Defense Education Act of 1958. It required schools to submit plans on how they would identify academically gifted students. This act led to the proliferation of guidance counselors in the United States.
MCSJCC	The Multicultural and Social Justice Counseling Competencies. This series of guiding professional standards from the American Counseling Association requires counselors to be competent in addressing concerns of power, privilege, and oppression, both within systems and in the counseling room (Ratts et al., 2016).
LGBTQ+	Members of the Lesbian, Gay, Bisexual, Transgender, Queer/Questioning, and additional sexual/gender identity communities.
Social Justice	The promotion of equitable access to education, opportunity, safety, security, social resources, and legal rights within society

REFLECTION EXERCISES

Reflection exercises are designed either to be done individually within the reading or to be used as group discussion questions within the classroom setting. A series of reflection questions will be presented at the end of every chapter.

1. Analyze a school you attended in the K–12 years.
   a. What type of career development was provided and during what years?
   b. Was your school more welcoming and accepting of some types of students than others?
   c. What local social norms and cultural systems influenced how your school treated students?

    d. What would you have changed about the career development interventions your school offered? How would you do it?

2. How has the environment in which you were raised influenced who you are least comfortable working with and why?

    a. How does this influence your future work?

3. What careers were you interested in as a child?

    a. What experiences influenced what was originally interesting to you?

    b. What experiences impacted which directions you took?

    c. Were there any negative influences that made you believe a certain path or educational field was not for you?

    d. What relevance does this have for your future work as a school counselor?

4. What career development intervention ideas do you have?

    a. What types of lessons, activities, or programs would you love to bring to a school?

    b. How might your identity, background, and experiences help you create and deliver comprehensive career development services?

    c. What type of community partners would you love to work with and why?

CASE STUDY

Willowview High School is a large suburban 9–12 high school with 2,000 students and five school counselors. Willowview historically had a high percentage of White students in its population, but the demographics have been shifting in the local community across the last ten years. Now, approximately 60% of the student population is students of color, with a high percentage of Black and Latinx students. Despite these shifts in demographics, the faculty at Willowview High School is 90% White. A significant portion of the student population of color resides in lower-income sections of the district, while the majority of the White student population resides in a higher-income section of town. Career development initiatives are focused on getting students into four-year colleges. A major focus of this is providing after-school tutoring in preparation for the SATs and state standardized tests. Every year, one school counselor meets with each grade level to discuss the career and college application resources available in the counseling office. School counselors meet once a year with the students on their caseload for college and career planning.

Students of color are disproportionately represented in classes in the lower academic tracks. They also make up a vast majority of the discipline referrals in the school. Students of color have significantly lower rates of college applications than White students. Even students of color with strong grades or test scores are applying and matriculating to college at lower rates than White students. In fact, White students with lower GPAs and SAT scores are applying to more schools than students of color with higher GPAs and SAT scores. During a recent faculty meeting to discuss college outcomes, several teachers expressed that students from Latinx and Black backgrounds appear "uninterested" in college and career and are more focused on "causing trouble." Several teachers expressed that the economics of certain parts of the district have students dealing with stress outside of school and that these students have "limited role models." This block of teachers attributed the disparity to the lack of the ability of people in these communities to keep their children focused on academics and career outcomes.

Given the above dynamics at Willowview High, address the following questions:

1. What cultural dynamics are influencing educational and career development practices at Willowview High?

2. How are the current practices at Willowview High impacting the college and career aspirations of its students?

3. What is your evaluation of the current slate of career development initiatives available at Willowview High?

4. Which students are benefiting from the practices at Willowview High? Why is this the case, considering the history of the town?

5. How can the local community positively inform and influence educational and career development programs at Willowview High?

6. What types of reform are needed at Willowview High for the career development programming to serve all students?

7. What specific interventions would you develop in order to accomplish this? List the action steps and necessary partnerships required.

References

Ali, S. R., & Saunders, J. L. (2009). The career aspirations of rural Appalachian high school students. *Journal of Career Assessment, 17*(2), 172–188.

American School Counselor Association. (2018*). The school counselor and equity for all students.* https://www.schoolcounselor.org/asca/media/asca/PositionStatements/ PS_Equity.pdf

Arum, R., Beattie, I., & Ford, K. (Eds.) (2015). *The structure of schooling: Readings in the sociology of education* (3rd ed.). Sage.

Biddle, C., & Azano, A. P. (2016). Constructing and reconstructing the "rural school problem" a century of rural education research. *Review of Research in Education, 40*(1), 298-325.

Bowles, S., & Gintis, H. (2011). *Schooling in capitalist America: Educational reform and the contradictions of economic life.* Haymarket Books.

Carnevale, A. P., Fasules, M. L., Quinn, M. C., & Campbell, K. P. (2019). *Born to win, schooled to lose: Why equally talented students don't get equal chances to be all they can be.* Georgetown University Center on Education and the Workforce. https://files.eric.ed.gov/fulltext/ED599947.pdf

Clark, G. (2015). *The son also rises: Surnames and the history of social mobility.* Princeton University Press.

Gysbers, N. C. (2012). *Embrace the past, welcome the future: A brief history of school counseling.* American School Counselor Association. https://www.schoolcounselor.org/getmedia/52aaab9f-39ae-4fd0-8387-1d9c10b9ccb8/History-of-School-Counseling.pdf

Harper, S. R., & Davis, C. H., III. (2012). They (don't) care about education: A counternarrative on Black male students' responses to inequitable schooling. *Educational Foundations, 26*(1–2), 103–120.

Holcomb-McCoy, C. (2007). *School counseling to close the achievement gap: A social justice framework for success.* Corwin Press.

Irvin, M. J., Byun, S.-Y., Meece, J. L., Farmer, T. W., & Hutchins, B. C. (2012). Educational barriers of rural youth: Relation of individual and contextual difference variables. *Journal of Career Assessment, 20*(1), 71–87.

Jang, S. T. (2020). The schooling experiences and aspirations of students belonging to intersecting marginalisations based on race or ethnicity, sexuality, and socioeconomic status. *Race Ethnicity and Education,* 1–22.

Jones, L. K. (1994). Frank Parsons' contribution to career counseling. *Journal of Career Development, 20*(4), 287–294.

Kunjufu, J. (1990). *Countering the conspiracy to destroy Black boys* (Vol. 3). African American Images.

Li, X., Kim, Y. H., Keum, B. T. H., Wang, Y.-W., & Bishop, K. (2021). A broken pipeline: Effects of gender and racial/ethnic barriers on college students' educational aspiration pursuit gap. *Journal of Career Development.* https://doi.org/10.1177/0894845321994196

Liu, W. M., Soleck, G., Hopps, J., Dunston, K., & Pickett, T., Jr. (2004). A new framework to understand social class in counseling: The social class worldview model and modern classism theory. *Journal of Multicultural Counseling and Development, 32*(2), 95–122. https://doi.org/10.1002/j.2161-1912.2004.tb00364.x

McWhirter, J. J., McWhirter, B. T., McWhirter, A. M., & McWhirter, E. H. (1994). High- and low-risk characteristics of youth: The five Cs of competency. *Elementary School Guidance & Counseling, 28*(3), 188–196.

Murphy, M., & Zirkel, S. (2015). Race and belonging in school: How anticipated and experienced belonging affect choice, persistence, and performance. *Teachers College Record, 117*(12), 1–40.

National Career Development Association. (2011). *Career development: A policy statement of the National Career Development Association.* https://ncda.org/aws/NCDA/asset_manager/get_file/39958?ver=29369

Parsons, F. (1909). *Choosing a vocation.* Gay & Hancock.

Ratts, M. J., & Greenleaf, A. T. (2017). Multicultural and social justice counseling competencies: A leadership framework for professional school counselors. *Professional School Counseling, 21*(1b). https://doi.org/10.1177/2156759X18773582

Ratts, M. J., Singh, A. A., Nassar-McMillan, S., Butler, S. K., & McCullough, J. R. (2016). Multicultural and social justice counseling competencies: Guidelines for the counseling profession. *Journal of Multicultural Counseling and Development, 44*(1), 28–48.

Sue, D. W., Arredondo, P., & McDavis, R. J. (1992). Multicultural counseling competencies and standards: A to the profession. *Journal of counseling & development, 70*(4), 477–486.

Vontress, C. E. (1970). Counseling blacks. *The Personnel and Guidance Journal, 48*(9), 713–719.

Credit

Fig. 1.1: Manivong J. Ratts, et al., The MSJCC Model from "Multicultural and Social Justice Counseling Competencies: Guidelines for the counseling profession," *Journal of Multicultural Counseling and Development,* vol. 44, no. 1. Copyright © 2016 by John Wiley & Sons, Inc.

CHAPTER 2

Career Development in Schools

W hat guides your vision of the appropriate roles of school counseling? You might answer in a standard way, referring to a course you have taken or are currently taking. I encourage you to go back farther than that, however. Before you applied for a graduate program, what framed your view of school counseling and its appropriate roles? What influenced your concept of appropriate career development? Who made you aware of careers at all? At what point in life did this occur? How much of your career development was aided by the experiences and interventions you received in school? Could the school counselor or other stakeholders have been more present? Take a moment to honor your younger self … what did you need? What would have helped you make the most out of your educational experience?

You obviously have come far in your educational pursuits, and it's likely that your barriers contributed to where you find yourself today. Take a moment to appreciate your strength, resilience, and skills. You're in a profession dedicated to helping children learn, grow, and succeed. You are willing to take on hard hours, taxing moments, and challenges of all varieties to help make children's lives better. For you to get there, you must reflect upon what brought you to this route in the first place. The challenge, however, is to touch base with our view without letting it cloud our view of others. Our experience is important and valid—we must never lose touch with it—but we cannot assume that our view of the profession and appropriate counseling approaches is absolute.

So often, our view of appropriate roles and responsibilities relies upon what we have experienced within educational systems. Our expectations are filtered through our own experiences, resulting in us framing all subsequent interactions through our contextual lenses. Have you ever heard a teacher or a school counselor say something like, "that's just how it is," or "that's how we do things here," or mention that an innovative approach could not work due to some concern? These educators are likely grounded in a perception that comes from their work experience and perhaps in their educational perception as well.

Take a moment to imagine how that influences students going through school. Perhaps even you experienced this type of response earlier in life.

The beauty of professional ethics and standards is that they are grounded in more than individual experience and insight. They allow for a deeper examination of the appropriate role of the school counselor in career development, and for stronger backing when a counselor advocates for expanded roles and resources. Professional roles are rooted in research and consistent critical examination, making them wonderful guideposts towards better, more informed, and more intentional career development. To understand how to best begin to implement career development practices in schools, a school counselor must understand the professional obligation to career development rooted in school counseling identity.

A Professional Obligation

Promoting career development is essential for the school counselor to assure that students make the most meaning out of their educational experience and are empowered to take this knowledge the furthest they can. Professional organizations such as the American School Counselor Association (ASCA) emphasize the importance of comprehensive career development across the PK–12 years. The ASCA National Model establishes three major pillars of foci for school counselors addressing student needs: academic, personal-social, and career (ASCA, 2019). Each domain is a foundational tenet to the philosophy and practice of school counseling, regardless of the age group of students (Knight, 2015; Stone & Dahir, 2015). The ASCA (2017) introduced career development guidelines for school counselors laying out the appropriate scope of duties and responsibilities. These include:

- Introducing world of work exploration beginning in the PK–3 years
- Exposing students to the ideas of life roles including learner and worker (Gysbers, 2013)
- Working with students to identify their interests, their abilities, and how these link to specific career clusters (Stipanovic, 2010)
- Providing postsecondary career planning
- Helping students understand the connection between school and work
- Helping students transition to postsecondary training or the world of work
- Advising students on multiple postsecondary pathways such as college, technical schools, certifications, apprenticeships, military, service programs, and full-time employment
- Collaborating with all stakeholders to create postsecondary readiness
- Connecting students to dual-credit and dual-enrollment opportunities
- Providing and advocating for PK–12 career awareness through interventions, planning, and guided decision making
- Identifying gaps in career readiness and access through the use of data and evaluating the role of biases related to college and career interventions
- Integrating career development education into academic curricula
- Allowing students to develop the behaviors and skills necessary to succeed in career fields, such as positive attitude, lifelong learning aspirations, and work ethic

- Supporting the development of self-efficacy, identity, motivation, and perseverance related to career development (Savitz-Romer & Bouffard, 2012).

This list emphasizes the critical importance of school counselors developing comprehensive and integrated career development models across the PK–12 levels. By introducing the world of work to students at a young age and supplementing this work with exploration of identity, skills, barriers, resources, and pathways, counselors can empower students to find their passion and reach desired educational outcomes. Integration into regular school programming and curricula allows this work to be done proactively, intentionally, and in a manner relevant to students' lived experiences. Analyze the above list in reference to your own PK–12 career development experiences. Which areas were met by your schools? Which areas needed more effort? What difference might more comprehensive programming have made for you or others?

Statewide Career Development Responses

In line with the ASCA National Model, many states have developed their own career development standards across the K–12 levels, with schools often required to provide evidence of progress through individual career portfolios at grades 3, 5, 8, and 11 (Boyd, 2017). For example, Pennsylvania requires schools to implement the PA Career and Work standards, with clear benchmarks, in curricula at each of these grade levels (Pennsylvania Department of Education, 2018). Some states' education departments, such as Missouri's, have posted entire school counseling curricula online to assist schools in meeting career development standards, with many classroom lessons focusing on skill, interest, ability, and work exploration (Missouri Department of Education, 2021). Further, 45 states have opted into the United States Department of Education's Common Core College and Career Standards. These standards include guidance on how to assure that content relevant to careers is delivered in English and Mathematics across the K–12 levels (National Center for Education Statistics (NCES), 2021). While the standards set yearly goals related to academics and career awareness, they do not require specific evidence of completion, leaving the method of evaluation largely in the hands of schools.

The School Counselor and Career Development

The school counselor provides support to meet these standards in a variety of ways. Specific interventions will be covered in depth in later chapters; however, it is important to understand the basic approaches a school counselor takes when delivering career development interventions across the K–12 levels. The school counselor should be providing classroom guidance lessons across the K–12 levels including those focusing on career development (ASCA, 2017). These lessons can be exploration of the world of work (what are these jobs, what skills do these jobs require, what education do these jobs require), exploration of self (what do I like to do, what skills do I have, how do these match up to potential jobs), and exploration of action steps (how do I access resources related to college, how do I apply for college and aid, how do I successfully transition out of high school). These lessons vary in scope based on the developmental level of the students, the topics covered, and local community needs. Lessons should be part of comprehensive career development curriculum including programming and experiences (Knight, 2015). Programming includes events such as career days, where local people present to students about what they do in their jobs and about what skills and education are required for them. Programming can also include shadowing at local places of business, field trips to technical schools or colleges, or presentations from local graduates about their college and career journeys.

Individual career counseling can provide students with one-on-one attention regarding their processing of school and of the world of work. Students can be empowered to work through questions they have regarding systemic barriers along the path of their career journey, to be linked to appropriate financial and educational resources, and to plan an appropriate high school course and experience schedule. Individual counseling often occurs at the high school level regarding college and major choices; however, it should be implemented prior to these years so that students come into high school already having a sense of important career-related dynamics (Gibson, 2005; Knight, 2015). Consistent one-on-one counseling can allow students to explore multiple pathways and formulate back-up plans in case they hit any stumbling blocks. Similarly, career exploration can occur at the group level. Targeted career exploration groups can be held during free periods, during lunch blocks, or after school. Career search elective courses are growing in popularity throughout high schools and can be taught by the school counselor (Pascual, 2014).

Resource allocation is another way the school counselor provides career development services. Newsletters home to parents across the K–12 level provide access to information regarding the school's curriculum, career programming, and helpful resources. Resources can include financial aid information, college search information, major choice guidance, and invitations to school-based workshops centered on these issues. Parents who did not attend college may be confused or intimidated when it comes to understanding the financial aid and college application process (Bryan et al., 2015). By providing resources to families throughout a child's schooling, the school counselor empowers families to access the information and support they need in a preventive, proactive manner.

Forming partnerships is another way the school counselor contributes to comprehensive career development. Partnering with local businesses could provide practical work curriculum such as internships for students where they earn academic credit while experiencing the world of work. Grant-funded opportunities, such as school-run farms, demonstrate the application of academic principles to local industry and allow students to gain experience as workers (Schafft, 2010). Partnering with local colleges can provide students opportunities for dual enrollment, increasing their exposure to higher education and majors while potentially saving them money in the form of earned credits.

These approaches will be examined in more depth in later chapters. While these are all ideal functions of the school counselor, many barriers to enacting these programs in schools exist. In order for a school counselor to be prepared to enact some of these valuable systemic changes, they must be aware of what barriers exist and how to overcome them.

Barriers to Career Development

In many school districts, comprehensive career development is an afterthought due to the pressures and constraints of meeting state benchmarks and preparing for standardized testing. Teachers are required to cover certain content, and they face pressure from districts, which are evaluated by their achievement on standardized test exams. Schools may face budgetary consequences or even state takeover for consistently poor performance on these measures. It follows, then, that teachers and administrators focus on more readily teaching for the test rather than adapting career-integrated curricula. While the goal of education should be to inspire and empower students, the immediacy of meeting standards often serves as a constraining force in public schools.

Career exploration, however, can be integrated into academic curriculum so that the lessons meet academic standards while also inspiring a student to find their path in life. If career development is thought of as an extra add-on, it will not become a priority in a school district. If it can be demonstrated as a process which meets the required standards while enhancing the quality of education and experience for all students, it is much more likely to earn buy-in. Even when career development programming is supported, many schools lack time and resources to implement new initiatives (Godbey & Gordon, 2019). A lack of funding may prevent school districts from hosting after-school activities, having a full-time school counselor, paying faculty to update curricula, providing training for faculty, or providing transportation for students to field trips. It is critical that the school counselor consider how funding works within their district, understand what grant opportunities exist locally and beyond, and be willing to look for partners who are able to sponsor major school initiatives.

Communities that have not been historically served by school initiatives may be hesitant to involve themselves in new programming and activities while facing additional barriers to success (Amatea & West-Olatunji, 2007). Parents of color as well as those who did not attend college may avoid career programming due to a perceived lack of relevance or a lack of connection with programming that feels elitist or discriminatory (Vega et al., 2015). Many schools develop their curriculum and programming without input from the local community regarding needs, creating protocols which may be irrelevant or even harmful to students. For example, if a school counselor is sending a newsletter home to families regarding career development programming, this is an excellent step. However, if a large portion of the community speaks Spanish as their first language and the newsletter is only in English, a significant number of families are not receiving the assistance and may feel othered by the school. By connecting with the community through asset mapping, surveys, and community events, the school counselor can begin to understand what systemic and cultural barriers exist and how to overcome them while supporting comprehensive career development.

Given the professional responsibility towards providing comprehensive career development and the requirements put forth by state governments, establishing appropriate K–12 career development programming is perhaps more important than ever. Another important piece to factor into this is our own individual experience with, and understanding of, career development. As social justice advocates, school counselors must critically analyze their own biases in order to provide appropriate services to all students (Ratts & Greenleaf, 2017). A helpful place to begin this analysis is for a counselor-in-training to examine their own perceptions of college and career development.

The Counselor's Identity

List the top five identifiers of yourself. These may include your racial or cultural background, religious preferences, sexual or gender identity, familial roles, work title, or your major hobbies. When you picture yourself, what are the top five identifiers which come to mind? Analyze the list you came up with. What order did the identifiers appear in and why? Why are some parts of your identity more salient than others? Why might some of us list our job or family role as the top identifiers while others may list a piece of their cultural identity?

A major influence on how we view ourselves and the world is through the social construction of our identity. Our families, environments, communities, and life situations all contribute to how we are aware of identity, relation to others, and preferred roles in society (Bandura, 2002). If we are to become competent career development counselors, we must analyze how our identity has contributed to our worldview and what that means for our work within this profession. For example, when I write the profession "doctor," what image immediately comes to mind? List the qualities of the person who popped into your head. Who do you associate with this profession? Why is this the type of person you associate the profession with? How do our views of self, society, the world, and life experience influence how attuned we are to the career development needs of people who are different than us?

Next, imagine the type of client you would be MOST comfortable delivering career counseling services to. This client would cause you little to no stress and would make you feel confident that you could meet their needs. Now, describe the top five identifiers of this client. Analyze the list: what about them makes you comfortable? Are you from a similar cultural background? Do they have similar life experiences or career aspirations?

Finally, imagine the type of client you would be LEAST comfortable delivering career counseling to. Imagine that with this client you would feel uncertain, incompetent, overwhelmed, and incapable. What are the top five identifiers of this client? What about them makes you unsure? Are they from a different cultural identity background? Do they have a different set of life experiences? Do they have experiences or beliefs that make you uncomfortable? Does their intended field of study intimidate you?

Being a social justice advocate requires a critical analysis of our socio-cultural lens (Ratts & Greenleaf, 2017). What do your two analyses mean? Where are you comfortable and aware? What do you need to examine further and work on? If you are going to be an advocate for all students, where do you still need to learn and grow? What experiences could assist you on this journey? Until we engage in this type of reflection, we keep our blinders on and are often unaware of how biases and uncertainties cloud our professional development and practices. If we go into career counseling unaware, we are often ignoring major critical aspects of client needs or of how our own experiences/ viewpoints are guiding the conversation. We may unintentionally marginalize our clients, pushing them away from career interventions or steering them toward unhelpful paths. Take a moment to reflect upon how you view yourself and others, and what significance this has for your work as a school counselor.

Your Career Development History

What is your earliest recollection of your career aspirations? What jobs did you desire as a child? Why did you want those jobs? Did a parent have one of these positions? Did someone in television or a movie portray this role? Were you exposed to this type of job in your personal experience? Consider what influences shaped how you viewed career and what influenced the work you deemed most appropriate for yourself. Consider your next batch of career options. What jobs did you focus on? Why did you make this switch? Did you acquire new information? Have new experiences? Perhaps you encountered new role models? Maybe your interests simply changed as you got older? Were there any critical incidents you could now reflect upon?

Let's jump to high school. What options did you focus on and why? Who influenced some of these "final" pathways? Family? Friends? Teachers? Counselors? Media? Your economic background? Your cultural identity? Your life experience? Some combination of the above? How did it come together for your own unique experience? How might that lived experience be radically different from the lived experience of others you went to high school with and even your fellow students in class now? Within college, what did you learn that helped shape this outlook? What experiences stand out to you? What classes? What conversations? How do you make meaning of how all of that has come together up to this moment? How has this entire process shaped your vision and outlook as an advocate?

This sociocultural framework influences how you will approach individual and systemic career development planning. Consider the answer to these questions for yourself and consider what this will mean for you in the school and community where you will work. Personal lenses and experiences often explain what theoretical orientations we gravitate towards in counseling, with many of us leaning towards frameworks that feel similar to our lived experience. Keep these thoughts in mind as we transition into exploring various career development theories and what these might look like within a school setting.

CHAPTER SUMMARY

This chapter detailed how current professional and ethical standards require a school counselor to provide culturally competent career counseling and advocacy for all students. The American School Counselor Association has set PK–12 career development standards laying out the necessity of the modern school counselor integrating career development and social justice advocacy across each of these grade levels. State and federal mandates have also put an increased spotlight on the need for schools to engage in comprehensive career development programming. In order for a school counselor to create these interventions, they must analyze the community they work in, the barriers students face, and their own under-standing of career, education, and society, including individual career history, knowledge blind spots, and unexamined biases.

TABLE OF KEY TERMS

Term	Definition
ASCA	The American School Counselor Association. Founded in 1952, it is the leading professional organization establishing the standards and practices of school counselors.
The ASCA National Model	The foundational guiding philosophy of the American School Counselor Association. The ASCA National Model presents four guiding quadrants to guide modern school counseling practice across the three domains of academic, personal-social, and career development.
Identity	The construct of self, including awareness of self, life-role preferences, relations to others, and life aspirations as influenced by repeated interaction with family, environments, communities, and life events (Bandura, 2002).
Career Aspirations	The level of educational training and specific careers sought by an individual (Lent et al., 1994).

REFLECTION EXERCISES

Reflection exercises are designed either to be done individually within the reading or to be used as group discussion questions within the classroom setting. A series of reflection questions will be presented at the end of every chapter.

1. How did the school counselors you had during your education meet their professional obligations regarding career development?
    a. How could they have expanded their efforts?
    b. How did your school support/not support integrated career development?
2. How might career development programming also align with the academic and social-emotional domains highlighted by the ASCA National Model?
    a. Create an idea for a classroom guidance lesson that combines career with one or both of these other domains.
    b. Create an idea for a schoolwide event that combines career with one or both of these domains.

3. Consider the school you attended as a child. What local partners would have been helpful to work with regarding schoolwide career development?

   a. Develop an event or program for any grade range within K–12, utilizing these partners.

   b. Are there any other stakeholders who could be included in these initiatives?

4. Which career development theories stand out to you? Why do these resonate with how you understand career development?

   a. How might your theoretical orientation and life experience be helpful in your career counseling work?

   b. How might your theoretical orientation and experience be a drawback in how you conceptualize certain clients and situations?

CASE STUDY

Craigsville Middle School serves students in grades 5–8. Its career development programming is focused on state-mandated individual career plans. These plans are created and modified in individual meetings which occur once per year between each student and the school counselor. The school counselor provides once-a-month guidance lessons to each classroom, in which the school counselor may provide career development programming if they choose to. The main focus of Craigsville's administration is increasing student standardized testing scores. A significant portion of the academic and remedial services in the building focus on specific skill and content knowledge related to the state tests.

Students in Craigsville's special education program, who are diagnosed with severe learning or developmental disabilities, are removed from regular classroom learning and have their own classrooms. The special education students do not receive the monthly guidance lessons and are excluded from the individual career development plan meetings. Instead, their assigned special educator completes the plans for the students. These students do not receive the same academic services or support available to other students in regular education. When pressed about why these disparities persist, a school administrator expresses that there "are only so many resources available and we have to use them where they will be most productive."

Given the above dynamics at Craigsville Middle School, address the following questions:

1. How is the school counselor meeting the career development needs of all students? How is the school counselor failing to meet professional obligations?

2. What interventions would improve the state of career development programming at Craigsville Middle School?

3. How are the current career development practices impacting students in the special education program?
4. What sociocultural perspectives from faculty are influencing the way the special education program students are treated in the school? How should we analyze and address this?
5. How would you reform the current practices to include and empower all learners?
6. What specific interventions would you develop in order to accomplish this? List the action steps and necessary partnerships required.

References

Amatea, E., & West-Olatunji, C. (2007). Rethinking how school counselors work with families and schools: An ecosystemic approach. In J. Wittmer & M. A. Clark (Eds.), *Managing your school counseling program: K-12 developmental strategies* (3rd ed., pp. 211–222). Educational Media.

American School Counselor Association. (2017). *The school counselor and career development.* https://schoolcounselor.org/Standards-Positions/PositionStatements/ASCA-Position-Statements/The-School-Counselor-and-Career-Development

American School Counselor Association. (2019). *ASCA National Model: A framework for school counseling programs* (4th ed.). American School Counselor Association.

Bandura, A. (2002). Social cognitive theory in cultural context. *Applied Psychology, 51*(2), 269–290.

Boyd, S. (2017). Transparency on college and career readiness: How does your state measure up? *State Education Standard, 17*(3), 24–29.

Bryan, J., Young, A., Griffin, D., & Henry, L. (2015). Preparing students for higher education: How school counselors can foster college readiness and access. In J. L. DeVitis & P. Sasso (Eds.), *Higher education and society* (pp. 149–172). *Peter Lang.*

Gibson, D. M. (2005). The use of genograms in career counseling with elementary, middle, and high school students. *The Career Development Quarterly, 53*(4), 353–362.

Godbey, S., & Gordon, H. R. D. (2019). Career exploration at the middle school level: Barriers and opportunities. *Middle Grades Review, 5*(2), Article 2.

Gysbers, N. C. (2013). Career-ready students: A goal of comprehensive school counseling programs. *The Career Development Quarterly, 61*(3), 283–288.

Knight, J. L. (2015). Preparing elementary school counselors to promote career development: Recommendations for school counselor education programs. *Journal of Career Development, 42*(2), 75–85.

Lent, R. W., Brown, S. D., & Hackett, G. (1994). Toward a unifying social cognitive theory of career and academic interest, choice, and performance. *Journal of Vocational Behavior, 45*(1), 79–122.

Missouri Department of Education. (2021). *School counseling curriculum.* https://dese.mo.gov/college-career-readiness/school-counseling/curriculum

Pascual, N. T. (2014). Factors affecting high school students' career preference: A basis for career planning program. *International Journal of Sciences: Basic and Applied Research, 16*(1), 1–14.

Pennsylvania Department of Education. (2018). PA career standards. https://www.education.pa.gov/K-12/PACareerStandards/Pages/default.aspx

Ratts, M. J., & Greenleaf, A. T. (2017). Multicultural and social justice counseling competencies: A leadership framework for professional school counselors. *Professional School Counseling, 21*(1b). https://doi.org/10.1177/2156759X18773582

Savitz-Romer, M., & Bouffard, S. M. (2012). *Ready, willing, and able: A developmental approach to college access and success.* Harvard Education Press.

Schafft, K. A. (2010). Economics, community, and rural education: Rethinking the nature of accountability in the twenty-first century. In K. A. Schafft & A. Y. Jackson (Eds.), *Rural education for the twenty-first century: Identity, place, and community in a globalizing world* (pp. 275–290). Pennsylvania State University Press.

Stipanovic, N. (2010). Providing comprehensive career guidance services through a career pathways framework. *Techniques: Connecting Education and Careers, 85*(7), 32–35.

Stone, C., & Dahir, C. A. (2015). *The transformed school counselor* (3rd ed.). Cengage Learning.

National Center for Education Statistics. (2021). Common core of data. https://nces.ed.gov/ccd/

Vega, D., Moore, J. L., III, & Miranda, A. H. (2015). In their own words: Perceived barriers to achievement by African American and Latino high school students. *American Secondary Education, 43*(3), 36–59.

CHAPTER 3

Career Development Theories

W here do you develop your impressions of how to help others? Take a moment to reflect upon what has informed your opinions on helping behaviors and appropriate career development approaches. Did you come up with these ideas on your own? Have any experiences or education influenced your approaches?

Let's imagine that a school counselor utilizes only their own beliefs to guide the career development process. What do you think the benefits of this approach would be? What about the drawbacks? An advantage to someone using the lens of their experience is undoubtedly the ability to connect with those in similar situations and act as a mentor. How about yourself? Are there any students you feel you could particularly connect to? Does your own life and career development experience have relevance for your work as a school counselor?

We must also consider the drawbacks of these situations. If a school counselor relies solely on their experience and intuition, they are not addressing the blind spots in their vision. One's experience may have valuable takeaways for some students but not necessarily for others. In fact, solely utilizing one individual framework may put students into inappropriate boxes, guide them in the wrong direction, or alienate them from seeking help entirely. Has anything like this ever happened in your educational experience?

Think of those who were most helpful to you on your career development journey. What approaches did they use? What insight did they share? How much seemed informed by their own experience? How much was rooted in knowledge of other approaches? While it may be difficult to determine this, it is important to recognize that we rarely actualize in our career development efforts due to a single perspective. Often, a multitude of experiences and ideas have influenced us, channeled in varying degrees by different sources.

Imagine you're a school counselor. A student who had a radically different childhood than yourself approaches you for career development advice. Their life and belief systems are different than yours. What do you lean upon when attempting to conceptualize the best approach for this student? How do you establish a rapport and get going? By understanding major career development theories, we can utilize interventions rooted in research across various populations to provide students meaningful counseling experiences.

Career development theories allow for conceptualization rooted in research rather than simply our own subjective opinions. Career development theories provide intentionality and a guiding framework to our targeted interventions. While there are hundreds of career development theories, with more being developed each day, this chapter will focus on those more influential in current career development practice and apply their tenets directly to work within school settings. As you read, evaluate how each theory applies and does not apply to your own experience, and conversely evaluate how these theories may in fact strongly apply to people with different perspectives or lived experiences than yours.

Career Development Theories: A Timeline

Trait and Factor Theory

Frank Parsons, the father of vocational guidance, developed the *trait and factor theory of vocational guidance,* a foundational theory which still influences career development practice to this day. Revolutionary for the time, Parsons suggested that an individual's traits and skills should be aligned to potential vocations to find the best fit. Parsons suggested a three-part framework in which a career counselor understands 1) the abilities of the individual seeking employment, 2) a knowledge of the available labor market, and 3) how well an individual's traits fit with a particular job opportunity (Parsons, 1909). Parsons advocated for a counselor to get to know a client on a deep level by investigating topics including personal facts about their life and career path, the self-analysis conclusions of the client, and the client's reflections on decisions and the fit of current prospects. While many of these tenets influence career counseling to this day, career counselors eventually noticed gaps in Parsons's theory. For example, little emphasis was placed on passions, aspirations, values, or sociological context within his framework. As time progressed, practitioners added additional layers to this foundation, developing more complex and comprehensive theories.

Developmental Theories

Ginsberg et al. (1951) proposed the *theory of occupational choice.* They claimed that career choice was a lifelong process influenced by developmental stages within one's life. During young childhood, a person is in the fantasy stage, where imagination and play help them find their preferred activities. During adolescence, an individual is in the tentative stage, where they explore how their likes, interests, and abilities correspond with potential career choices. Finally, a person enters the realistic stage, running from adolescence through adulthood, in which they go through a process of exploration (examining opportunities), crystallization (making a vocational decision), and specification (pursuit of necessary education/training required to obtain their career). This final stage may be one that an individual goes through again as they make a career change and are required to examine what options they have and how to achieve such employment (Ginsberg et al., 1951).

Donald Super created his largely influential *life-span, life-space theory* in 1954 and updated it throughout his career (Super, 1990). This theory advocated for the idea that the roles people play across different spans in life influence what careers they aspire towards and how they view career in relation to their concept of self. The life span was five career-focused developmental stages of their lives, while the life space portion covered how their self-concept (social roles and personal beliefs) influenced their career choice and maintenance (Super, 1990). While more particulars of this theory will be covered shortly, it must be noted that these developmental approaches were a major leap forward in career development theories. Traits were not looked at as stagnant, and the decision-making process was evaluated as occurring over time, with many different influences. While this change was positive for career development theories, critical aspects such as cultural identity were still left out of the conceptualization process.

Sociological Theories

Throughout the 1970s, 1980s, and 1990s, several theories emerged that considered the impact of societal trends, social systems, and cultural identity on career decision making. Krumboltz's (1979) *theory of planned happenstance* emphasized how the changing realities of society and the job market dictated what career options were available and how a client could best adapt (Mitchell et al., 1999). Within this theory, exploring client flexibility, persistence, adaptation, and optimism is essential in helping a client find which available job is best for them and how to maintain this career in a healthy manner.

Bandura's *social cognitive theory* claimed that self-efficacy, or belief in one's ability to succeed at a task, greatly influenced life direction. Within this theory, self-efficacy is formed not only through trying out tasks and experiencing success or failure, but also through absorbing the impressions and feedback put forth by others. This holistic view on how our beliefs in our abilities develop allowed social cognitive theory to contribute to several other career development theories, most notably social cognitive career theory (Bandura, 2005).

Gottfredson's *theory of circumscription and compromise* conceptualizes individuals according to how they process career choice based upon social influences (Gottfredson, 2005). Gottfredson contends that awareness of social processes delineates for children which careers are appropriate and attainable, most notably which jobs are perceived as appropriate based upon gender lines and which jobs hold the most prestige and desirability. Children are therefore influenced by common stereotypes about workers (such as which jobs are appropriate for men or women, which workers have more prestigious jobs) and select pathways depending upon their relation to these concepts. This is the circumscription portion of the theory, in which a child aligns to a job based on an idea of who they are. The compromise portion entails a child limiting career options based upon perceived barriers to career choice, such as societal gender expectations, income, and the prestige of a position. Career becomes about not just what a child desires, but also what they perceive as realistic and attainable based upon who they are (Gottfredson, 2005).

Social cognitive career theory integrated the ideas of self-concept, self-efficacy, aspirations, and values with the impact of contextual influences under a comprehensive career developmental model (Lent et al., 2002). This theory opened the door for career development to be a continuous system or feedback network, where an individual's beliefs about self were filtered through life experience and feedback from others. This creates an ever-evolving sense of self as related to the world of work. Social cognitive career theory's emphasis on social systems and feedback, including oppression and racism, has made it a popular guiding theory in research across many diverse populations.

Personality Theories

Personality theorists advocate for the idea that individual personality traits such as interests and values indicate which types of careers someone pursues. Personality theories suggest that occupations attract people with specific skills, interests, and values, and that by mapping these clusters a client can explore potential career opportunities well aligned with their personality. The most influential of these theories, Holland's *theory of career choice,* assigns clients a three-letter code using the initial letters of six categories: Realistic, Investigative, Artistic, Social, Enterprising, and Conventional (Holland, 1997). Each category is made up of characteristics related to populations. For example, individuals who score in the artistic category enjoy creative endeavors such as painting, writing, or acting. The three highest-scoring categories become the client's RIASEC code, which aligns to potential career options. Due to Holland's theory being popular and often being utilized in career counseling assessments, this theory will be covered more extensively later in the chapter.

While all the above-mentioned theories have provided meaningful contributions to career development and practice, it is important to consider how some of these major theories translate into the school setting. How applicable are some of the major tenets and approaches of these major theories? How can this guiding knowledge be helpful within a school? What limitations exist, and what might a school counselor need to be aware of? We'll begin this exploration by diving deeper into Super's (1990) life-span, life-space theory.

Super's Life-Span, Life-Space Theory

Donald Super's theory relies on the tenet that our career development takes places across five stages in our lives, by age: growth (birth to 14), exploration (15–24), establishment (25–44), maintenance (45–64), and decline (65+) (Super, 1990). The *growth* stage entails a person developing their self-concept, attitudes, and beliefs related to the world of work. The *exploration* stage has a person exploring entry-level jobs and hobbies to help them develop career options. The *establishment* stage is when a person enters the job or field of their career and earns valuable work experience. The *maintenance* stage involves a person improving their position within this job or field by earning promotions, salary advancements, and meaningful achievements. The *decline* stage is when a person prepares for retirement, reducing both their push for promotions and their amount of work and moving towards their post-career life (Super, 1990).

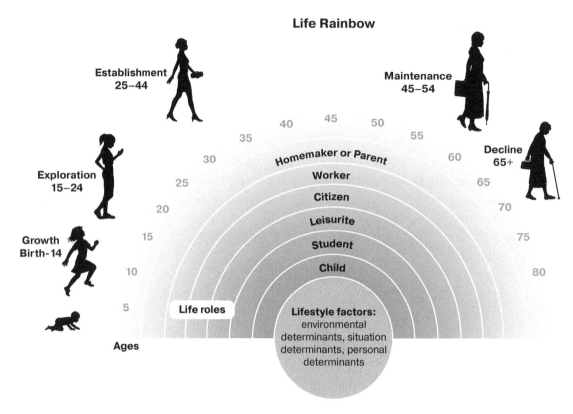

FIG. 3.1 Super's Life-Rainbow.

Super also detailed how life roles such as being a child, student, learner, citizen, worker, and parent influenced our world of work and concept of self. Growth, exploration, establishment, maintenance, and decline occur not only in our career functions but within our personal hobbies and life roles as well. This theory contributed the idea that self-concept is fluid and can change depending upon life stage and role. Put simply: career is an expression of self.

A great deal of career development work has been centered around Super's (1990) theory. In schools, counselors and teachers can assist students in working through their growth stage, where they explore self and the world of work through fantasy and play. Encouraging lessons in which children can imagine themselves in different occupations and introducing games revolving around career exploration can assist children in making sense of how they may relate to careers. This may also provide gradual exposure to self-concepts and work concepts that can link to Super's concept of life roles. If a student is empowered to imagine how they view themselves in the present and future, they can embark on a deeper level of self-exploration while also examining potential career options.

Application of Principles in Schools

Super's (1990) model can directly be applied to the grade ranges school counselors work with. The *fantasy* sub-stage (ages 4–10) would be most appropriate for elementary students. Lessons could focus on imagination and exploration rather than concrete alignment of self to a particular career.

Examples include students sharing what they'd like to be when they get older, detailing what they like to do and why, sharing what jobs their family does, and exploring local jobs in the community through speakers or field trips. More concrete interventions taking these approaches will be explored in later chapters.

The *interest* sub-stage (ages 11–12) aligns well with students identifying how their personal preferences and skills link to career fields. For example, students can take interest inventories, match their traits to career fields, present on potential career options, explore what type of learner they are and how this might relate to future education, detail the training required to obtain jobs, and more. This segues well into the exploration stage (mid-teens through early 20s), in which exploration becomes more solidified and specific. Here, lessons and individual counseling can direct students to identify specific careers and educational pathways and directly align their interests as well as make academic progress towards these goals in comprehensive plans. These plans can be portfolios that allow the school counselor to check in with students and help guide them as they change their mind or path, while also allowing the counselor to provide the student and their family guidance and resources. The counselor should be along every step of the way as the child works towards a college and career decision point, helping make sure the student has the most concrete information and access to helpful resources in transitioning towards the establishment stage.

Interwoven throughout these approaches should be an acknowledgement that an individual's needs change throughout their life. Conversations about transferable skills, career and major clusters, and transitioning to a new career path can proactively empower a student to understand these complicated steps before major decision moments are upon them. These lessons and individual counseling sessions can detail examples from the student's own life, or even include the counselor appropriately self-disclosing, to illustrate the dynamism of the career development process. This focus makes the world of careers more tangible by providing students real-world examples rather than simply providing them basic career information and tasking them to find their route on their own.

Super's (1990) theory might be particularly applicable during the high school years. Students may be uncertain what career development and growth looks like. By utilizing Super's model, counselors can help students understand that they are in the stage of their life where they are aligning themselves toward a particular career path. Further, they can understand that establishment in a career path requires certain skills, performance, experience, and continued education. For example, a high school student interested in becoming a medical doctor may not understand the full array of education and experiences required to advance in the career. Typically, after completing an undergraduate degree and the academic portion of medical school (a process that takes approximately eight years) a candidate must complete a paid residency of three to seven years to officially become a doctor. This will push back the establishing portion of their career into their 30s and may also compete with other priorities such as securing a home or starting a family. Based on a student's view of intended life roles and progress, they may also wish to consider other careers within the medical field which provide earlier access to career or family establishment, such as becoming a nurse, a nurse practitioner, or a physician assistant. Exploring a student's view of their future life and career holistically can empower them to know themselves and know the options available if they desire to make a switch during their college years. Providing this information proactively through established elective courses, community events, and resource letters to home can have students and families contemplating these important dynamics well in advance of major life decisions.

Potential Drawbacks

While Super's (1990) theory lays out an intentional structure and flow to career development which can be useful in work with students, critiques have centered upon the idea that the world of work has evolved in a way no longer represented in the model. When this theory was originally proposed in the 1950s, jobs in adulthood often became long-term careers lasting decades. In modern times, however, it is much more common for a worker to change companies, jobs, or even career fields several times throughout their career journey. This trend has further been exacerbated by the COVID-19 pandemic, in which workers find themselves leaving careers they are unsatisfied by due to burnout or transitioning to new remote working opportunities. Further, the erosion of local factories and small businesses as part of economic globalization has replaced more stable career jobs with lower-paying part-time jobs such as retail, food service, and gig economy positions, all of which offer limited advancement opportunity. These factors make the progression of Super's career stages less clear and solidified, resulting in some people potentially cycling through the stages multiple times in their lives.

Further, the stages and progression of career and life roles may not resonate with those from non-traditional backgrounds. For example, this general model may miss the mark of a career journey for migrant worker families who immigrate to the United States. These families may have faced incredible hardship leaving their former country seeking uncertain and insecure opportunities, majorly disrupting this traditional career development timeline for parents and children alike. Individuals in these situations may experience employment as a means of day-to-day survival rather than as an intentional progression with clear establishment. Life roles may also dramatically shift due to challenging situations or traumas. While Super's (1990) theory can still be adapted for these situations and have utility within schools, other theories more directly address the social and cultural realities influencing holistic career development.

Holland's Career Types

Imagine one of the many online sorting quizzes you've seen or taken in your life, from which Harry Potter house you'd be sorted into, to which color represents your personality, to which movie character you are, to more complex ones such as the Myers–Briggs Type Indicator. These types of assessments are popular and for a reason. It's often comforting to have a tangible representation of our likes, feelings, and preferences. It feels empowering to have the language or symbols necessary to represent who we are. Holland's career types offer this advantage for working with students— you'll often find that students have an enthusiasm for discovering which code they are and which careers fall into their cluster.

Holland (1997) developed his RIASEC codes based upon the personality characteristics of those working in specific fields. Holland reasoned that specific likes, dislikes, and qualities would align with different work in different fields. For example, people who like concrete facts, step-by-step approaches, and working with their hands may prefer jobs involving physical labor, such as those within the automotive, construction, repair, or athletic industries. Holland recognized that it was likely certain personalities were attracted to certain jobs, and that by recognizing how these traits clustered in real-world occupations, a counselor could assist a client in discovering their own personality type and aligning it to potential jobs (Holland, 1997).

Holland (1997) used his research on the personality characteristics of workers in a variety of jobs to develop six career types, which were designed to be combined into a three-letter code. For example, it is not only

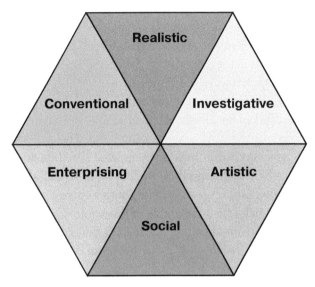

FIG. 3.2 The Holland Hexagon

one's major preferences that determine what they want to do in a career. Other aspects of their personality may also be salient. If the person from above who liked to work with their hands also enjoyed hypothesizing, solving problems, and practicing science and math, their top two types (Realistic and Investigative) might well suit them for a career in engineering, where both sets of skills are utilized. The top three scoring domains provide a code that more specifically corresponds to careers. In addition to these results, analysis of the differences between scores (such as one domain scoring well above the others, or all domains being nearly identical) can provide meaningful topics of conversation within the counseling room. Analyzing why the scores happened, how accurate they feel, and how certain a client is about their results can assist in making the most use of the RIASEC code.

The six domains include Realistic (the doers who enjoy practical and hands-on work), Investigative (the scientific types who enjoy using theory and solving problems), Artistic (the creative types who enjoy the arts, such as acting, music, and writing), Social (the people persons who enjoy helping others), Enterprising (the business types who enjoy influencing and persuading), and Conventional (the organizers who enjoy straightforward tasks such as office filing, data management, and analysis) (Holland, 1997). A counselor would expect a client to have their three results be adjacent within the RIASEC hexagon. If a client's highest score is in the Social domain, it is more likely that they also have high scores in the Enterprising and Artistic domains because these areas have overlapping skills and interests. For example, a teacher must not only be social in their desire to connect with and teach students, but also be persuasive and creative in their teaching methods. It is much less likely for someone who scores highly in the Social domain to have their second-highest domain be Realistic, as this has many opposite qualities of the Social domain. It is important to note, however, that while these incongruencies should be noted and explored, plenty of clients may still have legitimate top three domain scores on opposite ends of the hexagon.

The RIASEC hexagon is arranged in such a way that the direct opposite qualities are represented as across from one another. This does not make unusual scores impossible or inaccurate, but often is a sign that the counselor should do further exploration with the client about their score and why it came up that way. The same can be said about client scores in which all of the categories are nearly even, or only one of the scores is high. These might be indicators that the client is not quite sure of their full range of interests and abilities. These types of clients sometimes benefit from activities such as internships and job shadowing, where they can more clearly apply their interests and skills to develop clearer lines between what they like and dislike in a work setting.

When a person takes the formal RIASEC assessment, the three-letter code (and strength of each domain) is provided along with a corresponding list of potential careers in order of their likely match. Below is an example of just some of the results of the RIASEC code SAI (Social, Artistic, Investigative) taken from O*NET, a governmental college and career search website. O*NET is a wonderful free tool to explore potential options and pathways with students and should be in every school counselor's toolbox.

TABLE 3.1 SAI Job Results

3 Letter Code	Matching Occupations
SAI	Music Therapists
SAI	Recreational Therapists
SAI	Art Therapists
SAI	Art, Drama, and Music Teachers, Postsecondary
SAI	Communications Teachers, Postsecondary
SAI	Education Teachers, Postsecondary
SAI	English Language and Literature Teachers, Postsecondary
SAI	Foreign Language and Literature Teachers, Postsecondary
SAI	Marriage and Family Therapists
SAI	Philosophy and Religion Teachers, Postsecondary
SAI	Substance Abuse and Behavioral Disorder Counselor

*Note. From "Interests Search for Social, Artistic, Investigative," by O*Net Online, 2022 (https://www.onetonline.org/explore/interests/Social/Artistic/Investigative).*

Application of Principles in Schools

Whether the formal assessment or any of the dozens of free adaptations of these principles is used, the RIASEC model is a handy tool in K–12 career development. While elementary students may not understand the complete nuance of the linkage between personality and career, RIASEC activities can assist them in beginning to make the connections. Guidance lessons focused on how people choose jobs based on likes, dislikes, and skills can help students analyze what traits workers in certain jobs must possess. A helpful exercise might be asking the students what type of personality and skills are required for the school counselor and the teachers to do their jobs effectively. This direct example can make the conversation meaningful and ground the principles in the real world. An intentional curriculum (detailed in later chapters) can build upon these foundational lessons across the school years to include activities where students take a RIASEC assessment designed for elementary students. Earlier grades may have the students simply represent their highest score and what that means for them. Students can gather in groups according to their highest-scoring domain and discuss what jobs they might be interested in. The school counselor can present different options for each group and hear what the students think and why. While these lessons would not be intended to pipeline students in any direction, they could encourage students to think critically about who they are and what types of things they'd like to do and prepare for later in life.

As the lessons and years go on, students can retake the assessment and compare how their three-letter code aligns with potential jobs. Students can utilize O*NET or similar resources to explore what job opportunities align with their RIASEC code, what the outlook for those jobs is, and what education is required. This examination can become more specific and concrete through individual career counseling and portfolio building throughout the middle school years. All results, exploration efforts, and potential career paths can be chronicled in a career portfolio, which can travel with the student into high school. This model assures the student has already examined themselves and several options before getting to high school and can assist the high school counselor in determining the most appropriate individual counseling approach. During high school, additional attempts at the assessment should be utilized to help solidify potential careers and major paths. The assessment and its principles would be effective in the individual setting but also easily could be integrated into classroom programming as a single lesson or as part of a comprehensive career search elective course. In all of these ways, the language of the RIASEC code could travel with students, providing them a tangible way to link their own self-reflection with a variety of career choices.

Potential Drawbacks

While Holland's (1997) career types are a useful tool for students to explore themselves and the world of work, the RIASEC codes may simply be just that: a tool. Rather than providing a comprehensive framework identifying how to work with students as they progress through the years, Holland's model may best be used as a supplement to a primary theoretical framework. The ideal use of this assessment and its results may greatly differ from student to student, classroom to classroom, and community to community. Further, the formal assessment comes with a cost that many schools are unable to bear. Therefore, if a school counselor chooses to use a free version of this assessment, they must be critical in examining if it is appropriate and well-constructed. The school counselor must also be creative in their design of activities and lessons centered around these tools. This shows that the proper use of Holland's career types, especially across years of development, needs to be planful and nuanced, requiring a specific skill set. Our final in-depth examination of a career theory focuses on one with a more comprehensive framework of the social dynamics influencing students. This framework can easily integrate principles of Super's (1990) and Holland's (1997) theories, utilizing techniques from all of the approaches.

Social Cognitive Career Theory

Social cognitive career theory (SCCT) was designed to bring self-concept, self-efficacy, aspirations, individual abilities, personal values, and contextual influences together under a comprehensive career development model (Lent et al., 2002). This makes it a valuable theory in assessing how experiences and environment have influenced an individual's growth and career path. As a model, it is effective both for a counselor's self-analysis and a conceptualization of students' career development interests. SCCT addresses not only which variables are involved in making career decisions, but how these variables interact through a network of social experiences, feedback, and trial and error. Unlike previous career development models which took a unidirectional approach to variables, SCCT takes a fully bidirectional view of variables, in which people's thoughts, beliefs, and experiences all impact and are impacted by their behaviors and social environments.

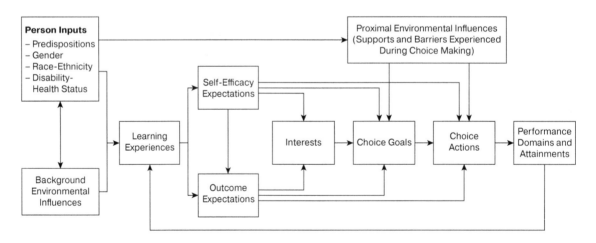

FIG. 3.3 The Social Cognitive Career Theory Model

Constructs of SCCT

Self-efficacy is the series of beliefs centered on one's capability to organize and execute actions related to goal attainment (Bandura & National Institute of Mental Health, 1986; Lent et al., 2002). These beliefs are not fixed traits or mindsets but rather are dynamic and consistently interacting with other personal, social, and environmental factors. Self-efficacy beliefs are developed through 1) personal performance accomplishments, 2) vicarious learning, 3) social persuasion, and 4) physiological and affective states. These beliefs develop through personal, social, and environmental feedback provided by individual effort and learning experiences and continue to reshape and refine throughout the life experience. More success in a role leads to belief in the ability to accomplish similar tasks, establishing higher self-efficacy and career aspirations (Lent et al., 2002).

An individual has greater levels of interest associated with areas in which they have higher self-efficacy and outcome expectations (e.g., a child is strong in math and science and believes they could succeed in a STEM field). Life experience and interaction with social systems impact the beliefs one has about what is appropriate for them, what they can achieve, and how likely they are to achieve it (Lent et al., 1994). These beliefs then drive what action (or inaction) someone takes when pursuing a career goal, with social systems potentially influencing an individual the entire time.

Outcome expectations are the "personal beliefs about the consequences or outcomes of performing particular behaviors" (Lent et al., 2002, p. 262). While self-efficacy focuses on whether or not an individual can accomplish a task, outcome expectations are the imagined outcomes of performing a behavior (i.e., if I attempt this, what will happen?). Outcome expectations include beliefs about positive outcomes (such as rewards for performance), self-directed consequences (such as pride or shame dependent upon success or failure), and the direct outcome of performing the task (such as skill in the task itself, and/or knowledge or skills learned). Outcome expectations are derived from similar experiences as self-efficacy, with both variables impacting one another. For example, self-efficacy may convince one of their ability to accomplish a goal, influencing their outcome expectations and corresponding beliefs (Lent et al., 2002).

Goals are the drives to engage in an activity with a particular desired outcome (Bandura & National Institute of Mental Health, 1986; Lent et al., 2002). Goals help organize and sustain individual behavior. While environment and genetic factors influence behavior, goals are the drives that develop amongst these and strongly influence how one acts and behaves. Self-efficacy and outcome expectations affect an individual's goals and the effort they put forth in attempting to achieve them. Goal attainment or failure then influences self-efficacy beliefs and future outcome expectations, illustrating a cycle at play. These three variables go through a network for informing and shaping one another, which then impacts how an individual pursues their career interests, aspirations, and choices.

Contextual influences are the personal, environmental, and contextual influences on social cognitive and career development (Lent et al., 2002). These include gender, race, ethnicity, ability status, genetic endowment, socioeconomic status, and any other category or condition which impacts the messages a person receives about what they can and cannot accomplish (Lent et. al., 2002). SCCT looks at these things under a social constructivist lens where the meanings of these attributes are interwoven into the social interpretation of the individual and society they interact with. For example, a boy may live in a rural town which holds traditional socially constructed views of gender roles within career. Under these views, the career of a nurse would not be considered masculine or appropriate for the boy to aspire to, despite his full capability in accomplishing the tasks. Even if the boy personally values the roles and tasks of a nurse, the societal messages and feedback he receives may dissuade him from pursuing this career or create barriers preventing him from attaining it. Thus, the networks of feedback occurring between self-efficacy, outcome expectations, and goals are all ecologically influenced by the social backdrop in which they are operating.

In fact, Lent and colleagues (2000) suggested that contextual supports and barriers may be the most powerful predictors of career choice behavior as they influence access to learning experiences. Aspects such as perceived gender roles, cultural role models, disability status, and income level may frame the experiences an individual has with learning and career planning, as well as influence the feedback a person receives from social systems (Lent et al., 1994).

Application in Schools

What elements impact students from a SCCT perspective? Let's consider contextual elements. Let's imagine you are working with a student, Gina, who has a physical disability and requires a wheelchair for transportation. While Gina has strong academics and support from teachers regarding her education, she demonstrates low self-efficacy and aspirations regarding higher education. When you inquire as to why this is, Gina reveals that she doesn't see many professionals out there who are in wheelchairs, and that negative comments from other students have made her doubt her ability to succeed. From a SCCT perspective, the influences of environment and ability status have informed self-efficacy and aspirations even though Gina has received significant academic praise.

The social aspect of career is a major factor with SCCT. How can a school counselor hope to provide competent career development if they are not considering the student's lived reality? If we try and provide educational and career guidance that solely focuses on academics, we are ignoring a major aspect influencing Gina's (and other students') career paths. Gina may have benefited from exposure to role models with a similar ability status who have completed college and transitioned to higher education. Whether through in-person connection or access to video resources, Gina may have found some inspiration and belief that she could achieve. Schoolwide career programming which included representational content could proactively address this concern and remove barriers influencing student aspirations. Field trips to institutions of higher learning could provide Gina with a connection to a campus and a visit to the disabilities service office, which exists on most college campuses and strives to provide students with equitable opportunities to learn on campus through supportive counseling, assignment accommodations, and linkage to resources. Newsletters and emails home to all families covering these support services could open minds as to what can be possible for students and how to achieve it. These potential interventions proactively provide students information that can positively influence their social reality, hopefully boosting what they see as possible.

A SCCT approach would integrate critical examinations of social realities within classroom and group lesson planning. How do the realities of income, race, and gender identity impact the opportunities available to individuals? What jobs are students aware of and interested in, and what societal views or biases may be presently influencing them? By processing these things with increasing complexity throughout the years, learners are empowered to more deeply evaluate how their view of self and work is linked to social systems, and what this means for their passion and path moving forward.

Potential Drawbacks

SCCT is a theoretical model that evaluates individual progression through experiences and social feedback. Thus, it could appear messy or disorganized within larger group settings, where even those from similar backgrounds may have radically different life experiences, perspectives, and expectations of education. SCCT also is not inherently linked to specific interventions, leaving the construction of lessons, activities, and individual interventions in the hands of the school counselor. In this way, it is ideal to integrate techniques developed from other theoretical frameworks, such as Holland's. In order for SCCT to be a culturally competent approach, the school counselor must not only know the individual student but also have a thorough understanding of the school and community culture framing their students' lived experiences.

Community Context

It would be impossible to utilize a SCCT framework without understanding and analyzing the community context of a school. It is important for a school counselor to have a deep understanding of the cultural dynamics of the community in which they serve (Grimes et al., 2013). By understanding the local population, a school counselor can be more greatly in touch with their needs and with how the school can provide services relevant to the community. This would allow a counselor to more keenly meet students and stakeholders where they are and to provide guidance that is appropriate given lived experiences and present barriers. For example, if a school counselor was unaware of students and family members experiencing systemic racism, their lack of awareness would likely result in tone-deaf guidance and an approach not suited to address the true barriers impeding academic and career growth. The important practice of connecting with the community and conducting asset mapping is presented in the following chapter.

CHAPTER SUMMARY

This chapter presented several prominent career development theories, their history, their tenets, their limitations, and how to apply them in a school setting. While all of the covered theories have value and applicability within K–12 education, each must be evaluated for its utilization with the specific student population a school counselor is working with, the age level of these students, and the scope of the theory. Certain theories, such as Holland's, may provide excellence guidance for structured activities and assessments but may lack a comprehensive framework through which to understand students and communities. Social Cognitive Career Theory is a major career development theory that allows for an evaluation of students through an investigation of their interests, beliefs, and experiences, the social feedback they receive, and environmental factors such as community context. Due to the broad and inclusive scope of the theory, SCCT is a majorly influential and beneficial framework for career development in schools.

TABLE OF KEY TERMS

TERM	DEFINITION
Trait and factor theory	Theory originally developed by Frank Parsons (1909) which advocates for the idea that a person's personality traits and vocational skills should align with their potential career options.
Theory of occupational choice	Theory developed by Ginsberg and colleagues (1951) which postulates that career development is a lifelong process influenced by the developmental stages and roles of one's life.
Life-span, life-space theory	Theory developed by Super (1990) which postulates that career development occurs throughout developmental stages across the life span, with career choice additionally influenced by the personal values of the individual and the roles they play in their familial, social, and career lives.
Theory of planned happenstance	Theory developed by Krumboltz (1979)which emphasizes how the changing realities of society and the job market dictate what career options are available and how a client adapts to these available choices.
Social cognitive theory	Theory developed by Bandura & National Institute of Mental Health (1986) which postulates that the belief to succeed at a task and the impressions developed based upon social feedback from these efforts strongly influence career choice.
Theory of circumscription and compromise	Theory developed by Gottfredson (1981) which conceptualizes individuals according to how they process career choice based upon social influences, with a heavy emphasis on role appropriateness as influenced by perceived gender norms and role prestige.
Social cognitive career theory (SCCT)	Theory developed by Lent and colleagues (1994) which integrated the ideas of self-concept, self-efficacy, aspirations, and values with the impact of contextual influences under a comprehensive career developmental model with a particular emphasis on the influence of social systems.
Self-efficacy	The series of beliefs centered on one's capability to organize and execute actions related to goal attainment (Bandura & National Institute of Mental Health, 1986; Lent et al., 2002).

Outcome expectations	The "personal beliefs about the consequences or outcomes of performing particular behaviors" (Lent et al., 2002, p. 262).
Goals	The drives to engage in an activity with a particular desired outcome (Bandura & National Institute of Mental Health, 1986; Lent et al., 2002).
Theory of career choice	Theory developed by Holland (1997) that assigns clients a three-letter code based consisting of letters across six categories: Realistic, Investigative, Artistic, Social, Enterprising, and Conventional. These categories align with the interests and skills of workers currently in various occupational fields.
Contextual influences	The personal, environmental, and contextual influences on social cognitive and career development. These include gender, race, ethnicity, ability status, genetic endowment, socioeconomic status, and any other category or condition which impacts the messages a person receives about what they can and cannot accomplish (Lent et al., 2002).

REFLECTION EXERCISES

Reflection exercises are designed either to be done individually within the reading or to be used as group discussion questions within the classroom setting. A series of reflection questions will be presented at the end of every chapter.

1. What theoretical orientations (from this chapter or beyond) resonate with you and why?

    a. How may this inform your work in career development?

2. How do career development theories align with the ASCA National Model and other professional standards?

    a. How can we use these professional guiding models to justify our career development work in schools?

3. How do the career development theories presented in this chapter align (or misalign) with your own career development journey?

    a. Does one theory fit your experience more than others?

    b. Is there a combination of theories which helps explain your experience?

4. Consider an intervention you might create using a career development theory as a foundation.

    a. What would this intervention look like and what grade level would it be intended for?

    b. What steps would you need to take in order to create this intervention?

    c. What stakeholders would you need to partner with?

CASE STUDY

Brandon is a 16-year-old white, straight, cisgender junior in your high school who has strong grades in all subjects. Like most of the students in this community, he comes from a rural low-income background. Brandon's parents were high school dropouts and now work retail and construction jobs locally for low wages. They have experienced employment instability throughout their lives. Your school district does not currently have comprehensive career development programming. Brandon comes to your office after deeply considering his educational and career path for the first time. Brandon expresses that he doesn't know much about what it takes to get into college and isn't sure what he would study. The local community has limited job availability due to its rural impoverished status, with most available opportunities being low-paying retail, service, construction, or agricultural jobs. The only visible jobs in the community requiring a college education are those at the hospital and the school.

Brandon says that he had some interest in nursing because he likes "helping people and finds health really interesting." He also knows that nursing takes less schooling than becoming a medical doctor, and this appeals to him because of his family's financial situation. However, Brandon's father strongly discouraged that route because he believes it is a "job for women." Brandon was upset by the comment and now doesn't know what route to choose. He is particularly good at and interested in science and views himself as a people person. He's on the basketball team and plays the trumpet in the school band.

Brandon believes in his academic ability, but the thought of trying to figure out financial aid and the college search process feels overwhelming. This is especially so since he knows his parents cannot provide financial support for college and are not capable of providing him guidance about the college search and application process. Brandon feels immense pressure in his career decision process because if he chooses the wrong path, it is unlikely he can afford to stay in college beyond four years, and he feels he would be "stuck" with a bad decision. Brandon feels "hopeless" and "confused" and isn't sure if he'll be able to make sense of all the complexities of deciding what to do with his life. He hopes that you can help him figure things out and start planning before senior year sneaks up on him.

Given the above dynamics, address the following questions:

1. How would you conceptualize Brandon's situation? What is contributing to his career development challenges?

2. Which career development theory(ies) would be useful in conceptualizing Brandon's situation?

3. What type of approach or interventions would be helpful to use with Brandon? Describe your full intended work with him.

4. What type of integrated and proactive interventions can be put in place within the district in order to preventively assist students in a situation similar to Brandon's?

References

Bandura, A. (2005). The evolution of social cognitive theory. In K. G. Smith & M. A Hitt (Eds.), *Great minds in management* (pp. 9–35). Oxford University Press.

Bandura, A., & National Institute of Mental Health. (1986). *Social foundations of thought and action: A social cognitive theory.* Prentice-Hall.

Ginsberg, E., Ginsburg, S. W., Axelrad, S., & Herma, J. L. (1951). *Occupational choice: An approach to a general theory.* Columbia University Press.

Gottfredson, L. S. (2005). Applying Gottfredson's theory of circumscription and compromise in career guidance and counseling. In S. D. Brown & R. W. Lent (Eds.), *Career development and counseling: Putting theory and research to work* (pp. 71–100). John Wiley & Sons.

Gottfredson, L. S. (1981). Circumscription and compromise: A developmental theory of occupational aspirations. *Journal of Counseling psychology, 28*(6), 545.

Grimes, L. E., Haskins, N., & Paisley, P. O. (2013). "So I went out there": A phenomenological study on the experiences of rural school counselor social justice advocates. *Professional School Counseling, 17*(1). https://doi.org/10.1177/2156759X0001700107

Holland, J. L. (1997). *Making vocational choices: A theory of vocational personalities and work environments* (3rd ed.). Psychological Assessment Resources.

Krumboltz, J. D. (1979). A social learning theory of career decision making. Revised and reprinted in A. M. Mitchell, G. B. Jones, and J. D. Krumboltz (Eds.), Social learning and career decision making (pp. 19–49). Cranston, RI: Carroll Press.

Lent, R. W., Brown, S. D., & Hackett, G. (1994). Toward a unifying social cognitive theory of career and academic interest, choice, and performance. *Journal of Vocational Behavior, 45*(1), 79–122.

Lent, R. W., Brown, S. D., & Hackett, G. (2000). Contextual supports and barriers to career choice: A social cognitive analysis. *Journal of Counseling Psychology, 47*(1), 36–49.

Lent, R. W., Brown, S. D., & Hackett, G. (2002). Social cognitive career theory. In D. Brown (Ed.), *Career choice and development* (4th ed., pp. 255–311). Jossey-Bass.

O*Net Online. (2022). Interests search for social, artistic, investigative. https://www.onetonline.org/explore/interests/Social/Artistic/Investigative

Parsons, F. (1909). *Choosing a vocation.* Gay & Hancock.

Super, D. E. (1990). A life-span, life-space approach to career development. In D. Brown & L. Brooks (Eds.), *Career choice and development: Applying contemporary theories to practice* (pp. 197–261). Jossey–Bass.

CHAPTER 4

Community Context

We reflected upon what influences individual perceptions of career development in earlier chapters. Much of the writing leaned into how individual experience provides us a series of beliefs and lenses through which we view ourselves and the world of work. These lenses are often influenced by the educational systems we engaged in and what help (or oppression) they offered us. Take a moment to go beyond your educational system. When you evaluate who you are and why you chose the career of school counseling, what aspects of yourself come to mind?

Envision the community in which you were raised. Think about its sociodemographic make up. Think about who lived there. Think about what the individuals in that community needed and if their needs were being met by social systems such as schools. Where were you and your family in this community? What did you believe about yourselves, society, schooling, careers, and the world? How did environmental context influence who you became and what you are experiencing now?

Imagine you get a job out of graduate school in a community starkly different from the one in which you were raised. How do you think your students view education? Careers? The future? How do they view themselves and relationships? What dynamics might influence this? How does what you know and understand about these things apply or not apply to their situation?

If you find yourself drawing some blanks, I commend you. This is a situation where having all of the answers might actually pull you further away from the truth. As school counselors, we must be willing to understand our students and the populations we serve. If we do not make the effort to fill in the gaps in our knowledge, we may be unknowingly pushing our biases on students or even extending systemic oppression. Even well-intentioned counselors can do this if they do not take the time to critically analyze the needs of their local community, their own biases, and what exact experiences and programs are beneficial for the student population. Think about how you'd work with students in a community very different from the communities you are used to. What are your knowledge gaps, and what are the first steps in filling them? Let's utilize an example from the previous chapter to begin this journey.

Community Challenges

Consider Brandon's situation from the previous chapter. How were the realities of his community influencing his understanding of self as related to the world of work? If a school counselor were to work with Brandon without considering the influence of community culture and dynamics, would their work be on the mark? Brandon was experiencing a situation many rural low-income students do: uncertainty regarding career development due to a lack of exposure to influences, isolation from institutions of higher learning, limited exposure to potential career options, limited financial means, and parents' unfamiliarity with the college and career process. If a school counselor from an affluent suburb were to come to this school and approach career development the same way they had previously, they would likely miss the opportunity to connect with students and families and to develop interventions specifically designed to meet the needs of this particular community.

Barriers in Rural Communities

Career development barriers in rural communities include isolation from training programs, cost of higher education, uncertainty regarding the college process, and student concern that going to college means they will have to leave home for good since there are limited work opportunities available at home (Ali & Menke, 2014). A vast majority of rural communities are not located near institutions of higher education, limiting student exposure to postsecondary programs, professional fields, and educated role models (Grimes et al., 2019). The lack of exposure to higher education also increases the logistical and financial challenges of traveling to attend college. Further, a lack of familiarity of college due to geographic isolation increases the cultural barriers of attending college, including knowing how the college process works and accessing available support systems (Grimes et al., 2019). In a study of 12,000 rural students from 73 school districts, Byun and colleagues (2015) found that rural students faced statistically significant disparities regarding postsecondary attendance including lower attendance at selective institutions and matriculation into graduate programs.

Rural high school students experience tension between the school's goals of pushing higher education and their own desires to live close to their families and communities (Corbett, 2007, 2010). The availability of low-skill jobs in the community exposes students to more practical, achievable jobs close to home, thereby contributing to lower student career aspirations (Corbett, 2010; C. W. Howley, 2006). Students interested in careers not available in the community may face tension and stress over these conflicting goals, resulting in a failure to attend or complete college (Corbett, 2010; Elder & Conger, 2000).

Not only do rural students feel rooted in their communities, but their ideas and conceptions of what success and achievement mean may also differ from those of their urban and suburban counterparts. Studies show that rural parents have lower educational and career expectations for their children than do parents of non-rural backgrounds, impacting what careers students aspire towards (Byun et al., 2012). Careerist definitions of success, including social prestige, income, and identity through the title of one's work, may seem out of touch in rural communities, which place a higher emphasis on community and relationships than on material gain or social status (Ali & Saunders, 2009; Corbett, 2010; C. W. Howley, 2006). In a study of rural Appalachian high school students, Ali and Saunders (2009) found that students had a negative view of education and its relevance to their lives due to a perception that education was a vehicle for White middle- and upper-class individuals, a group in which they did not feel included. These barriers and social processes are important to consider when counselors evaluate the career development needs of a particular school, and similar considerations must be taken into account when they create interventions for urban communities.

Barriers in Urban Communities

Students in low-income, inner-city schools face significant barriers to career development including risks for lower educational attainment, limited employment opportunities, and lower lifetime income than individuals from outside communities (Jackson, Kacanski, et al., 2006; Turner & Lapan, 2003). These challenges particularly affect students of color, who face the challenges of systemic racism in addition to the barriers of less funded schools, limited employment opportunities, and low-income family backgrounds (Howard et al., 2010). These barriers lead to a lower self-efficacy in educational and career attainment in many inner-city youth, who experience little benefit from educational systems or have internalized negative stereotypes placed upon them by those systems (Jackson, Potere, et al., 2006; Kenny et al., 2007).

Students of color may be dissuaded from pursuing higher education due to inequity in school funding and in educational and career opportunities, a lack of school safety, prejudicial teacher attitudes, and a lack of professional jobs in their home community (Diemer & Blustein, 2007). Inner-city students may also lack support from home, due to either similar attitudes towards schooling or a lack of experience in higher education (Kerpelman et al., 2008). High levels of community and generational trauma may have students and families dealing with complex familial and emotional challenges, greatly diverting student effort from academics (Blitz et al., 2020). A lack of representation in teachers and counselors, along with a lack of role models, also leaves many students in urban communities without a sense of connection or mentorship (Hurd et al., 2009). When these students do aspire and even transition to college, many experience continued racism at the higher education level, potentially having their college aspiration and completion diminished as a result (Jackson, Kacanski, et al., 2006).

One study found that when urban teenagers were aware of the systemic inequities present throughout education and knew how to overcome them, they had a deeper sense of vocational identity and commitment to their future career path (Diemer & Blustein, 2006). The researchers suggested that this critical consciousness is necessary to help students understand what barriers exist in society and how students can navigate these for the betterment of self and the world. The findings suggest that by directly providing opportunities for students to analyze the state of society, both in relation to work and not, schools can empower students to explore the reality of work, develop coping strategies, link to resources, and find their paths. These skills are particularly important for urban youth of color, who will face future oppression at the collegiate level. In order for school counselors to properly develop career development education that integrates social realities, they must thoroughly understand the community in which they are working.

Conducting Needs Assessments

One of the major tasks for ongoing school counseling programmatic upkeep is data collection and analysis. Data analysis revolves around both evaluating the effectiveness of ongoing interventions and conducting needs assessments to determine new areas of concern and growth (Stone & Dahir, 2015). Needs assessments entail creating a quantitative, qualitative, or mixed-methods data collection instrument to gather responses on particular areas of focus within a school. Areas of focus often include academic development, social climate and connectedness, career development, school equity, perceptions of bullying and school violence, and other major issues impacting students and families daily. Students are a major group who should be consulted through needs assessments to gather data on their perceptions and suggested areas of improvement. Because students are the ones experiencing the education day in and day out, their voices are critically important to consider when educators and counselors are framing holistic and culturally appropriate career development interventions. Families are stakeholders who can provide meaningful data about the needs of a school district, but their opinions are often under sought. Families not only know their child and have a deep understanding of the presenting concerns they face but also are inextricably linked to a student's progress in domains such as career development. By understanding and connecting with parents, a school can better shape its career development practices to be more intentional and effective.

What Assessments Look Like

What could a career-driven needs assessment look like? For students, a survey could include questions scored on a 1–5 Likert scale asking about: their familiarity with different career options; their awareness of their personal likes, dislikes, and skills; their perceived alignment of academic curriculum to their future lives; their awareness of college, financial aid, and major choice processes; and much more. Open-ended response sections could survey the students' beliefs about how school could better meet their academic and career needs, what types of lessons or programming would be helpful, how represented in and connected to school they feel, and what has most influenced their academic and career journey. Means, medians, modes, frequencies, t-tests, and regression models could be run to represent the students' Likert scale scores across each question or conceptual domain. These numbers could easily be disaggregated by group, such as classroom, grade level, gender, or ethnicity, in order to get a deeper picture of what's occurring at school and what disparities may exist. Qualitative analysis of the short answers could provide guiding themes and ideas for how to philosophically realign the efforts of the school to match the needs of the students and the community.

The constructs present on the survey, and the language utilized, depend upon what type of career development work is being done at a school and what age levels are being served. For example, the language of a survey will vary greatly between a 3–5 school and a 9–12 high school. In addition, there is likely to be much less focus on questions pertaining to college and major choice in the 3–5 elementary school. While the language of the survey needs to be adjusted by grade level, it is still possible to solicit meaningful information from students as young as the K–2 years. Simple smiley-face drawings provide an easy substitute for a 3- or 5-point Likert scale, and simple questions about how much students like school, feel connected to teachers, and know what they like to do in school can provide meaningful guidance for classroom lessons and programmatic activities.

Research and Assessment

Research literature is a wonderful place to start when we explore the domains that influence career development. As a case in point, school connectedness is a major indicator of academic success and high school completion (Liu et al., 2020). The barriers influencing the college and career process are major predictor of college attendance and success, and it is important to gain a critical understanding of this influence (Diemer & Blustein, 2006). Self-efficacy, or the belief in one's ability to achieve, is the major indicator of academic and career aspirations in students (Bandura et al., 2001). If working in a rural community, a school counselor may want to examine how a student's connection to their home community in the form of place attachment may hinder their desire to leave home for college (Bright, 2020; C. B. Howley, 2009). Sexism, transphobia, and racism all influence how students feel about what jobs and education are appropriate for them and why (Dispenza et al., 2019). The presence of these and other social barriers dissuades students from connecting to school and getting the most out of career exploration. By acclimating to one's school and community, the school counselor can read through the literature with an eye towards what domains are most worthy of examination within their district. Another major benefit is that many of these studies have statistically reliable and valid scales which can be directly used or adapted for the counselor's building. In order to make these intentional decisions in developing a needs assessment, a school counselor must increase their understanding of school and community through targeted outreach.

Community Outreach

A common critique heard from those who had a poor experience with school counselors in their life was that they never saw their counselor. The school counselor remained in their office, served only select students (often those with the highest needs or the highest academic performance), or only focused on one aspect of their job (college prep rather than social-emotional needs, for example). This reactive model of counseling is more akin to the guidance counseling of old. It is understandable that many counselors remain busy in their offices, considering growing responsibilities and large ratios of students to counselors. However, a school counselor cannot effectively serve their school and community if they are not interfacing with them. The role of a school counselor can become more streamlined, intentional, and efficient through some proactive planning, partnership building, and programmatic development (Dahir & Stone, 2009).

Outreach With Students

Outreach with students entails the counselor being visible in the school building. This includes the counselor being out in the hallways or outdoors when students are coming into or leaving school, being present at recess (not as a disciplinarian), meeting with students outside of presenting concerns, teaching regularly scheduled guidance lessons (weekly or monthly), and participating in schoolwide clubs and activities. When a school counselor is not visible in the building, students may be uncertain about how the counselor can be a resource or may feel too shy or intimidated to seek them out (Stone & Dahir, 2015). This prevents students from accessing resources that can help them succeed and disconnects the counselor from the lived experiences of students in their school. If the school counselor bases their interventions solely upon those few students actively seeking assistance, they may have a skewed picture of the reality of the school and of what would be helpful for other types of students.

Outreach With Faculty

Even as the school counseling profession continues to grow and prosper, many K–12 educational staff have little or inaccurate knowledge about the role of the school counselor (Cholewa et al., 2016). Therefore, going into a school building expecting supervisors and co-workers to know what a school counselor should be doing is a mistake. It is imperative for the school counselor to meet and make connections with faculty, starting on day one. A great way to make an impression on your new co-workers would be to give a presentation during the commonly held faculty in-service days just before the start of the school year. This presentation can introduce who you are but also detail what you believe your role in the school should be, what types of things you'd like to accomplish, how you'd like to collaborate with your co-workers, and how they can best contact you. This not only helps establish a joint understanding of the ideal function of your role but also plants the seeds of collaboration (Stone & Dahir, 2015). Co-workers interested in advocacy and unique projects may find it easier to come to you and establish professional bonds after hearing such a presentation.

Next, a school counselor should make time to individually meet each teacher and staff member. This personalization allows for an understanding of each faculty member's style, needs, potential collaborative ability, and perceptions of needs for school growth. A school counselor can learn about formal and informal power systems (who has clout in schoolwide decision-making initiatives, who socializes and collaborates with who) as well as analyze which faculty members may have expertise or interest in an area that can foster new programs. For example, a conversation with the art teacher may reveal that they are passionate about introducing students to the many careers in the arts or to how many careers can be supplemented by creative talents. Such a conversation could lead to a jointly constructed classroom lesson, schoolwide program, career day, or small group, allowing students to benefit from both of your expertise areas combined.

Finally, these meetings can also provide meaningful assessment data (Stone & Dahir, 2015). The school counselor can provide each faculty member with an initial needs assessment survey (printed or digital) and ask them to complete it at their convenience. This needs assessment can be general or be geared toward any particular domain. If the counselor has previously established relationships with co-workers, it is more likely that they will complete the assessment and give honest feedback.

These steps should be taken with administrators as well. Administrators' perceptions and willingness to engage as advocates will allow a school counselor to evaluate which initiatives may be easy to get off the ground faster and what work needs to be done in order for them to be trusted with major programmatic construction.

Outreach With the Community

Imagine you are a parent who had a negative experience with schooling. You felt underserved, mistreated, marginalized, or all of the above. Imagine that your child is having some type of challenge in school. How would you naturally feel about the school's ability to solve the problem, and how comfortable would you be with constructive outreach? All too often, parents are hesitant to engage with the school community due to their own negative experiences, uncertainties, experiences with racism, or feelings of intimidation (Holcomb-McCoy, 2010; McKenna & Millen, 2013). By proactively connecting with families, the school counselor can bridge them to resources and form meaningful partnerships, for the sake of the entire community.

School counselors should strive to be visible at school events. During parent–teacher conference nights, the school counselor can hand out brochures detailing who they are and what services are available to students. This is a productive way to foster individual conversations with parents about their child's needs and what services they believe would be effective. The school counselor can also be present within the room during parent–teacher conferences, sharing the perspective of a student beyond the classroom and offering support in addition to what the teacher provides.

In addition to being visible at regularly scheduled events, the school counselor should create new outreach events, particularly those related to career-related domains. For example, the school counselor can consistently host a monthly coffee hour, where parents are invited to the school for free coffee and donuts, with the school counselor and other important school stakeholders available for conversation around what school needs are and what programmatic shifts may be necessary (Griffen, 2019). Community resource fairs are another great way to connect with the community and empower families to succeed (Bryan et al., 2017). During this event, the school counselor invites community partners—who may address communal needs such as mental health, drug treatment, social services, career development, tutoring, extracurricular activities, and more—to the school for a fair. Parents are welcomed to come and see what assistance and activities are available for their family. This type of fair establishes the school as a place of helping and resource coordination, a model which may allow more families to come forward to discuss their needs. Targeted events, such as community summits, can allow community voices to be heard on issues such as curriculum, career development, equity, social justice, and present concerns within the school system (Bryan & Holcomb-McCoy, 2010). College application and FAFSA completion nights can offer valuable services to families, helping inform and boost their child's career development (King, 2012).

A step that can be taken early in and throughout a school counselor's tenure is monthly letters (or e-mails) to every family in the school (Bryan et al., 2017). These flyers can cover what programs or groups the school counselor is running, provide information about community and school resources, highlight school or student achievement, and provide referral contact information for families. These can also include, or be separate from, needs assessment forms (or links) sent to families. These needs assessments can gather data on perceptions of academic, social-emotional, career, or other school needs. By collecting data from students, staff, and families, a school counselor can gain a holistic sense of the needs of a school building across all major domains.

Data-Driven Advocacy

A school counselor's practice should be grounded in data (Dahir & Stone, 2009). Data allows the school counselor to be intentional in reforming a school and its programming. When analyzing data, the school counselor should keep in mind whose needs are being met and whose are not. Are there groups of students (by race, gender, socioeconomic background, etc.) who perceive their needs are not being met at a higher rate than other groups do? Are there groups of students with lower academic or career-related achievement? Does how the teachers perceive these things align or misalign with students and parents? Where are the gaps, why might they be there, and what must be done within the context of this school? How can this data be presented to administrators to illustrate need and to propose programmatic intervention? These considerations will allow a school counselor to design comprehensive programming to truly meet the needs of all students.

Data-driven advocacy builds upon itself. After data is used to develop interventions, data should be collected to evaluate the effectiveness of the programs and tweak them moving forward (Dahir & Stone, 2009). This is all aligned with the *accountability* domain of the ASCA National Model, which requires school counselors to consistently evaluate their efforts and remake programs for the betterment of the school community (American School Counselor Association, 2019). The more a school counselor engages in data collection, the more surveys, assessments, and measures they will have prepared for their upcoming projects, allowing them to quickly analyze data and present the findings to stakeholders. These efforts are essential in programmatic management and upkeep and allow the school counselor to make nuanced arguments in favor of systemic changes grounded in data instead of opinion. Data can also change the culture of a school, especially of a school where previous decisions were made based on historical norms that may have never considered the needs or perspectives of minoritized students (Stone & Dahir, 2015). Data is a central piece of advocacy which can shed light on issues previously not discussed and help form holistic interventions to better the entire schooling community.

Community Asset Mapping and Partnerships

If a school counselor is to use data to inform appropriate interventions, where do they get the resources necessary to provide comprehensive career development experiences to students? School districts are often strapped for financial and human resources, and the services available are not enough to allow students to experience critical programming in career development. Luckily, many community members and organizations are happy to partner with schools for unique programming and experiences. In order to establish these partnerships, a school counselor must conduct a community asset map (Stone & Dahir, 2015).

A school counselor can develop a deeper sense of understanding about the community they serve by using the research skills they developed in their graduate program. From a career development perspective, it is critical to analyze what types of businesses and jobs are available locally. What type of industry is present? What is the diversity of job opportunities? Are there single industries that dominate the local economy? What exposure do students have to higher education and to jobs which require it? A school district that is isolated from an institution of higher education, and that has limited available jobs requiring a college education, may lack role models showing students a diversity of careers. Students may not consider certain career fields or develop their understanding of the roles of certain jobs through inaccurate media portrayals. Within the full process of asset mapping, understanding the local economic framework and career development influences empowers a school counselor to truly connect with their community.

Asset mapping further entails identifying community partners for strategic interventions (Griffin & Farris, 2010). For example, a school counselor can identify a diverse array of businesses and professionals in the area and reach out to them for participation in a career day or fair. This type of outreach can further solidify more in-depth partnerships, such as field trips and job-shadowing opportunities, for middle and high schoolers. To take this a step further, high schools can work with local places of work to establish formal internship programs which allow students to experience the world of work for academic credit. This type of partnership (described in more depth in a later chapter) can provide incredibly valuable experience to students trying to decide what work they enjoy and would like to pursue.

School counselors need not partner only with local professionals and businesses; they can partner with institutions of higher education as well (Arriero & Griffin, 2018). Colleges often have students who require internship hours in social services fields such as education and counseling. These students can be utilized to help provide comprehensive services to students within a school district in conjunction with a local university. To take this a step further, the school counselor can partner with these interns to help deliver career education, counseling, outreach, and events. Interns provide more human resources, allowing more projects to be taken on, more data to be analyzed, and more valuable experiences to be shared by all. If successful, internship work can eventually become programmatic itself, with school counseling interns running career development groups, chaperoning field trips to university tours, acting as counselors in an immersive summer camp, or providing extensive outreach to families.

Community colleges and four-year universities are also wonderful resources to collaborate with for dual-enrollment experiences (Bryan & Henry, 2012). This is when a high school student takes a college course for both high school and college credit. These agreements benefit both the college and the high school, and students receive valuable exposure to college content, course expectations, campuses, and potential career fields while also saving money due to earning transferable credits. The school counselor should intentionally evaluate which business and educational resources are being tapped into within the community and which are not, in order to facilitate the development of meaningful partnerships and programs for the sake of holistic career development. Once the considerations from this chapter and those previous are considered, a school counselor can work on creating the appropriate career development interventions for their learning community.

Multitiered Systems of Support

Multitiered systems of support (MTSS) are evidence-based frameworks implemented in K–12 schools that integrate interventions across three tiers to meet the targeted needs of all students (Goodman-Scott et al., 2019). MTSS should be implemented across academic, social, and career-based interventions. *Tier 1 interventions* are intended to service 80% of the student population. Tier 1 interventions are proactive and preventive programming available to all students. For example, a series of guidance lessons given to every single classroom in a high school about the college search and major selection process would be a tier 1 intervention. This intervention provides information and assistance to all students and helps address concerns before they become more severe. If a school counselor did not provide these lessons (and similar programming available to all students), more students would have more intense needs. Imagine a high school in which there was no proactive education around the college search and application process—we can clearly guess that many more students would be rushing to their school counselor at the last minute trying to figure things out, resulting in an overwhelmed school counselor and a lack of effectiveness in service delivery. Tier 1 interventions help alleviate this concern by systemically meeting the needs of many students. From a career development perspective, tier 1 interventions can include classroom lessons, schoolwide presentations, recurring fieldtrips, newsletters sent home to families, schoolwide speakers, and many more interventions.

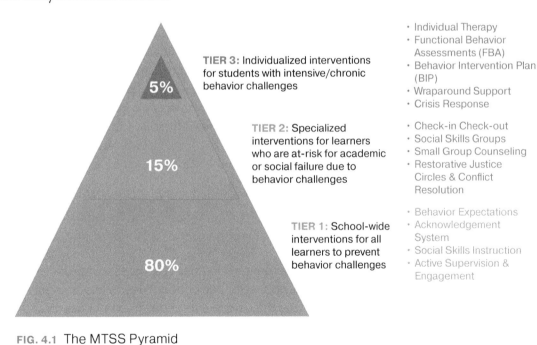

FIG. 4.1 The MTSS Pyramid

Tier 2 interventions are for the approximately 15% of students at higher risk for social-emotional, academic, and/or career challenges. These interventions are more specifically targeted and tailored for these students, providing more direct approaches to meeting their needs. From a career development perspective, these interventions may be focused on students who are facing academic challenges, barriers to graduation, or great uncertainty regarding their college and career path. Examples of these interventions can include individual career counseling/check-in sessions (with homework regarding class, college, or major search), small group counseling for academics (study habits, test anxiety management, standardized test preparation), small groups for career development (school transition anxiety groups, college exploration groups), after-school clubs or activities centered around career development, academic or career mentorship/shadowing programs targeted towards specific students or needs, and many more. For these interventions it is key to have a sense of the needs of the students and community and to have a keen sense of what community partners can be utilized to develop appropriate interventions.

Tier 3 interventions are for the 5% of students facing the highest level of challenges to their success. These students often have individual plans related to their academics or behavior, which may include more frequent structured check-ins or sessions with the school counselor. These students often are at the highest risk of dropping out of school. Tier 3 students may benefit from more intensive academic and career counseling, including enrollment in academic support programming (additional work with teaching specialists or tutors), repeated academic/career development counseling (including portfolio work), and specialized individual programs such as individual school-to-work programs, an individually designed internship meant to provide work experience and high school graduation requirements, individual visits/tours of new schools the student will be transitioning to, or alternative high school/college options (technical high school, community college, vocational programs). These interventions are more intensive and time consuming in order to meet the increased needs of these students, but it is important to keep the percentage balance of the MTSS framework in mind. If we are waiting to provide intervention until there are intense needs, the percentage of tier 3 students will be above 5%. This means a school counselor (as well as other staff) will become overwhelmed with these responsibilities and be unable to dedicate their efforts effectively to the entire student population. By establishing integrative and intentional support systems for tiers 1 and 2, a school counselor creates the environment necessary for a school to meet the needs of every learner.

CHAPTER SUMMARY

This chapter presented the educational and career development barriers facing rural and urban communities. It detailed how a school counselor can conduct needs assessments and community outreach to better understand the unique career development needs of their student population and can also partner with relevant stakeholders to enact comprehensive career development programming. Through community asset mapping and the intentional use of data, the school counselor can identify what programs are needed to benefit the community, how to enact them, and who to partner with to benefit the career development of all students.

TABLE OF KEY TERMS

Term	Definition
Needs assessments	Utilizing data to evaluate the needs of a school and community for the sake of student success, wellness, and growth (Stone & Dahir, 2015).
Community outreach	The process of a school counselor connecting with relevant stakeholders including school faculty, families, and community partners to gather relevant data, develop partnerships, and create interventions addressing student needs.
Data-driven advocacy	The process of using data to inform, reform, and evaluate the effectiveness of a comprehensive school counseling program to provide equitable access to success for all students (Dahir & Stone, 2009).
Community asset map	A list or graphic representing current and potential school and community programmatic partnerships addressing student academic, social-emotional, and career needs (Griffin & Farris, 2010).
MTSS	Multitiered systems of support. A research-backed model providing a framework for intervention design to meet the needs of all students.

REFLECTION EXERCISES

Reflection exercises are designed either to be done individually within the reading or to be used as group discussion questions within the classroom setting. A series of reflection questions will be presented at the end of every chapter.

1. What needs were present in the schools you attended in the K–12 years?
    a. Were those needs different for various groups of students?
    b. Did some student groups have their needs met more than others? Why?
    c. How did your schools conduct needs assessments?
2. What barriers existed in your school or community regarding career development?
    a. What programs or interventions did your school have available?
    b. How did the interventions you experienced vary by grade level?

3. Conduct an asset map of your local community.

   a. What businesses or professionals would be helpful career development partners?

   b. What institutions of higher education would be helpful partners?

   c. How could these partners fill perceived gaps in career development?

4. Consider an intervention you might create using these community partners.

   a. What would this intervention look like, and what grade level would it be intended for?

   b. What steps would you need to take in order to create this intervention?

   c. How would you collect data on the effectiveness of this intervention?

CASE STUDY

Ridgeview High School is a rural 9–12 school in a community with limited career opportunities. Physical labor such as working on natural gas pipelines and road construction is one of the major industries, while low-paying retail and service jobs make up most of the available positions in the sparsely populated community. The Ridgeview school district has no central town or downtown, and instead has goods, services, and businesses spread out across many miles of rural roads. Ridgeview's student population is largely Native American and Caucasian in heritage and has many students of low socioeconomic status. The staff at Ridgeview are primarily made of up individuals who are not from the immediate area. Many teachers come to Ridgeview due to how it qualifies for specific loan forgiveness programs, as an area of high need. Many of these teachers are from cities in the state several hours away. A majority of the staff do not live in the district community and instead live in or near the closest city, approximately a 35-minute drive from the school.

The administrator's goal is to send as many students as possible to college. She views this as the mark of success of the school. The White students at Ridgeview are currently going to college at higher rates than the Native American students. You've heard that generally the teachers (who are majority White) believe this is because the White students have more role models and express a deeper interest in school and higher education. The outcomes of students who go on to college are not known, and college-going rates are the only metric measured by Ridgeview High School.

Career development programming is based upon a grade-wide meeting with the school counselors held once a year. After this, students meet with their assigned school counselor twice a year for scheduling and college planning. Students are expected to seek out their counselors for any other questions or concerns. No data is kept on these interactions. School counselors have reported that the White students do show more interest in college and career development, since they seek out the services more frequently. As a new school counselor at Ridgeview, consider the following questions:

1. What types of needs assessments are needed at Ridgeview? Design the types of questions you'd ask to each stakeholder population. How would you analyze this data?
2. What types of outreach events might be helpful? How would you run and advertise these events?
3. What types of problems do you identify with the way career development practices are conducted at Ridgeview? What are some potential solutions?
4. What type of interventions do you believe you could create from your use of assessment data?

References

Ali, S. R., & Menke, K. A. (2014). Rural Latino youth career development: An application of social cognitive career theory. *The Career Development Quarterly, 62*(2), 175–186.

Ali, S. R., & Saunders, J. L. (2009). The career aspirations of rural Appalachian high school students. *Journal of Career Assessment, 17*(2), 172–188.

American School Counselor Association. (2019). *ASCA National Model: A framework for school counseling programs* (4th ed.). American School Counselor Association.

Arriero, E., & Griffin, D. (2018). ¡Adelante! A community asset mapping approach to increase college and career readiness for rural Latinx high school students. *Professional School Counseling, 22*(1). https://doi.org/10.1177/2156759X18800279

Bandura, A., Barbaranelli, C., Caprara, G. V., & Pastorelli, C. (2001). Self-efficacy beliefs as shapers of children's aspirations and career trajectories. *Child Development, 72*(1), 187–206.

Bright, D. J. (2018). The rural gap: The need for exploration and intervention. *Journal of School Counseling, 16*(21), 1–27.

Bryan, J., & Henry, L. M. (2012). A model for building school–family–community partnerships: Principles and process. *Journal of Counseling & Development, 90*(4), 408–420.

Bryan, J. A., & Holcomb-McCoy, C. (2010). Editorial introduction: Collaboration and partnerships with families and communities. *Professional School Counseling, 14*(1), ii–v.

Bryan, J. A., Young, A., Griffin, D., & Holcomb-McCoy, C. (2017). Leadership practices linked to involvement in school–family–community partnerships: A national study. *Professional School Counseling, 21*(1). https://doi.org/10.1177/2156759X18761897

Blitz, L. V., Yull, D., & Clauhs, M. (2020). Bringing sanctuary to school: Assessing school climate as a foundation for culturally responsive trauma-informed approaches for urban schools. *Urban Education, 55*(1), 95–124. https://doi.org/10.1177/0042085916651323

Byun, S.-Y., Irvin, M. J., & Meece, J. L. (2015). Rural–nonrural differences in college attendance patterns. *Peabody Journal of Education, 90*(2), 263–279.

Byun, S.-Y., Meece, J. L., Irvin, M. J., & Hutchins, B. C. (2012). The role of social capital in educational aspirations of rural youth. *Rural Sociology, 77*(3), 355–379.

Cholewa, B., Goodman-Scott, E., Thomas, A., & Cook, J. (2016). Teachers' perceptions and experiences consulting with school counselors: A qualitative study. *Professional School Counseling, 20*(1), 1096–2409.

Corbett, M. (2007). Travels in space and place: identity and rural schooling. *Canadian Journal of Education, 30*(3), 771–792.

Corbett, M. (2010). Standardized individuality: Cosmopolitanism and educational decision-making in an Atlantic Canadian rural community. *Compare: A Journal of Comparative and International Education, 40*(2), 223–237.

Dahir, C. A., & Stone, C. B. (2009). School counselor accountability: The path to social justice and systemic change. *Journal of Counseling & Development, 87*(1), 12–20.

Diemer, M. A., & Blustein, D. L. (2006). Critical consciousness and career development among urban youth. *Journal of Vocational Behavior, 68*(2), 220–232.

Diemer, M. A., & Blustein, D. L. (2007). Vocational hope and vocational identity: Urban adolescents' career development. *Journal of Career Assessment, 15*(1), 98–118.

Dispenza, F., Brennaman, C., Harper, L. S., Harrigan, M. A., Chastain, T. E., & Procter, J. E. (2019). Career development of sexual and gender minority persons living with disabilities. *The Counseling Psychologist, 47*(1), 98–128.

Elder, G. H., Jr., & Conger, R. D. (2000). *Children of the land: Adversity and success in rural America.* University of Chicago Press.

Goodman-Scott, E., & Ockerman, M. S. (2019). Integrating school counseling and MTSS. In E. Goodman-Scott, J. Betters-Bubon, & P. Donohue (Eds.), *The school counselor's guide to Multi-Tiered Systems of Support* (pp. 29–61). Routledge.

Griffen, J. (2019). Families and counselors taking action to transform culture: An action–inquiry case study of an urban high school. *Education and Urban Society, 51*(4), 501–525.

Griffin, D., & Farris, A. (2010). School counselors and collaboration: Finding resources through community asset mapping. *Professional School Counseling, 13*(5). https://doi.org/10.1177/2156759X1001300501

Grimes, L. E., Arrastía-Chisholm, M. A., & Bright, S. B. (2019). How can they know what they don't know? The beliefs and experiences of rural school counselors about STEM career advising. *Theory & Practice in Rural Education, 9*(1), 74–90.

Holcomb-McCoy, C. (2010). Involving low-income parents and parents of color in college readiness activities: An exploratory study. *Professional School Counseling, 14*(1). https://www.jstor.org/stable/42732754

Howard, K. A., Budge, S. L., Gutierrez, B., Owen, A. D., Lemke, N., Jones, J. E., & Higgins, K. (2010). Future plans of urban youth: Influences, perceived barriers, and coping strategies. *Journal of Career Development, 37*(4), 655–676.

Howley, C. W. (2006). Remote possibilities: Rural children's educational aspirations. *Peabody Journal of Education, 81*(2), 62–80.

Howley, C. B. (2009). The meaning of rural difference for bright rednecks. *Journal for the Education of the Gifted, 32*(4), 537–564.

Hurd, N. M., Zimmerman, M. A., & Xue, Y. (2009). Negative adult influences and the protective effects of role models: A study with urban adolescents. *Journal of Youth and Adolescence, 38*(6), 777–789.

Jackson, M. A., Kacanski, J. M., Rust, J. P., & Beck, S. E. (2006). Constructively challenging diverse inner-city youth's beliefs about educational and career barriers and supports. *Journal of Career Development, 32*(3), 203–218.

Jackson, M. A., Potere, J. C., & Brobst, K. A. (2006). Are success learning experiences and self-efficacy beliefs associated with occupational interests and aspirations of at-risk urban youth? *Journal of Career Assessment, 14*(3), 333–353.

Kenny, M. E., Gualdron, L., Scanlon, D., Sparks, E., Blustein, D. L., & Jernigan, M. (2007). Urban adolescents' constructions of supports and barriers to educational and career attainment. *Journal of Counseling Psychology, 54*(3), 336–343.

Kerpelman, J. L., Eryigit, S., & Stephens, C. J. (2008). African American adolescents' future education orientation: Associations with self-efficacy, ethnic identity, and perceived parental support. *Journal of Youth and Adolescence, 37*(8), 997–1008.

King, S. B. (2012). Increasing college-going rate, parent involvement, and community participation in rural communities. *The Rural Educator, 33*(2).

Liu, Y., Kim, H., Carney, J. V., Chung, K. S., & Hazler, R. J. (2020). Individual and contextual factors associated with school connectedness in the context of counseling in schools. *Journal of Counseling & Development, 98*(4), 391–401.

McKenna, M. K., & Millen, J. (2013). Look! Listen! Learn! Parent narratives and grounded theory models of parent voice, presence, and engagement in K–12 education. *School Community Journal, 23*(1), 9–48.

Stone, C., & Dahir, C. A. (2015). *The transformed school counselor* (3rd ed.). Cengage Learning.

Turner, S. L., & Lapan, R. T. (2003). The measurement of career interests among at-risk inner-city and middle-class suburban adolescents. *Journal of Career Assessment, 11*(4), 405–420.

Credit

Fig. 4.1: Source: https://www.mpusd.net/apps/pages/index.jsp?uREC_ID=1012305&type=d&pREC_ID=1322797.

Needs Assessment and Systemic Response Plan

Caitlin Pastore, MS

P
ractical Resources are examples of work school counselors can do in applying the concepts of this textbook to their own school districts. They are also an example of assignments counselor educators could assign to their students. All practical resources were contributed by school counselors in training working toward their master's degrees.

SECTION ONE

Demographics

The school this paper will focus on is Westport Elementary, my current practicum placement site. Westport Elementary is a public school located in Jackson Valley, NY and is part of the Jackson Valley School District. The Jackson Valley School District is composed of two elementary schools (grades K–3), one intermediate school (grades 4–6), one middle school (grades 7–8), and one high school (grades 9–12). Westport Elementary is the larger of the two elementary schools in the district. The following demographic information was collected in order to paint a broad picture of who Westport Elementary is serving, and to give context to the needs they have.

According to data from the New York State Education Department, Westport Elementary is comprised of a mostly White student population. Of the 303 students enrolled at the school, 86% of students identified as Caucasian, 8% identified as Hispanic or Latino, 2% identified as Black or African American, 2% identified as Asian or Native Hawaiian/other Pacific Islander, and 1% identified as multiracial. Student-to-faculty ratios vary across the district, but the average student-to-teacher ratio at Westport Elementary is 13:1. There is one school counselor for the building, so the ratio of students to counselor is about 303:1. This student-counselor ratio exceeds the ASCA National Model's recommended ratio of 250:1.

Westport is classified as a rural-fringe setting. In the 2019–2020 school year, 49% of students in the Jackson Valley School District were classified as economically disadvantaged, and 46% of students at Westport were economically disadvantaged. Students classified as economically disadvantaged were eligible for free or reduced-priced lunch, or other forms of financial assistance.

Other notable demographic information includes the following. In the 2019–2020 school year, 20% of the students in the Jackson View Valley School District had some form of disability, 15 students (or about 1% of the student population) were homeless, and another 1% of students were in foster care. At Westport Elementary, 11% of students had some form of disability, and about 2% of the student population were English Language Learners.

Area of Need

After researching demographics for Westport Elementary and the larger Jackson View Valley School District and consulting with my supervisor, I identified one area that seemed to negatively affect a large portion of the population: the economic disadvantage that nearly half of all students face. As is shown above, this is an area of need both at the elementary level and on the broader district level.

A large indicator of economic disadvantage in a school community is the percentage of students who qualify for free or reduced-price lunch. When a student is eligible for a free or reduced-price lunch, it means that their family has an annual household income below the federal poverty line. In New York State, the 2020–2021 income eligibility guidelines were updated. According to these guidelines—for a family of four—the annual household income must not exceed $48,470 to be eligible for reduced-price lunch and must not exceed $34,060 to be eligible for free lunch (New York State Office of Temporary and Disability Assistance, n.d.).

Although the Westport Elementary student and educator reports for the 2021–2020 and 2019–2020 academic years have not yet been published, the report from 2018–2019 shows a more in-depth breakdown of students receiving free vs. reduced-priced lunch. Of the 41% of students classified as economically disadvantaged in the 2018–2019 school year, 36% of students were receiving free lunch while 5% were receiving reduced-priced lunch. The Jackson Valley School District student and educator reports of years past show that this trend in breakdown has been consistent over the years—there is a significantly higher percentage of students receiving free lunch than there is receiving reduced-price lunch. Using the information from these reports, it can be determined that the families of a majority of the students classified as economically disadvantaged in the Jackson Valley School District and in Westport Elementary are earning below the federal poverty line.

There are several reasons why this is an area of need that should be addressed through school counseling curriculum, all revolving around holistically supporting the child. Students who come from economically disadvantaged backgrounds are more likely to face obstacles in the school setting than their peers, and these obstacles can result in poorer educational outcomes. Studies show that children from homes of low socioeconomic status (SES) develop academic skills more slowly than their more affluent peers and are more likely to drop out of school (American Psychological Association, 2014; Harless & Stoltz, 2018). This may stem from a lack of educational resources that parents are able to provide for their children, such as computers, books, and other related school supplies. These students are also more likely to struggle in developing a positive work identity, which impacts the development of their career identity down the road (Harless & Stoltz, 2018). The struggles they face throughout their time in K–12 schooling impact their ability to transition from school to work settings, and can limit their career opportunities and success. For all these reasons and more, this particular demographic of students should be receiving more school support—namely, a school counseling curriculum that is intentionally addressing their specific needs.

Although students at Westport Elementary have only recently begun their academic careers, it is crucial that inventions to support economically disadvantaged students begin at this age. When the obstacles mentioned above compound over time, the result is often significantly decreased educational success. By adding programs to the existing school counseling curriculum that more directly address the needs of this student population, Westport Elementary would be investing in these students' future and improving their likelihood of achieving academic and career success down the line.

SECTION TWO

The Multi-Tiered System of Supports (MTSS) is a framework utilized in K–12 schools to provide interventions that address the needs of students. The MTSS consists of three tiers of interventions that vary in size and scope. The first tier consists of interventions that serve the broad student population—the majority of the school. The second tier consists of more targeted interventions addressing a smaller group of students. The third and final tier contains highly targeted, specific interventions meant for the students whose needs are not being met at the first or second tier. The use of the MTSS often goes hand in hand with a comprehensive school counseling curriculum.

Tier 1

The tier 1 intervention for the proposed area of need is a series of professional development opportunities for teachers and other professional school staff that outline relevant community resources.

A. Professional Development for Teachers and School Staff

1. Outline of the delivery of services including action steps

Westport Elementary should establish mandatory training sessions for its teachers and staff to educate them on the available resources at the county level that can support their students. These resources should be specifically tailored to address the needs of economically disadvantaged students. Some resources that should be discussed in these training sessions include but aren't limited to: the Jackson Valley Community Action Committee, Family of Jackson Valley, the Jackson Valley Food Pantry, and RJVPCO (formerly Rural Jackson Valley Company).

These training sessions should also be created and delivered as professional development. Teachers are very busy and are often bogged down by mandatory meetings that have little to no importance to them. For this reason, they don't always have the time to attend informational meetings that do hold importance. If forced to attend yet another meeting, staff could feel upset or frustrated. But counting these training sessions as professional development opportunities would give additional meaning and purpose to staff who are already required to attend. Teachers holding professional certification in New York state are required to complete 175 hours of professional development every five years. Marketing these training sessions as professional development would increase staff cooperation and compliance. The content of the meetings is impactful, and staff are being compensated for their attendance.

The training sessions would be created through the school counselor's collaboration with outside resources. The school counselor would compile information on relevant community resources and should reach out to them directly to see if someone from some (if not all) of the organizations would be able to attend the meeting in person. The more involvement there is with each of the community organizations, the more beneficial the training sessions will be. And the more connected these organizations feel to the school system, the more likely they are to want to partner with the school in the future.

These training sessions should be offered at the start of each school year. As the years go on, the school counselor should make sure that all information originally gathered about the community organizations is still accurate and should also search to see if any new resources have become available. Making these training sessions annual would ensure that each staff member, whether new or returning, is knowledgeable about the community resources that can be beneficial to students and families. And making these training sessions mandatory guarantees that each staff member who is interacting with students is equipped with the knowledge they need to provide resources to students and families who may need it. Teachers in particular interact with students and families on the most consistent and frequent basis, so if each teacher is trained in this way, every student in the building will have a direct connection to someone who is prepared to provide them these invaluable resources.

2. Resources/stakeholders/partnerships required

- Teachers
- School administrators
- Other school staff
- Selected community resources

3. Intended outcomes/ways this intervention addresses the problem

The intended outcome of this intervention is that every single person in the school working with students will be fully equipped and prepared to provide resources when a student or family needs them. As mentioned above, this is especially important for teachers. Teachers work with their students on a daily basis, which is far more consistently and more often than a school counselor gets to see students. If a school counselor is prepared to give these resources (as they should be), it is beneficial to the students they see, but it does not necessarily help the students they don't see. On the other hand, every student in the building has a primary teacher who they spend most of their day with. These teachers also interact with parents and guardians on a far more regular basis than school counselors do. If these teachers are prepared to provide these resources, the dissemination of information about these resources will be far more widespread.

If students and families are being connected with these community resources more quickly and on a more regular basis, it reduces the likelihood that they will struggle with issues typically associated with families who are economically disadvantaged. They will have more consistent access to food and housing security, childcare, and educational resources. The more access families have to resources like these, the more stable the life of the student will be. Expected outcomes of this connection to resources include improved attendance, better academic achievement, and increased connection to the school community.

4. Methods of measuring effectiveness

One way of measuring effectiveness would be to deliver pre- and post-tests to faculty and staff to see if the professional development opportunities increased their knowledge about community resources, their confidence in speaking about these resources, and their likelihood to share these resources. If results showed that the answer to one or more of these measures was "yes," it would mean that they were better prepared to relay the information to students and families in need.

Another method would be to collect data from teachers and other school staff at the end of each quarter to see how many referrals they gave to students or families about the resources discussed in the training sessions. Ideally, each faculty member would be able to disseminate this information on a widespread level, but even if each faculty member gave one student or family a referral, it would be meaningful and worth the effort it took to put the intervention together.

One more method of measuring effectiveness would be to assess academic, attendance, and discipline data for students who received information about or referrals to these community resources. If academic or attendance outcomes improved, or discipline referrals declined, it could show a link between access to resources and overall student success.

Tier 2

The tier 2 intervention for the proposed area of need is the creation of a peer mentor program within the district that aims to serve the economically disadvantaged students at Westport who are struggling with academics, attendance, or discipline issues.

A. Peer Mentor Program

1. Outline of the delivery of services including action steps

Westport should create an after-school peer mentor program that pairs students at the elementary level with students in the intermediate school. The first step of this process would be creating a thorough description of the goals and intended outcomes of this program. The next step would be approaching the intermediate school counselor to discuss the proposed program and assess the degree to which they would be willing to help. The intermediate school counselor could provide recommendations and valuable insight as to which students would be well suited to mentoring. They could also help train/inform the intermediate school students of the rules that would come along with being a mentor, such as: schoolwork must always come first, any disciplinary issues would result in removal from the program, certain topics would be appropriate or inappropriate to discuss with the elementary school kids, etc. Next, the program would need approval from administrators to allow the partnership between the elementary school and the intermediate school.

Once these steps have been taken and the program is officially approved, it is time to select which students will participate in the program. At the elementary level, data should be used to determine which students could benefit the most from having a peer mentor. One way of making these decisions would be to pull information for students who have the lowest SES in the building. Once that list is generated, it can help to identify which of these students has struggled the most while in the school setting. This can be ascertained by looking at academic performance, school attendance, and disciplinary referrals. It can also be ascertained through firsthand observation and teacher referrals. The goal is to find the students who need additional support and who could benefit from having a positive peer influence in their life. Once these students have been selected, mentors from the intermediate school should be selected through collaboration with the intermediate school staff. Students selected at this level do not need to be struggling with the same issues as the elementary school students are, but they can be.

Once students have been selected, it is time to get parental approval. This approval could be obtained through a form sent home with the students or a phone call. For all students whose parents signed off on their participation in the mentor program, they can now begin. There should be one big meeting with all mentees and mentors where ground rules are covered, and then the pairs can break off and begin getting to know each other.

Since this is being offered as an after-school program, there should be some form of transportation provided to students who participate. Another step in the action plan would be to ensure that this transportation is available so that any student who wants to attend would be able to, regardless of their ability to have a guardian pick them up at the end of the day.

2. Resources/stakeholders/partnerships required

- Intermediate school (students and school counselor)
- Administrators
- Teachers (at both schools) for referrals
- Parents (for approval)
- Transportation department/office

3. Intended outcomes/ways this intervention addresses the problem

There are several intended outcomes for this intervention. First, that the elementary school students who are struggling will be able to build more social connections within the school system. Giving them something to look forward to will increase their desire to come to school, therefore improving their attendance. Once they are feeling connected to their mentor and the program, discipline referrals will likely go down as well, since they've been told they can only participate in the program while behaving well. Broadly speaking, another goal is to increase favorable attitudes towards school. Some secondary outcomes would benefit the intermediate school students. Being a role model for younger students is something that would likely improve their own performance and could give them an increased sense of pride and investment in school.

As described earlier, students from homes of a low SES are far more likely to struggle with attendance and academic achievement than their peers and are more likely to drop out of school altogether. Creating interventions like these at an elementary level will enable students to create positive ties to the school community and to hold more positive attitudes about schooling in general. These are factors which will hopefully set them up for greater success as they progress through their educational career.

4. Methods of measuring effectiveness

One method of measuring effectiveness would be to analyze academic, attendance, and discipline data for students involved in the program. If academics and attendance improve, or discipline referrals decrease, then the program could be linked to better school outcomes. Another way to measure effectiveness would be to have short check-ins with each student about their progress in and satisfaction with the program. Check-ins should occur twice in the first quarter, and then once in each quarter after. The counselor can ask questions like: How are you getting along with your mentor? Do you feel like your mentor cares about you? Do you think your mentor is being a good role model for you? Are you more excited to come to school since starting to meet with your mentor? Do you think you're doing better in school since meeting your mentor? These questions can help gather information about the students closeness with their mentor and how this relationship is affecting their daily life in school.

Tier 3

The tier 3 intervention for the proposed area of need is establishing a food backpack program such as Blessings in a Backpack. There are several backpack programs that exist to serve the same purpose, but for the sake of consistency, this section will focus on Blessings in a Backpack in particular.

A. Blessings in a Backpack Program

1. Outline of the delivery of services including action steps

Westport should begin a food backpack program for the children in school with the highest need. Blessings in a Backpack is a program that would pair well with this mission, as they "mobilize communities, individuals, and resources to provide food on the weekends for elementary school children across America who might otherwise go hungry" (Blessings in a Backpack, 2019).

The first step of creating a chapter of this program is to gain administrative support by meeting with the school principal and superintendent, explaining the purpose of the program, and explaining the benefits that it can have for student health, success, and performance. The next step is partnering with teachers, social workers, and other professional school staff who might have insight into which students are most in need. These can be students who frequently come to school hungry, whose parent(s) have recently lost their job, or who find themselves suddenly food- and/or housing-insecure. Whatever the reason for need may be, students identified should be of greatest need in the building.

The next step should be fundraising. A program manager from the national organization can pair with the school to determine what the budget should be, based on the number of students being served. In planning to raise money to assemble these backpacks, the school counselor should speak to administrators and see if there are any school funds that could be allocated to this project. Additionally, donations could be accepted, community fundraisers could be held, and grants could be applied for, depending on the total costs needed. Blessings in a Backpack has resources available to volunteers that can be helpful in this process, such as: grant proposals, fundraising tools, and templates for solicitation letters. They also provide the drawstring bags used to hold the food at no cost (Blessings in a Backpack, 2018).

Once the necessary funds have been obtained and the student recipients have been chosen, it will be time to find a food vendor to partner with. It could be the food provider used by the school, wholesale food suppliers, or a local food bank within the county. The vendor with best pricing and availability should be selected.

At this stage, the program is ready to begin. Backpacks can begin to be assembled and handed out on a weekly basis. In order to be respectful and discreet, staff and teachers can place backpacks in recipient student cubbies while they are out of the room. The first time backpacks are distributed, there should be an opt-out form for parents in the bag. The message will state that their child is eligible to receive these bags of non-perishable foods every Friday with no cost associated. If they wish to continue participating in the service they do not have to do anything, and if they wish to opt out, they only need to sign the form and return it to the school.

2. Resources/stakeholders/partnerships required

- Teachers, administrators, and other school professionals
- Blessings in a Backpack program manager
- Local food vendor
- Community members for funding support

3. Intended outcomes/ways this intervention addresses the problem

Food insecurity is a difficult reality that some students face. Studies have shown that food insecurity in young children has been linked to impaired academic performance, social skills, and overall development (Jyoti et al., 2005). While the federally funded free and reduced-price lunch program provided to students during the time they are in school is excellent, it is not always enough. If students do not have basic physiological needs being met at home, they can't be expected to obtain the same level of academic achievement as students for whom food insecurity is not a reality. For students not benefiting enough from the free or reduced-lunch program, or the other services outlined in tier 1 and tier 2, a more targeted intervention is necessary. Students should be able to access nutritional meals at all times—weekends included. The at-risk students eligible for this intervention would benefit from access to nutritional meals seven days a week. By removing this barrier from the student's life, it would help give them more equitable access to school success.

4. Methods of measuring effectiveness

One way the effectiveness of this intervention could be measured is through monitoring of student data for those who receive this service. Monthly or quarterly reports could be made on the attendance, academic, and discipline data for each student. If any or all of these areas improve, then the intervention could be considered effective. Another way to measure this would be to talk to the classroom teacher for each student, and see if they observe any notable change since the student began to receive this service. The change could be academic, social, or emotional in nature—anything that would contribute to the student's overall functioning and success in the school.

REFERENCES

American Psychological Association. (2014). *Education and socioeconomic status.* http://www.apa.org/pi/ses/

Blessings in a Backpack. (2018). *A volunteer's guide to leading a Blessings in a Backpack program site.* https://www.blessingsinabackpack.org/wp-content/uploads/2018/09/A-Volunteers-Guide-to-Leading-a-Blessings-in-a-Backpack-Program-Site-9-18.pdf

Blessings in a Backpack. (2019, January 25). *Start a program.* https://www.blessingsinabackpack.org/get-involved/start-a-program/

Harless, A. M., & Stoltz, K. B. (2018). Integrating narrative approaches with early recollections to provide career counseling with low-SES secondary students. *The Journal of Individual Psychology, 74*(1), 117–133. https://doi.org/10.1353/jip.2018.0007

Jyoti, D. F., Frongillo, E. A, & Jones, S. J. (2005). Food insecurity affects school children's academic performance, weight gain, and social skills. *The Journal of Nutrition, 135*(12), 2831–2839. https://doi.org/10.1093/jn/135.12.2831

New York State Office of Temporary and Disability Assistance. (n.d.). *School breakfast and lunch programs.* https://otda.ny.gov/workingfamilies/schoollunch.asp

PART II

Practical Applications

CHAPTER 5

K–2 Interventions

T ake a step back into your K–2 years. What do you remember about school? What excited you? What upset you? What seemed relevant and what seemed amiss? What were your earliest thoughts on what you wanted to be when you grew up? What influenced those thoughts? What barriers were in place that discouraged exploration? Did you always feel heard and represented in school? How about at home or in the community? What messages did the community send you?

If any of those things remain salient in your mind, imagine how students in the K–2 years are influenced in their thinking about themselves and the world of work today. With constant media in their lives and societal challenges due to the COVID-19 pandemic, children are experiencing complex challenges on the road to finding and becoming who they are. Would it be wise to ignore these salient realities when engaging in district-wide career development? The truth is: Career development is a lifelong process, even if academic development is not, and children go through their early schooling years developing harmful impressions that may solidify and become concrete if they are not addressed and processed in a safe and helpful way. Think about a kindergarten student in today's world. What types of experiences and school programming are necessary to make their K–2 years meaningful in terms of career development? What types of information, experiences, and processing could empower a child to make sense of it all, and to engage in and see relevance in their learning? These questions must guide career development efforts in the early elementary years.

This second section of this textbook delves into specific approaches to implement across the K–12 years. Before diving into more concrete interventions, however, a school counselor must consider how interventions are established and maintained. Intentional and integrated career development does not entail simply piece-mealing various interventions together when the counselor sees fit. After considering the dynamics presented in previous chapters, a school counselor should begin constructing a comprehensive curriculum to ensure that the intended programming and interventions are organized, have a logical flow, and are appropriate for the students being served.

Establishing a Curriculum

School counseling is programmatic, meaning that each intervention and activity a school counselor participates in should be consistently evaluated and updated to best meet the needs of students (Stone & Dahir, 2015). If a school counseling program had completely different interventions and programs each year, it would be impossible to evaluate the effectiveness of these approaches across multiple years. Further, jumping to completely new interventions ignores the reality that previous programming can be altered and improved upon. A comprehensive curriculum includes all major programs across the academic, social-emotional, and career domains (ASCA, 2017). A school counselor should know what groups are being hosted each semester, for how long, when and where the groups will be held, and which students qualify for each group. A school counselor should be well aware of the schedule of special events, such as career days or FAFSA nights, and supplement these programs with guidance lessons, field trips, or guest speakers related to the topics. A school counselor should have a comprehensive guidance curriculum prepared in which lessons build upon previous ones, link to programming, and effectively transition to the curriculum students will experience in the next academic year. As stated in previous chapters, this cannot be done if the counselor is not familiar with the history of the school, the dynamics of the students and community, the cultures and attitudes encompassing these facets, and an asset map of potential school and community partners. Once the foundational information has been acquired, however, a school counselor should set their mind to laying out their counseling curriculum for the following school year.

When you consider a comprehensive career development curriculum, what aspects come to mind? First and foremost, we must understand the variety of interventions we can utilize as school counselors. School counselors provide individual and group counseling, guidance lessons, field trips, guest speaker events, leadership of schoolwide initiatives, facilitation of after-school activities, family and community nights, informational outreach, resource coordination, and systemic advocacy. A shorter way to think about this might be: 1) Counseling interventions; 2) Guidance lesson curriculum; 3) In-school events; and 4) Community events. These four categories can include the above-mentioned interventions and provide an easier way to organize all of the initiatives planned.

A school counselor can consider which individual counseling methods they will use throughout the year. A high school counselor might consider what resources (websites, brochures, referrals) they might use with their junior class for the next school year. They might also consider the frequency of when they meet with students individually for college and career planning as well as when these meetings occur. With this information in hand, the school counselor can plan specific interventions with these students (such as having them look up occupations on O*NET, take a career inventory, or search colleges on CollegeBoard), and give students homework assignments to be reviewed during their next scheduled meeting. Having these individual counseling sessions and assorted resources built into the schedule in advance allows for more intentionality, follow-up, and follow-through.

Similarly, the school counselor can have all career development exploration groups planned out, including their referral process, curriculum, length, location, and the time of year they will be held. The school counselor might intentionally schedule these types of groups early in the school year, since they are aware they planned for the next year's scheduling meeting to occur later in the school year. This would allow the groups to have an impact before students have to select their path for the following year. Here, individual counseling works together with group counseling to create a more intentional flow to the overall approach.

By dividing intended interventions into these categories and approximating when they will occur and for how long, a school counselor can better draw connections between interventions that complement and build upon one another. Fitting these interventions together, like pieces of a puzzle, can build the foundation of a career development program and allow for continuous re-evaluation.

Let's imagine that a school counselor is creating a career exploration guidance unit on the STEM fields. The school counselor knows a local engineer who is willing to give a presentation and interactive demo on mechanical engineering to their students. The school counselor has aligned this special event with the flow of their curriculum for the benefit of their students. The counselor can work the presentation into their lessons and have their lessons inform the type of questions the students ask the presenter.

The Guidance Lesson Curriculum

The overall guidance programming curriculum should also include within it a guidance lesson curriculum. The curriculum may lay out which units occur when, with what grades, and for how long, but the guidance curriculum itself should include individual lesson plans and resources. This curriculum should be constructed by the school counselor, borrowed from an appropriately used professional source such as a reputable curriculum or one available through a state department of education, or some combination of the two in which the school counselor takes sections of curricula and combines them with their own unique efforts. Key considerations are grade level, school and community dynamics, and the amount of time allocated to the school counselor for lessons.

Classroom lessons are necessary for comprehensive K–12 career development (ASCA, 2017). If limited time is allocated for classroom lessons, the school counselor should advocate for more time, using research literature proving the value of this intervention. For example, an integrated review of career development literature by Falco and Steen (2018) found that students using career development curricula that allowed them to explore the world of careers and apply academic concepts directly to work were more motivated to accomplish short- and long-term academic goals. Career development curricula ease the transition of students to post-secondary education and are especially impactful for low-income and minority students, who may have had little access to this comprehensive style of education (Bryan et al., 2011). Mariani and colleagues (2016) found that these types of interventions promote a deeper exploration of self and career and increase student motivation to pursue higher education later in life. Falco and Steen (2018) also found evidence that career development programming was more effective in assisting educational and career outcomes when implemented earlier in the schooling years (such as the primary and elementary years) and comprehensively built upon in the following years. These types of literature reviews, as well as individual studies, can provide a wealth of evidence supporting how a guidance lesson curriculum along with supporting programs will benefit outcomes throughout the district.

Career development curricula should be not only month to month but year to year, grade to grade, and building to building (Eliason et al., 2019). Imagine the benefits for a student who transitions from one school building to another and has their career development curriculum pick up where it left off. The student can take previous knowledge and experiences further, engaging in a deeper exploration of self and the world. All too often, students receive inconsistent career development across different buildings in the same school district. Imagine a student's disappointment or disengagement if they cover the same content again in the same manner, or if some aspect of career development they were excited about is never followed up on.

Through yearly meetings, a school counselor can partner with other counselors in the district to develop a lesson and programming curriculum that intentionally builds a pathway, collects valuable outcome data to inform programming, and fulfills state career portfolio requirements, all while motivating students to achieve academically. The work is challenging to complete, due to school counselors having high ratios and demands for their positions (Goodman-Scott, et al., 2018); however, the preventive work would be a worthy investment, saving schools time and effort in the long run and producing more beneficial outcomes for all. Once established, the efforts should begin during the very beginning of schooling, in the K–2 years.

K–2 Interventions

A common critique of career development programming in the K–2 years is that these children do not have the capacity to decide what jobs they want and will not be making the decision for a long time, and that therefore the effort is wasted. Career development, however, is a life-long process entailing views of self, the world, and ability, impacted by outlook and experience throughout life (Magnuson & Starr, 2000). Students who drop out without finishing high school may have been disengaged from school since as early as third grade (McWhirter et al., 1994). By the time students reach fifth grade, they have already developed the conceptual framework for understanding job requirements and begun making decisions about what is appropriate for them and their future (Blackhurst et al., 2003; Gottfredson, 2005). In a major review of the career development literature by Hartung and colleagues (2005), the authors found that: 1) Children can discriminate between occupations based on gender by age four; 2) Career aspirations based upon stereotypes tend to grow and remain stable throughout the elementary school years; 3) Childhood stereotypes included impressions of jobs based on perceived prestige, role, function, value, and for whom the jobs were appropriate; 4) Career development is affected by differences in cultural group norms and family socioeconomic status; and 5) Children from minority and low-SES backgrounds aspired to careers with less prestige and careers that required less education than students from white and higher-SES backgrounds due to experiences of racism, a lack of role models, and biased media representation.

Taken in sum: It is clear that children *are* making choices and sorting career options during the K–2 years. Even if they have not explicitly made decisions about their career choice, the social influences within society have impacted what options they believe are appropriate for themselves, while schooling experiences have determined how willing they are to use school as a method of life advancement. Knowing this, it is imperative that a school counselor begin addressing these dynamics within career development during the K–2 years.

Intervention Philosophy

Elementary career development must be developmentally appropriate (Akos et al., 2011). As children enter school, they are beginning to more concretely understand their relationship to self, others, and the world (Gottfredson, 2005). These students come into school new to structured learning but have wonderful ideas and impressions about academic content and even the world of work. During the elementary years, career development efforts should focus on building an awareness of self and the world of work (Akos et al., 2011).

For example, many kindergarten students can quickly answer the question, "What do you want to be when you grow up?" It is important to consider that the child is engaging in the world when they answer this question. They may also be engaging in fantasy thinking, relating to a concept through their use of play and imagination, as it is so natural for children to do (Gottfredson, 2005). The children may relate to a sports or media figure who they look up to, or emulate the career choice of their parents, imagining themselves in these roles. This style of thinking is related to the developing concept of self, including preferences, likes, dislikes, interests, hobbies, and aspirations. These critical facets of identity can be explored through a helpful career development lens within guidance lessons and programming experiences.

Elementary career lessons can also encourage a strengths-based view of individual talents and preferences, allowing children to explore who they are and why along with how, in the long run, these aspirations can tie into their career path (Niles & Harris-Bowlsbey, 2013). In addition to career development curriculum spanning the elementary years, events such as career days, where local workers and graduates of the school visit to present about their profession, can inspire students to consider possibilities, break stereotypes, and see what types of jobs are available in their community and beyond (Beale & Williams, 2000). School-counselor-organized field trips, to local businesses or institutions such as the hospital, can open students to the myriad of professions available in local spaces as well as the diversity of skill sets required for a workplace to function (Beale, 2003). Partnerships with universities expose elementary children to the world of higher education while also strengthening the school with resources, such as career development or mental health professionals in training (Knight, 2015). All of these approaches can be considered within three developmentally appropriate domains: exploration of interests, exploration of abilities, and exploration of careers.

Exploration of Interests

Across the K–2 years, children are choosing and developing the activities they like to engage in, alone and with others. During these pivotal years, children attach themselves to sports, video games, music, movies, television shows, and hobbies. From a Social Cognitive Career Theory (SCCT) perspective, these interests come with feedback from others including friends, family, and school faculty (Lent et al., 2002). By exploring how interests might align to what people do later in life, children can begin constructing the bridge from fantasy thinking to grounded self-exploration.

The Missouri Department of Education (MDE) provides an excellent online K–12 guidance lesson curriculum covering academic, personal-social, and career lessons (MDE, 2021). This comprehensive curriculum includes complete lesson plans and resources, all aligned to the ASCA mindsets and state career standards. Examination of this resource, and consideration of adopting lessons within this curriculum, is a must for any school counselor building a new curriculum.

An example of how an exploration of interests is covered within this framework comes from the MDE's Kindergarten Career Development Unit. The first lesson of the progressively building curriculum is titled "These are a Few of my Favorite and not so Favorite Things to do." The lesson objectives are for students to identify things they like to do at school and at home and also to identify things they dislike doing at school and at home. The lesson involves a puppet show dialogue expressing that all of us have things we like to do and things we don't, and how that is completely healthy. The dialogue brings students in with discussion questions around what people like to do at home and school and why. After this interactive period, students draw pictures on a provided worksheet of what they like and dislike doing, at home and school. Afterwards, students discuss what they drew and why in a sharing circle. The school counselor is tasked with validating the students' ideas and linking them to the concept that we all have different likes and dislikes, and that these things will probably change throughout our lives as we try new things. While this lesson may seem simple in composition, it is clear that it is laying the foundation for more in-depth exploration of self as related to the world of work. This is proven in subsequent lessons, which engage the student in analyzing how adults may like and dislike different things and how this might relate to the type of job they have. Later lessons in the curriculum emphasis how there are different career paths and how people sometimes choose different paths based upon what they like and dislike. Here, an exploration of interests is tangibly linked to academics and career at an early stage in schooling, allowing further introspection, growth, and development in later years.

Exploration of interests across the K–2 level can be accomplished in several ways. Guidance lessons can focus on a student representing who they are, what they like, and why in discussion, through art, or even through classroom role-plays. Students can discuss why they like these things and what experiences may have influenced them. Lessons can link to direct activities that occur in school (such as reading) and why students like or dislike it. These interests can be bridged to adults in the students' lives, including teachers. For example, a meaningful conversation could emerge when asking students what interests their classroom teacher has and what subjects in school they had to be interested in to become a teacher. School counselors can also offer themselves as a direct example. While student answers may not be 100% accurate, engaging in this creative thinking will open their minds to the linkage between self and the world of work.

Programmatic experiences can include career day events or classroom speakers who share not only about their job, but also about the interests they had growing up which linked them to their career. They can discuss what school subjects are needed to do the job and how the job remains interesting to them every day. This type of prompted presentation can ensure that the speaker represents a career possibility to students while also making the linkage between interests and career more concrete. The same model can be used on class field trips to local places of business. Older students within the building or district can be guest presenters, talking about how their interests have influenced their academic path and what they are considering for future careers. This type of role modeling can encourage young students to be more interactive with the meaning of education and how it can best align for their lives.

As students progress in lessons across the K–2 years, these experiences should move from a more general exploration (what are interests, what am I interested in, what are others interested in) to a more specific examination of self-interests as related to academic and career pursuits. Lessons should build upon previous experiences and encourage students to examine how their specific interests may align to careers one day. This can be done through concrete alignment of interests to career families (such as those in the RIASEC model), lesson assignments where students align careers in the community to the career families and explain their potential interest in each, and career fairs with representatives separated into specific career clusters.

As students move from fantasy to more concrete thinking, conversations around the social dynamics framing their interests and career choices should occur in lessons. Children can discriminate career choices based upon perceived racial, gender, and class appropriateness as early as the elementary years (Blackhurst et al., 2003; Gottfredson, 2005). Students should be empowered to resist and shed the negative influence of social barriers in their pursuit of holistic academic and career success. Lessons inviting a sharing of the feedback students have received about their interests from various sources, and how this made them feel, can allow for a deeper processing of relevant social dynamics. Students can explore the influence of family, teachers, and friends and experiences with racism, sexism, and classism on their likes, interests, and career aspirations. Similarly, guest speakers from select marginalized communities can share how their interests or paths were influenced by the views of others, including racism, sexism, or classism. These role models can also open the door for students to engage in meaningful sharing of their own. These efforts allow for the true lived experience of students to be honored, shared, and processed in a supportive atmosphere, in contrast to curriculum that ignores these crucial realities and allows children to make meaning of them solely on their own. Further, this lays the foundation for students to more critically examine the influence of systemic oppression on their community and society. These experiences can be further built upon through other educational and experiential initiatives throughout their schooling in the district, empowering students to be advocates for themselves and for marginalized populations.

It is critical to empower families to process career development with their children. By sending resources home, including summaries of lessons, experiences, or completed student worksheets, the elementary school counselor can involve parents in the career development process. Parental influence has a major impact on children's career choices (Hutchison et al.,2016); therefore, it is crucial that the school counselor loop them into the process as a partner in career development education. This approach and those outlined above should also be applied to the other major domains of career development, exploration of abilities and career paths.

Exploration of Abilities

Children begin developing a perspective on what they are good at and what they should pursue before and during their elementary school years (Bandura et al., 2001). Children who mentally disengage from school often feel they don't have the capability to succeed in school or that the system is stacked against them (McWhirter et al., 1994). A key transition point occurs as students move away from the primary years (K–2) and toward the intermediate years (3–5) where fantasy thinking gives way to understood concrete realities about job educational and skill requirements (Blackhurst et al., 2003). During these pivotal years, educational sorting occurs, whereby students determine what options they will keep their minds open to and which are dismissed as not applicable or not achievable (Blackhurst et al., 2003). It is pivotal to introduce exploration around abilities earlier than these years, to counteract any misinformation or stereotypes students have encountered. For example, harmful stereotypes related to race or gender may convince students they do not have the ability to succeed in certain subjects or fields. The school counselor is in a prime position to introduce lessons and activities surrounding self-efficacy before these negative influences have a deeply rooted impact.

Self-efficacy is the principal belief centered on one's capability to organize and execute actions related to goal attainment (Bandura & National Institute of Mental Health, 1986; Lent et al., 2002). These beliefs are not fixed traits or mindsets but rather are dynamic and consistently interacting with other personal, social, and environmental factors (Lent et al., 2002). More success in a role leads to belief in the ability to accomplish similar tasks, establishing higher self-efficacy and career aspirations (Lent et al., 2002). A school counselor can encourage the exploration of abilities in a manner similar to how they encourage the exploration of student interests.

Guidance lessons should focus on students representing what they like to do and feel confident doing, in and outside of school. For example, a student who is confident in their musical ability might also be excited to go to music class. This student will likely understand the connection between feeling good at musical activities and pursuing a job requiring these interests and talents. Even during the K–2 years, children can understand the linkage between confidence in their abilities and what preferences they choose to pursue. These lessons can offer important discussions around what impacts self-efficacy. A prompting question could ask students: How do they know they are good at something? What experiences do they have receiving feedback? What did that feedback feel like? Is feedback from others always accurate? In a safe environment, students can share their thoughts on how social feedback may have influenced what they feel confident doing. This segues well into needed discussions on media portrayal and systemic racism within society. With a foundation of this type of critical thinking established early, the comprehensive K–12 curriculum can become more advanced as students progress through their schooling.

Programmatic experiences such as speakers and field trips can offer an experiential component, where students feel excitement and accomplishment through completing a career-associated task. For example, a speaker telling students about the career of engineering could assist them through an engineering challenge such as supporting a certain amount of weight using supplies like toilet paper tubes. The speaker could work with the school counselor to have the lesson be developmentally appropriate while allowing students to engage in applied thinking. These experiences may show students that in a team setting they each bring skills to the table and can utilize their skills to one day obtain careers which may interest them. Skills necessary for certain jobs can be explored throughout lessons emphasizing an exploration of careers as well.

Exploration of Careers

The Missouri Department of Education provides an excellent example of an integrated curriculum bridging the domains of career exploration with exploration of interests and exploration of abilities. One of their first-grade units is a two-lesson series exploring jobs students like to do at home and school and what career paths exist in their community (MDE, 2021). The intentionality is clearly present, with the first lesson demonstrating what interests and skills the students have while the second lesson allows them to explore what careers exist, using local examples, and which of them the students may be interested in based upon their self-exploration (MDE, 2021). The first lesson covers identifying both interests and strengths while also prompting the students to consider why people have jobs at home and school and what would happen if we did not have jobs. The sharing circle model is once again used to allow students to share and process their perspectives. The second lesson uses a career paths mini-poster to identify six potential career fields. The paths are listed as business, creative, nature, fixing & building, technology, and helping, all of which align with a corresponding RIASEC domain. The counselor is to prompt students to think about the fact that they actually started their career path when they began kindergarten, and that they have developed skills and interests all along the way. Students then discuss and evaluate what they have become interested and disinterested in and why. The students are then broken up into six groups, with each group tasked with drawing local careers that align with their group's assigned career path. In the discussion portion, students share their drawings and identify what skills the job requires (MDE, 2021).

This lesson is an excellent example of integration at the first-grade level. Because the concept of career paths has been introduced, any future lessons focusing on interests and abilities can refer back to this knowledge. The local focus is also a wonderful way to offer a tangible exploration of career options. Students are much more likely to make sense of the relationship between skills, academics, and career by using examples they encounter in their everyday lives. Exploration of these dynamics can even begin with the school and community as examples, with students pondering what careers exist in the school and what skills are required. Students can further share the careers of their families and engage in similar analyses.

Field trips that take students around the local community to identify jobs help students realize how the world of work is alive around them (Knight, 2015). Walking through a local section of town and prompting students to identify jobs and how they fit into specific career paths can empower them to think more concretely about the work roles in their community. Specific places of work can be chosen as stops on this field trip, allowing students to interact with businesses, tradespeople, and professionals, all of whom can serve as role models and future job-shadowing supervisors. These specific experiences should be worked into the processing that occurs in guidance lessons and programming, allowing for a deeper dive into career development.

It is important to consider how the school counselor introduces the world of work to students. By processing what children see and interact with daily and linking these examples to career fields and other previously unknown options, the school counselor helps create a foundation of knowledge into which explorations of interests and skills can be integrated. Classroom lessons, activities, and experiences all provide more exposure to children, allowing new social feedback messages to develop while potentially countering the influence of harmful stereotypes. This work can go a step further by integrating career development not only into the guidance curriculum, but also into the academic curriculum.

Academic Integration

Let us return to the example at the beginning of the book. Let's imagine you are a student sitting in a classroom and you see no relevance between the academic lessons and your life. Why would you be inspired to give your best effort in school? A meta-analysis by Evans and Burck (1992) found that elementary students' academic achievement rose when it was paired with integrated career development interventions throughout their schooling. Researchers have also found that collaboration with teachers to integrate career education into the classroom results in higher career aspirations and academic achievement. Students who feel a sense of relevance in their education may be more hopeful and driven to pursue future academic and career endeavors, empowering them to gain the most from their schooling experience (Akos et al., 2011).

Why should the academic curriculum be separate from the reality of the school counseling curriculum? Imagine if the school counselor coordinated with the classroom teachers to create intentional and integrated lessons which build off of one another. For example, an academic lesson covering scientific principles can integrate what types of careers use this knowledge. At the K–2 level, lessons focusing on animals could mention the types of careers that work with animals. Guidance lessons could allow students to explore interests, abilities, and careers related to the animals and the types of science being learned in their class. Guest speakers or field trips could be planned related to this pairing as well. For example, while learning about animals, a guest speaker who works with animals (such as a veterinarian, game warden, or zookeeper) could visit the school and speak to the students. Instead of pulling students in various directions, the school counselor and classroom teacher can reinforce important principles and jointly help students find relevance and connection to academic learning.

A classroom teacher could also offer examples of careers related to the subjects students are learning. The school counselor could help the classroom teacher draft worksheets or activities providing examples of careers in the chosen academic field. Through these activities, students could understand how reading, writing, spelling, science, math, art, music, and computer literacy are integral to so many careers. Word problems within these classes could make explicit mention of the real-world utility of these academic principles in careers. Writing prompts could focus on students imagining what they want to be when they grow up and what interests and skills they will use to achieve their goal. With a little planning and collaboration, the school staff could lay the foundations for a truly comprehensive K–12 career development experience. Worksheets and reports from these experiences could be gathered for the sake of program data analysis and for the sake of inclusion in individual student career development portfolios—collections that easily could be used to prove to the state that the school is meeting career education standards. This means the school is not only meeting its requirements but also helping students understand that academic work links directly to future goals, hopefully inspiring them to learn, grow, flourish, and achieve.

CHAPTER SUMMARY

This chapter presented a model of career development beginning in the K–2 years. Integrated career development curriculum begins with a comprehensive guidance curriculum spanning years and school buildings. Career development curriculum includes guidance lessons, programmatic experiences, outreach to parents at home, and field trips. These activities should focus on developing students' awareness of their interests and abilities and of the types of careers available to them, at home and in the world. An analysis of social dynamics and societal oppression (such as discrimination, biases, and stereotypes) should be integrated during this period of career education. Integration of career programming into the academic curriculum offers a way to further reinforce the relevance of education in students' lives and springboard their career development early in their schooling.

TABLE OF KEY TERMS

Term	Definition
O*NET	A website run by the United States Department of Labor that includes up-to-date employment and training facts, statistics, descriptions, and job search tools. Accessible from: https://www.onetonline.org
Collegeboard	A non-profit organization that provides students access to standardized test preparation, scholarship applications, college search tools, and college application materials Accessible from: www.collegeboard.org
RIASEC	Realistic, Investigative, Artistic, Social, Enterprising, and Conventional. These Holland Code categories align with the interests and skills of current workers in various occupational fields (Holland, 1997).
Self-efficacy	Self-efficacy is the principal belief centered on one's capability to organize and execute actions related to goal attainment (Bandura & National Institute of Mental Health, 1986; Lent et al., 2002).

REFLECTION EXERCISES

Reflection exercises are designed either to be done individually within the reading or to be used as group discussion questions within the classroom setting. A series of reflection questions will be presented at the end of every chapter.

1. Consider how a guidance lesson curriculum focusing on student interests may grow and evolve in the K–2 years.

   a. Plan a lesson for the K level.

   b. Build upon this lesson and tailor a new one for the first-grade level.

   c. Build upon this new lesson and tailor a new one for the second-grade level.

   d. Consider what stakeholders you'd partner with, how, and what data you'd collect to evaluate the effectiveness of these lessons.

2. Design an academic lesson (using a core emphasis such as reading, writing, math, or science) that incorporates career exploration.

   a. How would the lesson engage students?

   b. How would the lesson link students to the world of career?

3. How comfortable are you discussing sociocultural dynamics (such as racism and gender identity) with K–2 students?

   a. What influences your comfort level?

   b. How do you see yourself incorporating these realities into career development?

   c. How do you evaluate whether or not your career development approaches are culturally appropriate for your student population at the K–2 level?

4. Locate a K–2 career development intervention online. Evaluate it in the following ways:

   a. Is the intervention aligned to school counseling ethics, philosophy, and national/state standards?

   b. Is the intervention developmentally appropriate for this age level?

   c. Does the intervention cover the exploration of interests, abilities, and the world of work?

   d. How could the intervention be improved or further integrated into a comprehensive career development programming framework?

CASE STUDY

Amy is an Asian American cisgender female second-grade student in your K–2 school building. During a career development guidance lesson, Amy shares that she is interested in careers that require skills in math because other students have told her, "Asians are good at math." Amy has also seen online videos that perpetuate this belief. Amy reasons that she should pursue careers she would be good at, so she's been trying harder during math class. During your class discussion, it is made apparent that other students have encountered this stereotype and believe it. This discussion prompts other students to ponder what they might be good at based upon their racial backgrounds. Your school is composed primarily of students of East Asian, European, and Latin American descent, and the stereotype about Asians and math appears pervasive across each group. You know that historically the school had a smaller Asian American population and that it has grown within the last decade to be about the same size as the other major demographic groups. As the sole school counselor in the building, you are tasked with addressing this career development dynamic and developing a comprehensive framework for the rest of the second-grade year. As the school counselor, consider the following questions:

1. What additional information would be helpful in your conceptualization of the situation? How would you obtain it?

2. How would you address Amy in the moment, during a classroom lesson? How would you address the class as this type of discussion occurred?

3. Would you take an individual approach with Amy? Would you solely utilize classroom or schoolwide approaches? Would you consider both?

4. What types of interventions would you create for students to process these dynamics related to stereotypes, ethnic background, and career choice?

5. Consider how you would create a guidance lesson related to this. How many lessons would it be? When would this lesson curriculum begin? What approaches and experiences would you incorporate into it?

References

Akos, P., Charles, P., Orthner, D., & Cooley, V. (2011). Teacher perspectives on career-relevant curriculum in middle school. *RMLE Online, 34*(5), 1–9.

American School Counselor Association. (2017). *The school counselor and career development.* https://schoolcounselor.org/Standards-Positions/PositionStatements/ASCA-Position-Statements/The-School-Counselor-and-Career-Development

Bandura, A., Barbaranelli, C., Caprara, G. V., & Pastorelli, C. (2001). Self-efficacy beliefs as shapers of children's aspirations and career trajectories. *Child Development, 72*(1), 187–206.

Bandura, A., & National Institute of Mental Health. (1986). *Social foundations of thought and action: A social cognitive theory.* Prentice-Hall.

Beale, A. V. (2003). It takes a team to run a restaurant: Introducing elementary students to the interrelatedness of occupations. *Journal of Career Development, 29*(3), 211–220.

Beale, A. V., & Williams, J. C. (2000). The anatomy of an elementary school career day. *Journal of Career Development, 26*(3), 205–213.

Blackhurst, A. E., Auger, R. W., & Wahl, K. H. (2003). Children's perceptions of vocational preparation requirements. *Professional School Counseling, 7*(2), 58–67.

Bryan, J., Moore-Thomas, C., Day-Vines, N. L., & Holcomb-McCoy, C. (2011). School counselors as social capital: The effects of high school college counseling on college application rates. *Journal of Counseling & Development, 89*(2), 190–199.

Eliason, G. T., Lepore, M., Samide, J. L., & Patrick, J. (Eds.). (2019). *Career development across the lifespan: Counseling for community, schools, higher education, and beyond.* IAP.

Evans, J. H., Jr., & Burck, H. D. (1992). The effects of career education interventions on academic achievement: A meta-analysis. *Journal of Counseling & Development, 71*(1), 63–68.

Goodman-Scott, E., Sink, C. A., Cholewa, B. E., & Burgess, M. (2018). An ecological view of school counselor ratios and student academic outcomes: A national investigation. *Journal of Counseling & Development, 96*(4), 388–398.

Gottfredson, L. S. (2005). Applying Gottfredson's theory of circumscription and compromise in career guidance and counseling. In S. D. Brown & R. W. Lent (Eds.), *Career development and counseling: Putting theory and research to work* (pp. 71–100). John Wiley & Sons.

Hartung, P. J., Porfeli, E. J., & Vondracek, F. W. (2005). Child vocational development: A review and reconsideration. *Journal of Vocational Behavior, 66*(3), 385–419.

Holland, J. L. (1997). *Making vocational choices: A theory of vocational personalities and work environments* (3rd ed.). Psychological Assessment Resources.

Knight, J. L. (2015). Preparing elementary school counselors to promote career development: Recommendations for school counselor education programs. *Journal of Career Development, 42*(2), 75–85.

Lent, R. W., Brown, S. D., & Hackett, G. (2002). Social cognitive career theory. In D. Brown (Ed.), *Career choice and development* (4th ed., pp. 255–311). Jossey-Bass.

Magnuson, C. S., & Starr, M. F. (2000). How early is too early to begin life career planning? The importance of the elementary school years. *Journal of Career Development, 27*(2), 89–101.

McWhirter, J. J., McWhirter, B. T., McWhirter, A. M., & McWhirter, E. H. (1994). High- and low-risk characteristics of youth: The five Cs of competency. *Elementary School Guidance & Counseling, 28*(3), 188–196.

Missouri Department of Education. (2021). *School counseling curriculum.* https://dese.mo.gov/college-career-readiness/school-counseling/curriculum

Niles, S. G., & Harris-Bowlsbey, J. (2013). *Career development interventions in the 21st century.* Pearson.

Career Goals Lesson Plan

Lindsay Weber, MS

Practical Resources are examples of work school counselors can do in applying the concepts of this textbook to their own school districts. They are also an example of assignments counselor educators could assign to their students. All practical resources were contributed by school counselors in training working toward their master's degrees.

Instructor: Lindsay Weber
Target Audience: Students grades K–2
School Counselor Mindsets and Behavior:

M4. Every student should have access to a comprehensive school counseling program; M 5. Belief in using abilities to their fullest to achieve high-quality results and outcomes; M 2. Self-confidence in ability to succeed
B-LS 9. Gather evidence and consider multiple perspectives to make informed decisions
B-LS 1. Demonstrate critical-thinking skills to make informed decisions
B-SS 1. Use effective oral and written communication skills and listening skills
B-SS 6: Use effective collaboration and cooperation skills

LEARNING OBJECTIVE(S)/COMPETENCIES

Students will: After group discussion and activity, students will be able to identify various careers and their jobs/roles in society as well as gain insight into the daily activities of each occupation. Students will be able to identify careers new to them as well as identify which careers interest them and fit with their personality.

Students will: All students will be able to identify multiple careers as well as discuss the future careers they might want to pursue, through discussion and bingo games. Students will also be able to match careers with their descriptions.

MATERIALS

1. Career Bingo cards (squares containing names and pictures of each career in each square and free space, set up like a typical bingo card)
2. Bingo markers
3. Prizes for winners

PROCEDURE: DESCRIBE HOW YOU WILL ...

Introduce

- Introduce the importance of thinking about careers and about what they might want to do when they grow up.
- Have students go around and discuss if they know what they want to be when they grow up.
- Initiate discussion on what they might want to do, and possibly on why, and/or on what people in their family do.

Communicate Lesson Objective

- We are going to match careers with their job description and picture and discuss careers of interest as well as new careers learned.

Teach Content

- Discuss the different jobs and what their different roles are. Talk about careers that you have been interested in, as well as about what family may do and if that influenced decisions.

Practice Content

- After discussing with students different careers and their roles, distribute bingo boards and pieces.
- Read the description of each job and see if the students can match it to the picture.
- Help students identify these jobs on the bingo board, based on a description of their role, and go over each one.
- When a student wins, they may come up and receive a prize.
- Discuss with each student a job they may be interested in and why.

Summarize

- Discuss the importance of there being different types of jobs and have students describe some of the jobs that were their favorite.
- Summarize the different jobs and discuss the unlimited options of the working world.
- Post-test: Can each student name and describe a new career?

Close: Questions and answers period.

DATA COLLECTION PLAN

Participation Data
Anticipated number of students: 15, from kindergarten through second grade.

Planned Length of Lesson: 45 minutes.

Mindsets and Behaviors Data

- Pre-activity discussion of knowledge
- Post-activity discussion of what they have learned
- Observation of who was able to correctly identify careers during the activity

Outcome Data

Achievement: Students will have to show they paid attention through discussion of careers in class. Each student will have to remember one career and what they do and share at the end of the activity.

CHAPTER 6

3–5 Interventions

ake yourself back to childhood, specifically somewhere between third and fifth grade. Picture a conversation with an adult, or a setting in which adults were conversing. Can you recall a time during this period where adults spoke down to you? Perhaps they treated you as though you were younger than you were, assuming you had little to no knowledge of concepts you thoroughly understood. Perhaps they assumed you had little to no exposure to certain types of media, ideas, culture, or slang terms. Perhaps they spoke to each other as if you weren't even there, brazenly assuming you couldn't understand their lightly coded language or references. Can you picture a situation like this?

How did it feel?

For so many children, the answer is: alienating. As we transition through the years from third through fifth grade we are exposed to more social and cultural elements in life. This has increased even more now, due to digital culture and smartphones. Children are constantly exposed to ideas, and as they age they more concretely understand what is going on, why, and what these things might mean. Unfortunately, rather than having the opportunity to process these things, all too often children are dismissed as lacking the capacity to understand the things they are commonly grappling with.

Career development is no different. The K–2 years may be marked by imaginative and fantasy-based thinking, but as children change developmentally and experience more of the world, their impressions about self and the world of work solidify. This solidification is why, by the fifth grade, most children have concrete impressions of which jobs are more desirable due to prestige, gender role expectations, and educational requirements (Blackhurst et al., 2003). These impressions are not only ideas, but also guiding frameworks to which children align their aspirations and efforts. Unfortunately, without critical conversations about career development, many students misunderstand college and career requirements, become discouraged by stereotypes, and believe certain careers are not attainable (Blackhurst et al., 2003). Throughout the years from third to fifth grade, comprehensive career development should focus on the exploration of interests, skills, and careers that will become more concrete and tangible as students springboard into the critical decision-making time of their adolescence.

3–5 Interventions

Intervention Philosophy

Interventions across the 3–5 grade level should build upon the foundation set in the K–2 years. An exploration of self and the world of careers becomes more specific and nuanced once children have background information and experiences to fall back on. As children advance from fantasy thinking, the reality of jobs, their linkage to skills, and the training required to obtain them become clearer. Children in the 3–5 grade level engage in a process of social sorting where they align themselves more directly towards potential occupations based on perceptions of social prestige, income potential, interest, ability, and perceived fit based upon their identity (Hartung et al., 2005). With these principles in mind, a school counselor should facilitate lessons and experiences that allow for a critical examination of self, education, careers, and societal messaging.

Exploration of Interests

Across the 3–5 years, students have had more exposure to the realms of academics, extracurriculars, and social experiences. This empowers students to identify careers they may be interested in due to a deeper understanding of what they enjoy, who their role models are, and what they perceive as appropriate for their identity. For example, few kindergarteners would likely list their future dream occupation as being a YouTuber, video game streamer, or influencer. However, ask any education professional in the modern age how many students in third through fifth grade list this as a future aspiration. Children in this age range have had more time exploring this type of content, more independent access to the technology required to view it, and more socialization with others who enjoy similar content. These students have had more conversations with their friends about the videos they like and the type of content they would produce, including their style of video and the humor infused throughout. Many students have even created and posted videos, receiving feedback from friends and (unfortunately) from online strangers.

These experiences form impressions in a child's mind about their interests and abilities. They look up to those who do this career due to finding the content creators entertaining or relatable. They find social community in the associated fandom of these individuals. They understand the basic skills required to embark on this career journey. These students can also cite how many of these content creators make significant incomes. While I'm sure many of us cannot wait to jump in to caution these students about the difficulty of this career path, how few of these individuals actually succeed, and how related skills easily transfer into many other career options if the content creation career doesn't pan out, it is first important to consider how these students have engaged in a social process and formed solid guiding impressions. These students have considered who they are, what they like, what is appropriate for them, the prestige of a career, its requirements, and its income. Think back to how this chapter began: We cannot underestimate how much children at this age understand, what they interact with, and how much influence these experiences may have on their career pathways.

Students' developing interests in being entertainers (such as actors and singers) and professional athletes also tend to solidify during this period. What a wonderful time for a school counselor to be involved in career development! While traditionally these aspirations have been categorized as unrealistic and even had students facing put-downs from teachers, the interest and passion students experience around careers as content creators, entertainers, and athletes can be utilized to propel students into a deeper exploration of self and career.

Imagine a conversation with students in which all of their ideas and interests are encouraged. How might it feel for those students to be heard and represented in their career dreams? What might it do for their levels of hope and motivation for the future? Further, what if we could link those aspirations to more careers and to the relevance of school? For example, students could discuss the interests and skills required for each of their dream careers. An actor needs to be interested in theater, the creative arts, reading, and history to understand their role and perform effectively. An online content creator needs to understand computer science, theater, the creative arts, marketing, and business to entertain their audience and manage their business. An athlete must be interested in physical education, have an intense commitment to physical training, and learn public speaking to successfully navigate their career.

Students should be prompted to engage with their level of interest across these domains and to learn how schooling experiences could facilitate their growth in these areas. The educational background of individuals in these fields could be used to show that many actors, athletes, and content creators have extensive educations which have contributed to their success. Further, students could collaborate with the school counselor to list careers that require similar interests and skills as these jobs. For example, a student interested in being a professional athlete may also enjoy the career of being a coach, athletic trainer, sports journalist, sports broadcaster, social media specialist, or sports agent. A student interested in acting might also be interested in writing, directing, costume design, set design, photography, editing, and many more careers. These types of lessons provide space for critical conversations exploring the depth of student interests and how they align with relevant educational and career options. This intentional curriculum design lays the foundation for deeper exploration of interests, skills, and careers throughout subsequent lessons and years.

The following is an example of an integrated series of lessons I used with fourth graders during my time as a school counselor. I had them take a modified version of a RIASEC assessment designed for elementary students. Each student was able to come up with their top category, corresponding to the Realistic, Investigative, Artistic, Social, Enterprising, and Conventional career fields (Holland, 1997). Students were then instructed to gather in groups based upon their results. Competition style, the groups were tasked to come up with a list of skills required to do jobs within their career category. The groups shared their lists aloud and were rewarded points based on every answer I accepted as correct. The next round had students list as many careers as they could that fell into this career category. Points were awarded in a similar manner. We displayed the lists of skills and careers within the classroom as a way to keep the learned concepts in mind. During the next lesson, students were tasked with selecting a career which interested them within their career field. Students individually listed what skills were required for this career and how much education they believed was required for the career. We discussed the results as a group and had students share their perspectives. After this lesson, I worked with their classroom teacher to include an academic writing prompt reflecting on their chosen career, what they thought about it, what challenges might get in the way, and how they planned to get there. The final lesson included information about what higher education was (apprenticeships, trade schools, community college, four-year degrees, advanced degrees) and how certain jobs require more training. Students were again divided into groups and were challenged to guess the level of education required for the list of jobs they had previously come up with. We processed the answers after each question, especially for those careers that required varying levels of education. Students were asked to identify anyone they knew in the local community who had this type of job. The competitive atmosphere and streamlined nature of the unit allowed students to build upon previous knowledge, understand the linkage between interests, skills, and career choice, and grasp the relevance of education for future goals. While the lesson unit was not perfect in composition, it allowed for an important examination of the critical elements of the elementary career development process.

In addition to these educational lessons, I coordinated guest speakers to correspond to each of the RIASEC categories. The timing of these speakers aligned with the lesson unit detailed above. The speakers spoke about how their educational and general interests aligned with their chosen career field, what skills they utilized to succeed in their career, and what education they had to get for their career. This intentionality allowed for more student connection to the speakers and more advanced question-and-answer sessions. Additional integration included writing prompts in each of their academic classes exploring how what they were learning in school related to the careers of the speakers.

For schools required by their state to submit evidence of career education and individual student career portfolios, worksheets from these type of guidance lessons and classroom activities serve two purposes. They not only engage students on their comprehensive career development journey, but also provide easy documents to catalogue within a portfolio. This type of portfolio isn't only about meeting state requirements. The contents of the portfolio could be shared with parents during parent–teacher conferences to keep them updated on their child's career development journey. The contents could also be used within future college and career counseling sessions, allowing the student to reflect upon their career development journey and process any changes in their paths. A career development portfolio allows for a record of the career development initiatives of a school and the steps along the journey for a student on their path to success.

Exploration of Abilities

During the K–5 years, an exploration of abilities should not focus on discouraging career options based upon skill level. Younger children have little exposure to the nuances of academic fields and the bevy of related skills required to succeed in careers. It would be a disservice to have children deny themselves true exploration of career pathways based upon perceptions of inadequate skills at a young age. Instead, an awareness of skills, their linkage to interests, and their connection to career should be encouraged and explored, with more refinement scheduled for later years.

While these chapters are divided into three sections, lessons exploring interests, abilities, and careers truly should be integrated. Any lesson examining interests at the 3–5 level should also integrate skill and career exploration. This does not mean, however, that some lessons, units, and experiences are not more specifically skill focused. For example, when I invited a mechanical engineer to speak to my fourth- and fifth-grade students, I asked him to emphasize what skills he needed to succeed in his job and what school subjects aligned with these. Students readily asked about what he needed to know and how difficult the subjects were. The speaker noted how the skill mastery could be challenging but also strongly encouraged any students interested in this field to believe in themselves and to pursue continued development of these skills.

Abilities-based career education across the 3–5 level should allow students to analyze what they feel confident in and good at, how their abilities link to careers, and what skills different careers need to succeed. As children move on from fantasy thinking within this stage, they can concretely understand the different abilities required to do well in various occupations (Gottfredson, 2005). An example of this focus was a series of guidance lessons I did with my fifth-grade students.

Utilizing what is around students in the local community is an excellent way to make career education tangible and accessible. For a lesson linking skills to careers, I utilized our school building as a prime example. In groups, students analyzed what academic skills and what people skills were necessary for individuals at our school to succeed at their jobs. The students analyzed the school counselor (myself), their classroom teacher, other teachers in the building, the principal, the custodian, the school nurse, the occupational therapist, and the bus drivers. We held a classroom discussion about which classes these individuals had to do well in when they were in school, the level of education this job required, and the personal qualities necessary to succeed in this job.

A breakthrough moment occurred when I compared the skills necessary to function within the classroom setting (as students) to the skills necessary to succeed in jobs. I prompted the students to analyze whether they believed everyone who worked at the school always got along. The students quickly identified that they believed some teachers would disagree about many things. I asked if this was obvious, or if it seemed to impact the teachers' work, and the students replied it did not. I then asked what skills the teachers were using (conflict management, emotional management, listening skills, planning skills) to ensure that any disagreements didn't prevent them from doing their jobs effectively. I asked what would happen if the teachers did not have these skills and the students replied that the school wouldn't function well, students wouldn't learn, and staff would end up getting fired. We then processed how behaviors we learn in school (listening, waiting our turn to speak, respecting other students, following teacher instructions) directly relate to social skills we need to succeed in jobs. Students expressed that it was much clearer to them why they had to practice teamwork behaviors in school and how these skills became much more relevant to their lives through this discussion.

Finally, each student selected a career they were interested in. The students catalogued what academic skills and general abilities they would need to succeed at the job and what social/team-work skills would be necessary for them to succeed at the job in the long term. The next lesson provided time for students to present on their chosen job and discuss whether they believed they had the required skills or would develop them as they got older. The key focus of this unit was to align skills with relevant life and career goals, to encourage students to foster hope for the future and get the most out of schooling.

The Missouri Department of Education (MDE) has two wonderful examples of units which capture the abilities exploration philosophy well. One third-grade unit prompts students to reflect upon what personal, work, and ethical skills they have. Later lessons have the students diagram these skills as they relate to school and career success. The final lesson of the unit involves students writing an essay about how they can apply these skills to particular jobs within the school setting. Finally, the students each participate in a job-shadowing experience in the school where they can analyze how these skills are being utilized. Another unit within their curriculum includes an academic skill component, where students analyze their academic performance and set goals for improvement. The students practice self-evaluation skills as they pertain to short- and long-term goals (MDE, 2021). The goal of the unit is to help students raise their academic self-efficacy, a major variable in career aspirations and achievement. By walking students through the strategies necessary to accomplish goals, the school counselor empowers students to better succeed in their academic career, allowing them to pursue a wider array of career options.

While there are many approaches that meet these emphases within ability exploration, a school counselor must be intentional in how these lessons and experiences are designed. Based upon school and community demographic and needs, a school counselor should tailor lessons that will be most impactful and relevant. The school counselor should align these experiences to state and national standards, gather data (such as the types of interests and skills, the careers identified, growth from early lessons to later lessons, student perceptions of the relevance of lessons, and parent perceptions of the impact of experiences) and intentionally have subsequent lessons build upon prior ones. While the examples of the lessons and experiences detailed in this section are good starting points, how they are utilized and how they flow in conjunction with the rest of the career development curriculum depends entirely upon the unique situation of an individual school building.

Exploration of Careers

As children transition throughout the 3–5 years, they are more able to understand the concrete realities of jobs and related careers, and the education required to obtain them. Career education centered around the types of jobs in each career path, the skills required for these jobs, and the education necessary is critical to help children understand the reality of the world of work. The idea of exploring what college is, what types of jobs require it, and why they require it should be introduced and built upon from the third to fifth grade. This grounds students in the requirements of certain jobs while also directly linking school success to their future aspirations. Research strongly supports the efficacy of these type of interventions, illustrating that these are imperative approaches.

Mariani and colleagues (2016) found that fifth-grade students had significant increases in their career awareness, career interest, college and career requirements, and aspirations to attend college after receiving a college and career readiness unit. Career development interventions also increase school engagement and reduce long-term dropout rates (Castellano et al., 2003; Kenny et al., 2006; Perry et al., 2010). Indeed, an exploration of college and career is not simply an "add-on" but a critical component of a holistic K–12 education. While the previous sections detailed interventions that cover career exploration based upon interests, skills, and educational requirements, this section shall focus on additional career interventions that can expose children to the possibilities of the world of work.

Online career websites such as Career Cruising offer career-focused games and activities for K–12 students (Career Cruising, 2021). Career Cruising Spark, designed for the K–5 population, has an animated and welcoming interface in which students can click around and explore a town filled with careers. The strength of programs such as Career Cruising Spark is that they engage with children on their level through the utilization of games, animation, and humor. The career exploration process becomes more immersive in this manner, rather than seeming to be yet another facet of classroom education. Students are exposed to activities linking social-emotional skills to career, the skills required for different careers, and different types of careers available overall. There is a cost associated with Career Cruising and similar programs; therefore, each school must evaluate if this cost is within budget. However, as an additional tool for comprehensive career development, this website and those similar can offer a fun, engaging, and organized way for students to engage with and track their career development journey.

Since students at this age are more able to understand the social processes impacting career, such as perceived gender, class, and racial appropriateness for differing roles, it is imperative that speakers and field trips are targeted and intentional. Choosing speakers who are representative of the many groups of people with various professions will open children's eyes to what is possible for them and provide them a potential role model moving forward. If a selected group of speakers in college-educated professional roles are all White males, for example, this may reinforce negative stereotypes that students from minority groups have received about their fit within these career fields. After conducting a thorough community assets map, a school counselor can invite various professionals from various gender, ethnic, socioeconomic, and other identity backgrounds to inspire every category of student to imagine themselves in those shoes.

I worked in a school district in which a majority of students lived in poverty. This rural, isolated district had little diversity in available occupations, few jobs around requiring higher education, and no institutions of higher education nearby. The district was also composed of small-town schools that sent students to a large combined high school. I thought it would be important for students in the 3–5 range to meet a career speaker who had gone to their elementary school, was raised in this local community, and understood how to overcome the barriers of economic hardship and geographic isolation in pursuit of higher education. I was fortunate to locate someone through community asset mapping and networking. This individual worked at the closest state university, approximately 50 miles away. She was happy to speak to our students about what it was like exploring her interests, considering careers, applying to college, and managing the finances to get there. The speaker also had spent time studying and working abroad, thanks to her college education. Since our student population was composed of many students who had not traveled much beyond the local community, many children were intrigued and inspired by these tales. They had never known that even just by going to college they could get to experience different countries. Since the speaker was originally a local, students were eager to connect with her and ask about her story, thoughts, feelings, and future plans. The connection was wholesome, and it was clear gears were turning in the minds of my students. I utilized this speaker across several grades as a resource to inspire students to think about how they too could get an education and experience much more in the world.

School counselors should work at finding speakers who could benefit their student community. These speakers may act as role models or future resources for job-shadowing or mentorship programs within the middle school and high school years. Job-shadowing opportunities can even begin within the 3–5 years on a more limited basis. As cited in the MDE's guidance curriculum, students can shadow professionals at the school to better understand what their jobs are and what skills are required to succeed. Field trips to local businesses can also include a mini-shadowing component where groups of students spend time with people in one or several different roles within an organization. Witnessing and walking through the world of work allows students to connect themselves to it, inspiring more thought, more contemplation, and a concrete foundation to build upon in future years. These efforts in conjunction with guidance lessons, career days, letters home to parents detailing the career development efforts, tracking of programmatic efforts in individual career portfolios, and academic integration all serve to continue the momentum of a comprehensive career development program as students approach middle school.

Academic Integration

What if a critical examination of self, society, and the world of work were not simply reserved for the occasional guidance lesson, speaker, or career-related event? What if this type of thinking were also applied regularly in the classroom to provide direct content linkage between academic skills and a student's future? Children across grades 3–5 have a deeper ability to understand and express ideas related to self and the world. For example, a guidance lesson detailing women role models in the science, technology, engineering, and math (STEM) fields could inspire children to combat stereotypical thinking and aspire for new career trajectories. Wouldn't it be wonderful if this could be paired with an essay examining what children thought about gender stereotypes in careers, within an English or social studies class? Could other essays focus on a critical examination of a student's interests, skills, and identity and how these might relate to what they wish to do in the future? Could computer class include information about how the skills being learned are used in various fields, including online streaming and influencing? Could every academic unit intentionally begin with a survey of the types of existing jobs that require the skills and information students are learning in the classroom?

While this integration should begin in the K–2 years, the process should become more ingrained and solidified across the 3–5 years. By meeting with the academic teachers and those developing curriculum in the district, the school counselor can help fully immerse career development into the school curriculum. A major stakeholder to be aware of is the school administrator. Administrators are under pressure to meet local, state, and federal governmental standards, including career development outcomes. If an administrator can have their building prove it is addressing core career development standards within its regular curriculum, this allows the administrator to streamline reporting, hold the district accountable, and represent the fruits of all personnel's labor. Meeting with district administrators can allow for necessary partnerships to create this structure surrounding an integrated academic framework. For example, a district-wide team of school counselors could be part of an official career development integration team who work with other curriculum teams to create, evaluate, and tweak career development lessons and experiences for the general curriculum on a yearly basis. This team would also be critical in making sure that any career development curriculum spanning grade levels and buildings is intentional and cohesive. This would be a streamlined use of human resources within the district to meet state standards and, more importantly, provide a comprehensive career development framework for all students. Given the benefits, it is likely that administrators within a school district would be open to the idea of school counselors leading these types of initiatives. These are important steps to help students truly get the most out of career development, which changes in focus and demands within the middle school years.

CHAPTER SUMMARY

This chapter explored how career development impressions become more concrete across the years from third through fifth grade. Students move from fantasy thinking regarding careers to being able to understand the skills, knowledge, and training necessary for different vocations. Lessons and experiences exploring interests, abilities, and careers should work on connecting and jointly exploring each of these domains. Continued conversations around the social aspects of career (the influence of oppression, stereotypes, and biases), along with representative career development speakers, should be utilized to empower students to pursue all that is possible for them. Instilling the connection between academic abilities, skills, and social cooperation can also serve to link school to a student's future in a positive manner. By integrating efforts into the academic curriculum and keeping track of the sum of these efforts in individual career development portfolios, schools can collect proof that they are meeting state career standards while setting the foundation for deeper career development exploration in the middle and high school years.

TABLE OF KEY TERMS

Term	Definition
RIASEC	Realistic, Investigative, Artistic, Social, Enterprising, and Conventional. These Holland Code categories align with the interests and skills of current workers in various occupational fields (Holland, 1997).

REFLECTION EXERCISES

Reflection exercises are designed either to be done individually within the reading or to be used as group discussion questions within the classroom setting. A series of reflection questions will be presented at the end of every chapter.

1. Consider how a guidance lesson on career interests may be similar and different in the third, fourth, and fifth grades.

    a. Plan a lesson for each of these grade levels.

    b. Evaluate how your lessons are developmentally appropriate at each level.

    c. Analyze how your lessons build upon one another across each year.

2. Create a community asset map of a local schooling community. Can you identify any potential career speakers who would be good representative role models across diverse careers for this community?

    a. How would you reach out to these stakeholders?

    b. What types of events or lessons would you create in conjunction with them?

3. How might your conversation of sociocultural dynamics related to career (such as racial and gender identity) change by level across the third, fourth, and fifth grades?

    a. How would your lessons or experiences differ conceptually across each of these levels?

    b. What stakeholders or resources would you utilize to provide comprehensive services in this domain?

    c. How would you respond to parent resistance to career lessons that critically evaluate the issues of racism, sexism, classism, transphobia, and other forms of discrimination?

4. What were your most formative career development experiences in your 3–5 years?

    a. How did these experiences inform your understanding of career at the time?

    b. How accurate or inaccurate were the impressions you formed from these experiences?

    c. How did the beliefs you developed from these experiences influence your educational and career trajectory?

    d. What type of career development interventions would have helped you better process and utilize the information you gathered from these experiences?

CASE STUDY

Shelby Intermediate school is a 3–5 building within an ethnically and culturally diverse urban center. As a new school counselor, you have advocated for the development of comprehensive career development programming and curriculum over your first few months on the job. Your building principal is open to the idea but has told you that there is an immense pressure on the teachers to meet state academic testing standards and that this type of curriculum is the priority. The teachers you know in the building feel burned out from teaching for the tests, due to how this limits their creativity and often results in students not being as well-behaved or engaged. Further, several teachers have mentioned that this type of education and focus appears to be least helpful for the economically disadvantaged students in the building, who disengage the most and are often mentally and emotionally preoccupied with challenges in their living situation. You understand the major pressures put on the administration to meet certain testing levels but also wish to advocate for your student population to receive the comprehensive education they deserve. As the school counselor, consider the following questions:

1. What type of research data would be helpful in advocating for a comprehensive and integrated career development curriculum? Search for and locate articles to build your case.

2. What type of data could you collect from within the school to help build your case? Who would you collect the data from, how, and how would you analyze it?

3. What other stakeholders would be helpful in designing the framework for a new career development curriculum in Shelby Intermediate? How would you reach out to and partner with them?

References

Blackhurst, A. E., Auger, R. W., & Wahl, K. H. (2003). Children's perceptions of vocational preparation requirements. *Professional School Counseling, 7*(2), 58–67.

Career Cruising. (2020). *Career cruising's spark! For grades 3–5.* https://help.careercruising.com/article/288-spark-3-5-usaca

Castellano, M., Stringfield, S. C., Stone, J. R., & Wayman, J. C. (2003). *Early measures of student progress in schools with CTE-enhanced whole-school reform: Math course-taking patterns and student progress to graduation.* National Research Center for Career and Technical Education.

Gottfredson, L. S. (2005). Applying Gottfredson's theory of circumscription and compromise in career guidance and counseling. In S. D. Brown & R. W. Lent (Eds.), *Career development and counseling: Putting theory and research to work* (pp. 71–100). John Wiley & Sons.

Hartung, P. J., Porfeli, E. J., & Vondracek, F. W. (2005). Child vocational development: A review and reconsideration. *Journal of Vocational Behavior, 66*(3), 385–419.

Holland, J. L. (1997). *Making vocational choices: A theory of vocational personalities and work environments* (3rd ed.). Psychological Assessment Resources.

Kenny, M. E., Blustein, D. L., Haase, R. F., Jackson, J., & Perry, J. C. (2006). Setting the stage: Career development and the student engagement process. *Journal of Counseling Psychology, 53*(2), 272–279.

Mariani, M., Berger, C., Koerner, K., & Sandlin, C. (2016). Operation occupation: A college and career readiness intervention for elementary students. *Professional School Counseling, 20*(1), 65–76.

Missouri Department of Education. (2021). *School counseling curriculum.* https://dese.mo.gov/college-career-readiness/school-counseling/curriculum

Perry, J. C., Liu, X., & Pabian, Y. (2010). School engagement as a mediator of academic performance among urban youth: The role of career preparation, parental career support, and teacher support. *The Counseling Psychologist, 38*(2), 269–295.

Student-Centered Career Day

Angelo Carpenter, MS

P ractical Resources are examples of work school counselors can do in applying the concepts of this textbook to their own school districts. They are also an example of assignments counselor educators could assign to their students. All practical resources were contributed by school counselors in training working toward their master's degrees.

School Counselor: Angelo Carpenter
Lesson Plan: Student-Centered Career Day
Intended Student Audience: Students in third to fifth grade

ASCA STUDENT STANDARDS

Mindset:	Behavior:
M 3. Positive attitude toward work and learning	Learning Strategies B-LS 2. Creative approach to learning, tasks and problem solving B-LS 6. High-quality standards for tasks and activities
M 4. Self-confidence in ability to succeed	B-LS 7. Long- and short-term academic, career and social/emotional goals Self-Management Skills B-SMS 1. Responsibility for self and actions
M 6. Understanding that postsecondary education and lifelong learning are necessary for long-term success	B-SMS 5. Perseverance to achieve long- and short-term goals Social Skills B-SS 1. Effective oral and written communication skills and listening skills B-SS 2. Positive, respectful and supportive relationships with students who are similar to and different from them B-SS 9. Social maturity and behaviors appropriate to the situation and environment

American School Counselor Association, Selection from ASCA Student Standards: Mindsets & Behaviors for Student Success. *Copyright © 2021 by American School Counselor Association.*

STUDENT LEARNING EXPECTATIONS

Students will be expected to:

- Manage their in-class work time effectively
- Use outside resources to find needed information
- Express an understanding of the basic duties and required schooling of their assigned careers
- Effectively communicate to/with their peers and educators
- Meet specific predetermined deadlines
- Use critical thinking to choose and successfully produce modality of expression

Students will gain:

- Awareness and understanding of life after secondary education
- Exposure to various career fields as well as different forms and levels of post-secondary education
- The opportunity to explore existing or possibly new interests
- Respect for all career fields, with the understanding that all careers are necessary for a fully functioning and diverse community

PROJECT SUMMARY

Students will be introduced to the idea of having a career in the future by randomly being assigned a career from a selection of popular/common occupational fields to research. They will then express what they have learned in a multitude of creative ways; these expressions will be presented at a culminating "career day." The reason behind the careers being randomly chosen is to avoid repetition of jobs represented and also to expose students to fields that they may have had no previous knowledge of. Hopefully, students will gain a respect for said fields, whether they would consider them as a future career option or not. The careers should span educational requirement levels, from doctoral degree to vocational school training, in order to avoid education/career bias. In order to avoid social class stigma, projected salaries for each career should not be included in this lesson for the recommended grade levels.

PROJECT GOALS

- Learn topic-relevant terminology
- Show an understanding of the required educational path and main responsibilities of assigned careers
- Get students thinking about their career future (it's never too early!)
- Garner respect for all working professions and understand the value each occupation contributes to their community

LESSON INTRODUCTION

Day One: Relevant Terminology and Career Assignment
Time: Approx. 45 mins.–1 hour

Recommended Materials:

- Slideshow/visual format for introduction and terminology
- Career assignment method (paper cut-out option provided within)
- Project packet (sample provided within, if chosen as method of delivery)

The instructor should begin the lesson by addressing the definition of a "career," then follow by inviting students' personal interpretations or experiences they have had in their lives with any and all careers. Consider the following discussion questions:

- What careers do your parents/guardians have?
- Can you think of popular careers in your community? **Instructor suggestions could/should include jobs students most likely have come into contact with, which may vary based on social environment**
- What sorts of careers do you see on TV or in movies? On social media?

After this brief discussion, instructors will then introduce the project the students are to partake in over the next few days (or more, depending on instructor discretion). After checking for understanding and answering any questions, the instructor should then move on to instructing students on terms that they may encounter during their research. Students may write this in the provided packet or through an instructor-preferred method.

Suggested terms to include are:

- Occupation
- Profession
- Vocation
- Vocational School
- Technical school
- Associate/bachelor's/master's/doctoral degree (Standard time to finish each degree; it would be positive to mention that not everyone completes these degrees at the same pace.)
- Trade
- Interview
- Resume

**Guided note sheet provided within

Once the definitions are covered and students have a personal access method for each of them, the lesson can move on to the career assignment. Once all students are "hired" at their new jobs, the instructor should go around and ask each student to introduce their career title. A discussion can be held about which careers sound presently familiar to students.

The lesson should then transition into an instructor-led discussion on why all jobs have value. Highlight the idea that each of the students' new careers will have different educational requirements and responsibilities, but that each and every one of them hold importance in all communities, which is partly what students are to discover through their research. (Discussion point example: Doctors cannot safely practice medicine without a sterile room for their patients, which sanitation workers provide.)

Day Two:** Research and In-Class Work Time
Time: By instructor discretion

**Amount of allotted in-class work time/days will vary based on various academic factors; instructors can decide as they go how much time is appropriate for this specific project in relation to their students' needs.

Recommended Collaboration:

- The school librarian can preemptively pull books related to careers for students to look through on research days, to eliminate the need for students to search the shelves and find books on their own. The librarian can also be a valuable instructional resource while students are in the library.
- Vetted, positive role models from the students' immediate community with relevant careers may be willing to publicly speak to your classroom about their career and education journey.

Recommended Materials:

- Guided research outline (sample provided within)
- Access to school library
- Books on various careers
- Computers, research databases

  - Recommended research sites (as of November 2021):
    - https://careerkids.com/pages/career-research
    - https://www.bls.gov/k12/students/careers/career-exploration.htm
    - https://www.mynextmove.org/
    - https://www.myplan.com/careers/index.php
    - https://collegegrad.com/careers/all

- Poster boards/construction paper
- Art supplies: crayons, markers, colored pencils, glue, scissors, etc.

The first day of research should begin with instructors going over the required information students need to move on to the expressive presentation projects. Best-evidence based practice would recommend instructors introduce a few of the research websites where students should be getting a majority of their information. The websites listed above host all information required in this project (as of November 2021), so recommending that students use only these sites would assist in the research process. If a school library is available, teaching students to research using books would be beneficial to future education prospects. Because the paths, accessibility, and daily responsibilities are more cut and dried for some careers than for others, students may need various levels of assistance with the research portion of the job.

The instructor should then cover the different methods of delivery the students have to choose from on their "career day."

Suggested delivery methods include:

- Poster board presentation
- Slideshow presentation
- "Day in the life" journal entry
- Job application poster
- Informational video
- Alternative methods upon instructor approval

Research and in-class work time will be vital to student success on this assignment. Expecting elementary grade students to do the bulk of the work at home on their own, where resources might be inequitably available, is unfair to the students. For many students, this may be one of the first, if not the very first, research-based project they have been assigned. The instructor should continuously make their way around the room to check on students' progress and provide hands-on guidance as needed.

Final Day: Career Day!

Time: Half of the school day, depending on instructor discretion (make an event of it!)

This is the day! All of the students' hard work will culminate in a short presentation, where students will represent their career and deliver their found information to their peers through whichever preferred presentation model they chose. Students will present for their classmates for 5–10 minutes, after which they can be asked questions by their peers or instructor(s).

Optional Part Two:

Because this project is extensive for elementary-level students, you should celebrate their hard work! Once students have presented for their classmates, you can have your students stand at their own "stations" and open your class's "career day" to the rest of the school. Invite other school staff, administrators, students, and maybe even parents/guardians (if you're feeling brave) to come down and admire your students' projects and ask them questions about their careers!

Recommended Materials:

- Snacks

Recommended Extra-Credit Opportunities:

- Dress up as your career! This does not have to be a complete costume (e.g., the "doctor" can wear a medical mask and gloves, the "teacher" can wear fake glasses or carry around a measuring stick, etc.).
- Bring in handouts/props that pertain to your career (e.g., the "nurse" can bring in tongue depressors (popsicle sticks), the "teacher" can bring in pencils or apples, etc.).

All supplemental materials provided can be adjusted based on students' academic needs, grade level, etc. Supplied materials are merely suggestions of delivery, and instructors can manipulate the project to fit their preferred methods.

CAREER CUT-OUTS

Cut these out and place them in a container. Have students choose them at random to assign careers.

Teacher	Electrician	Doctor	Nurse
School Counselor	Carpenter	Engineer	Computer Programmer
Sanitation Worker/ Custodian	Firefighter	Chef	Mechanic
Lawyer	Judge	Editor	Writer
Actor	Bus Driver	Nutritionist	Environmental Scientist
Farmer	Librarian	Graphic Designer	Bus Driver
Social Worker	Executive Assistant	Park Ranger	News Reporter
Speech Pathologist	Video Game Developer	Cashier	Architect

CAREER DAY!

New employee's name: _____

Boss's (teacher's) name: _____

Date of hire (today's date): _____

↓Drawing space below↓

Draw a picture of what **you** will look like in the future as an employee in your career!

Important Career Vocabulary Words

Word Bank		
occupation	technical school	master's degree
job	career	doctoral degree
vocational school	trade	interview
associate degree	resume	bachelor's degree
employed	employee	employer

A person who works somewhere is _____ there, and is often called an

_____ .

A person's _____, their _____, or their _____
are all <u>synonyms</u>* that refer to their _____ .
*<u>synonyms</u>: *words that mean the same thing*

_____ and _____ both
teach people about specific careers they are interested in, such as electrician, carpenter, or
automotive mechanic.

If someone is applying for a career, they will first have to have an _____, that they
will bring a _____ to, which is a sheet of paper that tells the _____
information about themselves.

Two years of college = _____
Four years of college = _____
Six years of college = _____
Eight years of college = _____

<u>Circle "Yes" or "No" for the answers below:</u>
Were there any vocabulary words that were completely new to you?

          Yes   No

If yes, which one(s)? _____

Were there any words that you have heard before but did not know the meaning of until now?

          Yes   No

Which one(s)? _____

Write any questions you have about the newly learned vocab below:

_____

_____

_____

ANSWER KEY/COMPLETED MODEL FOR VOCABULARY NOTES

A person who works somewhere is **employed** there, and is often called an **employee**.

A person's **occupation**, their **trade**, or their **job** are all _synonyms_* _(words that mean the same thing)_ that refer to their **career**.
*synonyms: _words that mean the same thing_

Vocational school and **technical school** both teach people about specific careers they are interested in, such as electrician, carpenter, or automotive mechanic.

If someone is applying for a career, they will first have to have an **interview**, that they will bring a **resume** to, which is a sheet of paper that tells the **employer** information about themselves.

Two years of college = **associate degree**
Four years of college = **bachelor's degree**
Six years of college = **master's degree**
Eight years of college = **doctoral degree**

PART 2: RESEARCH GUIDELINE

Use your researching skills to discover the information about your new career and log the information below!

What is your career? _____

What type of schooling do you need to get this career? _____

Which means (approximately) how many years of school? _____

Explain _at least 5–6_ responsibilities of your career below. (Remember to use complete sentences!)

_____

_____

_____

_____

_____

_____

_____

_____

Opinion Questions: Answer all questions below with your own thoughts! Please remember to use complete sentences for all of your answers!

Think! Would you want this career in the future? Give _2–3 examples_ of why you would or why you would not.

_____

_____

_____

_____

_____

_____

_____

_____

What are _2–3 responsibilities_ that you think make this job difficult?

_____

_____

_____

_____

_____

_____

_____

_____

What are _2–3 responsibilities_ that you think make this job fun or interesting?

_____

_____

_____

_____

_____

_____

_____

_____

Why do you think your career is valuable/important to your community/society? Explain your answer with _4–5 reasons_.

_____

_____

_____

_____

_____

_____

_____

_____

Try to recruit (hire) other people to join your career! In _4–5 complete sentences_, explain below why you think other people (not yourself) should want this career!

_____

_____

_____

_____

_____

_____

_____

_____

Wait!
If you reach this part, and all of your above research prompts have been completed, speak to your teacher to get your work checked before you move on!

PART 3: CAREER DAY PRESENTATIONS

Time to show off all your hard work by representing your career at our very own career day! Review the presentation options below and choose the one you think you would like to do the most! Be creative with your presentation, explain your career with specific details, and most importantly, have fun!

Poster Board

Create a poster board to set up and use during your presentation.

Must include:

- 4–5 picture examples of your job
- All of the details from your <u>research findings</u> and <u>opinion statements</u>
- Colors (in your drawings or printed pictures)

Slideshow

Create a detailed slideshow presentation to display and use for your presentation.

Must include:

- 4–5 picture examples of your job
- All of your research findings and opinion statements
- Colors and attention-grabbing details
- <u>Optional</u>: Max. of 1 video, no longer than 5 minutes

"Day in the Life" Journal Entry

Imagine you just completed your required education and are now home from your first day in your new career. Incorporate all of your research materials and opinion statements into a personal journal-style entry detailing your day of work.

Must include:

- What type of school you just graduated from and for how long you attended, including which degree or certificate you received
- The daily responsibilities of your job you completed that day (research findings)
- How you feel about your job (opinion statements)

Help Wanted Flyer

Create a "Help Wanted" advertisement for your career, as if you are a boss looking for new employees.

Must include:

- Daily responsibilities (research)
- Amount of schooling applicants must have (research)
- Why people should want to work in your career field (opinion)
- Creativity (company name, pictures, color, etc.)

Informational Video

Make an informational video for a new employee in your career field.

You must:

- Cover all of your research findings.
- Explain why your new employee should be excited about working there (opinion statements).
- Act as if you are a boss! Do not record yourself reading off of a script. Pretend like this is a real informational video.

If you have other ideas for your project, let me know! We can discuss any creative ideas you may want to do.

POST-TEST SAMPLE

Now that you have been an audience for your classmates' presentations, answer the following questions below:

Were there any careers you learned about other than your own that you would be interested in learning more about or maybe pursuing as a future career?

Yes   No

If yes, which career(s) were you interested in and why? If no, why not? Is there a career you are interested in that was not covered in this project?

_____

_____

_____

What was the best part of this project?

_____

_____

_____

Do you have any suggestions on how to make this project better?

_____

_____

_____

Overall, how do you feel about this experience?

Great!   Good!   Meh.

REFERENCES

American School Counselor Association. (2021). *ASCA student standards: Mindsets & behaviors for student success.* https://www.schoolcounselor.org/getmedia/7428a787-a452-4abb-afec-d78ec77870cd/Mind-sets-Behaviors.pdf

Career Kids. (2022). *Research careers.* https://careerkids.com/pages/career-research

CollegeGrad. (2022). *All career profiles.* https://collegegrad.com/careers/all

My Next Move. (2022). *What do you want to do for a living?* O*Net. https://www.mynextmove.org/

MyPlan.com. (2022). *Career exploration.* https://www.myplan.com/careers/index.php

U.S. Bureau of Labor Statistics. (2020, May 14). *Career exploration.* K-12: Student Resources. https://www.bls.gov/k12/students/careers/career-exploration.htm

CHAPTER 7

6–8 Interventions

magine a student in grades 6–8. What changes are occurring in their life? How are they changing physically, culturally, and emotionally? What type of media sources do they consume? How do they view themselves compared to peers? How do societal trends and norms influence them in a different way than younger students? Let's put ourselves in the shoes of a student who has not had a positive schooling experience. Let's imagine they have not had a comprehensive career development experience and in general have a negative perspective on schooling. What might this student's priorities be? How might they feel about exploring the usage of education as linked to their career path? Would they care about academics? How would they now make meaning of their negative schooling experiences?

For students who are left behind in educational systems, the middle-school years are a crucial period of disengagement (Anderson et al., 2019; Eccles & Roeser, 2011). As children reach adolescence, they are in the process of physically and emotionally establishing themselves as individuals with unique goals, interests, and aspirations. As they grow, they are more capable of handling life and academic tasks independently. In these processes, students develop self-efficacy, or the belief in themselves that they can accomplish school and life tasks. Self-efficacy is critical in determining whether students stay engaged in school or if they disengage due to a perceived lack of confidence or dissatisfaction from experiencing social barriers (Anderson et al., 2019).

This bridging period between early childhood and early adulthood comes with students exploring who they are, what they like, and where they would like to go. This time is often filled with great turbulence as students experience stress related to physical body changes, challenges in finding one's social group, dating pressures, and the difficulties of establishing a unique identity. Historically, teenagers have been labeled as angsty and rebellious, quick to argue and disagree with adults on principle. A more holistic perspective might be that adolescents are in the processing of figuring out who they are while juggling new pressures, challenges, and responsibilities. Exploring boundaries, asserting new opinions, trying new things, and associating with new people are natural parts of this process. It's important to realize that hobbies, media preferences, and friends may understandably hold a lot of weight in a teen's mind throughout this process. It is crucial for school counselors and other faculty to help students explore their beliefs and abilities to help them connect these to viable career paths. Self-efficacy and hope can only be developed if a student is heard, represented, and given access to available support systems.

6–8 Career Interventions

Intervention Philosophy

While the K–5 years are about planting the seeds of career development through repeated education and exposure, the middle-school years are more about sowing what blossoms from these efforts and refining student interest and direction. As a child learns more about who they are, what they like, and what they feel good doing, they begin to have a clearer sense of what feels right for them moving forward. Children in grades 6–8 are more able to concretely understand educational and career pathways, the barriers that might get in their way, and how to plan for the high school years in anticipation of further educational training. Experiences should move from more general (what careers/training exist, how do we obtain them) to more targeted (what does a particular student want, how do they plan and pursue that pathway). This intentional narrowing helps students more deeply understand themselves and learn how to plan their high school experiences.

Exploration of Interests

A student's career interests are influenced by academic experiences, but also by their general life experience, including their social, economic, and cultural background, family life situation, ability status, and life traumas experienced (Brown & Lent, 2017). For example, a seventh grader who experiences insecure housing and threats of domestic violence at home may have the ability to conceive how their interests and abilities relate to career, but understandably this long-term thinking process may be very far from their mind. It is here that a school counselor must remember that the career counseling process is not its own sector of the job. The counseling work school counselors do with children is always inherently academic, social-emotional, and career related (Levy & Lemberger-Truelove, 2021). In the example of the seventh grader noted above, a school counselor could not provide competent career counseling to this student without addressing the reality of their situation.

An example comes from my work with a seventh-grade student in a similar situation to the one detailed above. This student, whom we'll call Billy, had strong academic ability but often would be removed from class due to blurting out, goofing off, and arguing with the teachers. Billy reported he did this because of the strong anxiety he felt when he thought about home. Billy lived in a housing-insecure situation and was afraid of his mother's boyfriend, who had challenges with alcohol and violent outbursts. Billy preferred blurting out and interacting with others, rather than sitting in silence with his troubling worries. Since Billy was removed from class due to his response to anxiety, he became convinced his life was "bad" and that it was "pointless" for him to try in school because he was "destined" to get in trouble and be "poor forever." Billy could recognize his academic ability but also was aware that college cost money and required focusing skills he believed he lacked, so he had eliminated it as an option.

It would have been an utter disservice to simply focus on career exploration and academic alignment for Billy. How could I provide competent and holistic career interventions if I did not acknowledge and honor the whole student? By focusing on the relevant social-emotional factors using a trauma-informed lens, I helped Billy become more aware of his anxiety, work on communicating his distraction in a healthy way, and utilize mitigation strategies when he noticed it creeping up on him. We were able to bridge his social-emotional progress to career development using an empowering metaphor.

While Billy detailed how his esteem was impacted by his emotional challenges and confrontations in the classroom, I presented the idea that getting through school is often like running a track race. I suggested every student was running around the track, but some students had heavy weights strapped to their backs due to personal and family challenges. I asked Billy if this resonated with him and he agreed it did, adding that he felt like he was carrying "way more" than most of his classmates. I then honored Billy's strength by pointing out he was doing well in math class despite the weight on his back. Even though he was running with additional weight strapped to him, Billy was keeping up with or surpassing many of his classmates. When I asked him how other students might perform if they were dealing with all he had to at home, Billy responded that they wouldn't be able to get through class at all. He sat up straighter in his chair as a newfound appreciation for his resilience dawned upon him. I told him that he was quite impressive for doing as well as he did, and perhaps if he was able to do this well in school despite those challenges, he could overcome many barriers in life and accomplish amazing things. Billy began looking at himself in a new way. Rather than his narrative being one of a deficit-based perspective, he appreciated the inherent strengths and skills required for him to navigate his life situation. This reworked his narrative and allowed him to see the linkage between his qualities and future life endeavors, increasing his self-efficacy. Once hope was instilled in this manner, Billy was much more open to career-related discussions in our career counseling sessions.

In our individual sessions, Billy expressed interest in careers involving mathematics, including mechanical engineering and technician jobs. He was originally dissuaded from pursuing these interests by the cost of college. When Billy also mentioned the military as a career interest, I provided valuable information that inspired him to dedicate himself to school and to have a plan moving forward. Billy was overjoyed to hear that the military could partially or fully fund his education, or perhaps even give him relevant work experience while he was enlisted. He could complete his education and then serve, or serve first and then complete his education. Both technical colleges and four-year universities could be options if he kept his grades up and took the right high school courses. Suddenly, a student who was ready to disengage from school entirely found relevance to his life and found something meaningful to aspire toward. Honoring his history and taking a trauma-informed approach made all of Billy feel heard, represented, and guided toward a relevant life goal. Billy's behavior and academic performance both dramatically improved after this series of interventions. As the case of Billy shows, exploration of interests during this age needs to honor the client's holistic self while also making tangible connections to abilities and available career pathways.

As the career coordinator at our district, I was tasked with maintaining a career development portfolio for every middle-school student. Individual career counseling was a way to explore student interests as they progressed through their schooling years. This was a way to help track students' processing of academic and life experiences as they related to their career paths, and to provide them a place to make meaning of these, plan future steps, and access career-related resources. While regular career counseling is not common in the middle school years, it is helpful to establish a framework in which students are more regularly critically evaluating their academic and career paths using professional guidance (Trusty et al., 2005). A student could gain access to career interest inventories, such as the Strong Interest Inventory, the Holland (1997) RIASEC test, or the Myers-Briggs Type Indicator. These assessments allow for a more comprehensive examination of personality and interests as they align with potential careers. The assessments I utilized were recorded in each of my students' portfolios, which they carried with them to high school. This allowed for the high school counselors to more deeply understand each student and hit the ground running in their own individual sessions. Regularly scheduled career counseling during the middle school years allows students to make meaning of their academic journey and link their efforts to future hopes for their lives (Trusty et al., 2005).

Interests should also be explored through intentional programmatic events such as field trips. For example, I took my sixth-to-eighth graders to a career fair sponsored by the state agency of education. Students chose from a variety of interactive workshops led by individuals from diverse fields across the state. The jobs spanned each category of the RIASEC hexagon and allowed for students to hear from educators, those in social service, business owners, engineers, and many more. These workshops were engaging and fun and left plenty of time for questions and answers. Each student was allowed to attend multiple workshops throughout the day. I integrated this experience with my guidance lessons, allowing students to have more time to deeply process and analyze their experiences. We linked personal interests to the careers experienced at the event and processed what that meant for each student moving forward.

Similarly, events during this period should become concrete and filled with information. Children in this stage of career development are moving fully away from fantasy thoughts and are evaluating their experience with more realistic expectations (Patton & Porfeli, 2007). Speakers should cover how their interests in school aligned with their chosen career path and what skills and education were necessary for them to achieve their goals. Job-shadowing programs can allow middle schoolers to have direct experience in places of work, helping them solidify what they are or are not interested in (Lozada, 2001). With proper community asset mapping, local business owners and professionals can serve as both guest speakers and job-shadowing mentors, allowing for an expanded use of their valuable knowledge and experience.

Exploration of Skills

Individual career counseling should directly align academic strengths and abilities to career paths to empower students to see what abilities they can utilize to open doors in their lives (Trusty et al., 2005). Career inventories, such as the Strong Interest Inventory, allow for an examination of where a student feels competent and capable and of how these skills align with career opportunities (Harrington & Long, 2013). While these assessments come with associated costs, there are various free adaptations available online that can be appropriately used for student populations if the counselor selecting them is thoughtful, intentional, and informed in selection and application.

Experience-based workshops and job-shadowing programs, such as those highlighted in the previous section, allow students to practically explore their talents and to assess whether these roles could be linked to future career pathways. In addition to including academic skills, comprehensive career development during this time should highlight the soft skills necessary to succeed in a variety of fields (Succi & Canovi, 2020). Consider how important the qualities of respect, timeliness, flexibility, creativity, and attention to detail are to countless workplaces. Are students actively aware of how they are building and utilizing these skills during the school day? Are they aware of how these skills will benefit them in the long term?

Workplaces value transferable skills such as leadership, initiative, organization, outside-the-box thinking, respect, and appreciation for diversity (Mitchell et al., 2010; Succi & Canovi, 2020). These are skills schools often try to emphasize in their students to create connected and flourishing learning communities (Bradshaw et al., 2008). These practice skills can and should be linked to their relevance for the student's future career. An example of this is an intervention I utilized with my middle schoolers called Bright Bucks, modeled after a standard Positive Behavioral Intervention and Supports (PBIS) approach (Center on PBIS, 2021).

I selected a monthly theme related to personal skills and traits that would promote success, both now within the school and in the students' futures. Adults in the building were provided Bright Bucks to hand students (or entire classrooms) when they demonstrated the use of these skills. The Bright Bucks were used for individual, classroom, and school prizes at the end of the month in a ceremony celebrating student progress. The key to making this intervention relevant to career development was the integration of classroom content related to the practice skills. For example, during the month where teamwork was the emphasized skill, my weekly guidance lessons honed in on what teamwork was, what it looked like in school, what it looked like in careers, and how it was evaluated in career progression. Students examined their own teamwork skills, how these skills matched up with their current career path, and how teamwork looked across different career options. Students critically analyzed why these skills were necessary in chosen jobs and what would happen to individuals and organizations if teamwork was not practiced. We even considered the underlying skills necessary for teamwork (respect, listening, appreciation for others) and how a constellation of personal and professional qualities help an individual succeed in their everyday and work lives.

A key facet in career development is not only personal skills but also the skills required to overcome structural and systemic barriers, such as racism and classism, including the awareness of these barriers. Students who have increased awareness of these challenges develop skills and perspectives helpful in overcoming these obstacles, reducing their chances of being dissuaded from pursuing higher education (Ali & Menke, 2014). Interventions should focus on students analyzing the social barriers present on their career path, what resources can help them overcome the barriers, and how systems that impose these barriers can eventually change.

Intentionally chosen career development speakers—such as graduates from the local community, individuals representative of the cultural background of the community, and minoritized individuals who overcame barriers—could present to students on these topics. Such speakers could facilitate meaningful discussion and awareness, and even play a role as mentors to students. These types of programmatic mentorship roles have been shown to increase career aspirations and self-efficacy in minority students, who often lack representative role models (Holt et al., 2008). Universities increasingly employ equal opportunity advisors, multicultural counselors, and disability services counselors who could present to students about the supports available at colleges to open the doors to all types of learners from all backgrounds. Guidance lessons examining bias and career barriers in industries could allow students to process these barriers and their thoughts about career paths in advance of coming upon these types of barriers.

An example is an intervention I utilized with my middle-school students. In the lesson, I set a trash can in the center of the room and stated that this trash can was to represent a goal: enrolling in higher education. The task was to see if the students could accomplish this goal by throwing a paper ball into the trash can. I instructed the students to stand at different points in the room. Some were directly next to the trash can while others were across the entire room, with a mix of students in between. When the students threw their paper balls, the ones closest were overwhelmingly more "successful" in accomplish the goal of attending college. I celebrated these students as successful, capable, and having the skills necessary to get to college. My students were quick to see a ruse here; they identified that those closest had indeed succeeded but had started much closer to the goal. When I asked what the students thought this task represented, my middle schoolers responded that some people have advantages that put them closer to achieving these types of goals. This segued into a rich examination of privilege, oppression, and social barriers in America, in which the students analyzed what qualities impacted the ease or difficulty of trying to get into college (race, socioeconomic background, college generation status) and what that meant for each of them in their own career journey. The critical conversations illuminated the actual conditions of the path to college and career success, instead of only focusing on basic academic requirements. I was impressed by my students' deep reflection and introspection, and several commented on how transformational this activity was to their thinking in individual career counseling sessions. As should all activities at this grade range, the conversation did not solely include skills but also focused on interests and thoughts on available careers.

Career Exploration

Career exploration efforts should become more integrated, nuanced, and intentional during the middle-school years (Patton & Porfeli, 2007). Career exploration should be done in conjunction with examination of skills and interests. An example of a powerful resource to use in individual counseling or classroom activities is O*NET, found at https://www.onetonline.org. O*NET is a comprehensive website sponsored by the United States Department of Labor that includes career search options by abilities, interests, knowledge, skills, work activities, work contexts, work values, job outlook, job family, career clusters, career outlook, and other aspects (National Center for O*Net Development, 2021). Students can search for careers by industry, keyword, educational requirement, salaries, and much more. O*NET provides a comprehensive description of the job, related positions, salary description, and growth and outlook statistics, as well as the required education and training to obtain these positions. It is a helpful and free resource for schools aiming to provide their students access to quality information on available careers in the United States. During the middle-school years, a school counselor can assign tasks to be accomplished between career counseling sessions including exploring careers and reporting findings during the next meeting. Similar approaches can be taken during a career counseling session or in a structured classroom guidance activity where students are tasked with finding a career or careers and laying out the associated educational requirements, related jobs, and career outlooks of each selected profession.

An example of an integrated approach using O*NET as a resource comes from my work with seventh and eighth graders. The four-lesson unit included an updated examination of a students' skills and interests as they related to career options and an examination of the tangible realities of achieving and maintaining a career. In the first lesson, students took a Holland Code assessment to discover their career cluster (Holland, 1997). Students were tasked with looking up their three-letter code and identifying careers they might be interested in. As a class, we discussed results and the education or training required to earn these jobs. In the second lesson, students researched one of these careers on O*NET to compile a comprehensive report about the nature of the job, the skills required, the average salary, the outlook, and the training required. Students reported on these findings in front of the class. In the third and fourth lessons, students were tasked with researching the cost and application process for colleges/training programs that could allow them to achieve their selected job. Students were then to select a town or city they'd like to live in, explore the outlook for their job in that area, and analyze the cost of living. I provided the students with a workbook including associated life costs (utilities, internet, gas/car payment, dining out, various optional life expenditures) in which students had to check off and calculate their monthly living expenses. Students were provided several options of monthly rent or mortgage payments taken from local examples but were encouraged to search the market of where they were interested in living and use those figures. Students had to factor in the cost of the program they'd attend and consider if they'd likely have student loan payments, which were factored into the equation. Students calculated their monthly cost of living based on these factors and then calculated their monthly income based upon O*NET's reported salary for their position.

This activity was eye-opening for many middle schoolers. They witnessed the realities of how college and career location impact a career journey and how cost of living and salary influence the style of life one can live. Career no longer seemed academic or far away when students had to make concrete decisions (and lifestyle sacrifices) to successfully complete the activity with a balanced budget. Students were highly engaged with this activity and proud to share the results of their searches, all while asking deep and meaningful questions along the way.

One student in particular set out to prove me wrong. Her goal was to save a large amount of money per month, even straight out of college, which I told her could be a challenge. This student found a college to pursue a journalism degree, found a city in which she wanted to live, found a job posting that reported a salary higher than what O*NET provided (which also accepted applicants straight out of college) and located an apartment posting looking for a roommate to split rent and utilities, greatly reducing the monthly cost of living. After contending she could utilize public transportation (reducing transportation costs) and electing to forgo several elective entertainment options, the eighth grader proudly showed how much she could save monthly as an "in your face" moment. Of course, as her school counselor, I couldn't have been happier! The thinking and skills she utilized to make this plan were pivotal to college, career, and life planning. It was inspiring to see middle schoolers understanding these complex concepts and making tangible plans in their lives moving forward. We emphasized that these routes weren't their final routes, and that they would likely change their minds and make many turns along the way, but each student valued how these practiced skills were useful in their future exploration of careers.

Exploration of careers should be intentionally linked to educational and training options (Webb et al., 2014). Middle schoolers benefit from trips to technical schools, community colleges, four-year colleges, and apprenticeship programs. Immersion in these settings may make students more familiar with what these settings look and feel like, what support systems are in place, and what areas of study align with what career opportunities. For students from non-traditional backgrounds who may feel overwhelmed by the idea of college, visits can help them evaluate how they feel on a campus, pursue campus settings and sizes that align with their needs, become aware of financial aid and other student support services, and understand the linkage between majors and their career choices. In districts where students transition to high school after seventh or eighth grade, visits to the high school (and technical high school options where available) help students adjust to the transition and access available support systems, such as school counselors. A familiarity with school settings and resources helps students acclimate, adjust, and self-advocate for what they need (Cauley & Jovanovich, 2006). These coordination efforts could also benefit from the transfer of student career planning portfolios, to allow the new school counselor to hit the ground running with each student in individual sessions.

Academic Integration

Academic curriculum should join guidance lessons and curriculum to align with career development programming (Webb et al., 2014). Given that academic curricula are more complex during this stage of education, more in-depth integration is required. Experiential career development activities need not be an add-on to academic content, but rather can exist as a core component, further illustrating the reality and use of subject principles.

Schafft (2010) detailed an excellent application of these practices. Saint Mary's Area Middle School, in a rural Pennsylvanian district, won the prestigious Building Community award given for innovative educational practices benefiting the local community. Saint Mary's had cultivated curricula and programs centered around the reality of environmental conservation in the local area. The school went as far to develop its own environmental learning center through governmental partnerships with the Pennsylvania Conservation Corps, The Pennsylvania Department of Environmental Protection, the Workforce Investment Board Youth Council, and the Pennsylvania Fish and Boat Commission. The school developed specialized learning curriculum and experiential opportunities concerning careers in wildlife management and environmental preservation, exposing students to a variety of specialized careers requiring higher education that were available in their hometown or similar communities.

The environmental learning center provided a linkage between academic principles and real-life careers. Students received microbiology lessons in a local stream, developed an aquaculture facility on the school's campus, and even managed a trout nursery fed by hydroponics. The fish raised in this capacity were released into streams, illustrating the impact of education and specialized career functions on the environment of the local community. This hands-on learning allowed Saint Mary's to meet and exceed academic career standards while giving students quality experiences informing their interests and future paths (Schafft, 2010). Students were empowered to understand the relevance of academics and education to their home community and beyond, opening the doors to all potential pathways. The exposure to scientific principles, concepts, and activities also likely increased their academic self-efficacy in biology and related fields.

School counselors can assist in making academic lessons more connected to the reality of rural careers. This includes collaborating with teachers in the building to develop comprehensive curricula with room for guidance lesson integration. For example, what a teacher instructs about biology within the classroom can be supplemented by career exploration lessons with the school counselor directly related to what the students are learning about. Further, these principles can have a local focus, making ties to local biology, problems, needs, solutions, and the role of education through it all. Students are therefore empowered to see the relevance of education locally and beyond. Such work could easily be utilized to build personalized student career portfolios, increasingly required by state education departments throughout the United States (Boyd, 2017). Each academic lesson can tie to career development standards, while the school counselor's work can further explore student thoughts, feelings, and beliefs about these careers, tying to information and resources and making all paths seem open and acceptable. This type of intentional and streamlined career development effort would be less disjointed than efforts where career development is tacked on as an extra and foreign piece of a child's education (Boyd, 2017; Knight 2015).

It important for students to have conversations about which opportunities are available in the community and why (Gruenewald, 2003). A better understanding of the social and economic realities surrounding their community can help students to think more critically about what educational training would be beneficial to their home community. For example, the profession of a lawyer may not be highly visible in a geographically vast and sparsely populated rural area. Examining why (low consumer base/lower average salary in rural towns) will allow students to further think about if they would like to change that and how. Students considering law may not be aware of the many types of legal needs which exist, including social service advocacy, public defense, and work within local government. Students can explore this career from a local perspective in order to have a deeper understanding of what the job is, how it ties to where they live, and if they may be interested in pursuing this option. By using local dynamics as case studies, school counselors can inspire students to critically interact with the social processes impacting their personal beliefs related to career development.

CHAPTER SUMMARY

This chapter explored how career development efforts become more integrated throughout the years from grades 6–8. Exploration of skills, interests, and careers should become concrete through the sharing and processing of information and experiences. Individual career planning and counseling can be effective ways to track student progress and create portfolios, which can then transfer with them to high school. Programming and lessons should become deeper both in content and process, providing students with in-depth information and encouraging reflection upon the meaning of the content for their career journey. Lessons should not be designed as one-offs but rather should be structured to build upon themselves in an intentional format, incorporating exploration of knowledge, skills, and career options. Interventions that integrate local economic needs, track employment trends, and involve hands-on experience bridging academic content to the world of work can allow careers to become more tangible for students as they evaluate their preferences.

TABLE OF KEY TERMS

Term	Definition
O*NET	A website run by the United States Department of Labor that includes up-to-date employment and training facts, statistics, descriptions, and job search tools. Accessible from: https://www.onetonline.org/e

REFLECTION EXERCISES

Reflection exercises are designed either to be done individually within the reading or to be used as group discussion questions within the classroom setting. A series of reflection questions will be presented at the end of every chapter.

1. Recall the middle school you attended. What local community economic and career dynamics were present?
    a. How might these realities influence career development work in that school?
    b. What types of lessons or interventions would you build with this information?
    c. How might these types of interventions have influenced your own trajectory if you received them?
2. Consider your comfort in conducting individual career counseling sessions.
    a. What knowledge, skills, or experiences do you have that would be helpful?
    b. What are your shortcomings?

   c. Are there students you would be more comfortable doing this work with? Less comfortable? Analyze what dynamics (such as race, gender, SES, life situation) influence your comfort level.

   d. How could you improve your competence in working with these students?

3. Consider an intervention that integrates knowledge and experiences across the domains of interest, skill, and career exploration.

   a. What type of intervention would you design?

   b. How would you deliver this intervention?

   c. What other stakeholders would you require to successfully pull off this intervention?

CASE STUDY

High Falls Middle School has had an increase in students openly sharing their gender identity as transgender and non-binary. Students and their families have been advocating for more understanding and representation of these identities within social studies and social-emotional learning at the school. Other local families have been vocal about wanting no discussion of gender or sexuality to occur within the school setting. As a school counselor, you also realize that identity is a major concept influencing career development, and that social barriers stand in the way of gender minorities in the United States. During career development lessons, students have raised concerns regarding barriers, such as representation in careers and workplace expectations around professional attire. Students clearly have an awareness of how transphobia will be present at points in their educational and career journey and wish to have more nuanced discussions about this in lessons or groups. As the school counselor, consider the following questions:

1. How might any social-emotional work you do supporting this student population also integrate a career component?

2. What type of data could you collect from within the school to help you understand what types of experiences or career interventions could be helpful?

3. How might you utilize the above considerations in creating an intervention that would be helpful for your students? What types of knowledge, experience, or programs would assist them on their career development journey?

4. How would you design an intervention or interventions? Consider classroom guidance lessons, in- and after-school programming, school events, field trips, or any other possible approaches.

5. How would you work with other school stakeholders to address any concerns or backlash you'd receive from parents in the district opposed to these approaches?

References

Ali, S. R., & Menke, K. A. (2014). Rural Latino youth career development: An application of social cognitive career theory. The *Career Development Quarterly, 62*(2), 175–186.

Anderson, R. C., Graham, M., Kennedy, P., Nelson, N., Stoolmiller, M., Baker, S. K., & Fien, H. (2019). Student agency at the crux: Mitigating disengagement in middle and high school. *Contemporary Educational Psychology, 56,* 205–217.

Boyd, S. (2017). Transparency on college and career readiness: How does your state measure up? State Education Standard, 17(3), 24–29.

Bradshaw, C. P., Koth, C. W., Bevans, K. B., Ialongo, N., & Leaf, P. J. (2008). The impact of school-wide positive behavioral interventions and supports (PBIS) on the organizational health of elementary schools. *School Psychology Quarterly, 23*(4), 462–473.

Brown, S. D., & Lent, R. W. (2017). Social cognitive career theory in a diverse world: Closing thoughts. *Journal of Career Assessment, 25*(1), 173–180.

Cauley, K. M., & Jovanovich, D. (2006). Developing an effective transition program for students entering middle school or high school. *The Clearing House: A Journal of Educational Strategies, Issues and Ideas, 80*(1), 15–25.

Center on PBIS. (2021). Positive Behavioral Interventions & Supports. https://www.pbis.org/

Eccles, J. S., & Roeser, R. W. (2011). Schools as developmental contexts during adolescence. *Journal of Research on Adolescence, 21*(1), 225–241.

Gruenewald, D. (2003). The best of both worlds: A critical pedagogy of place. Educational Researcher, 32(4), 3–12.

Harrington, T., & Long, J. (2013). The history of interest inventories and career assessments in career counseling. *The Career Development Quarterly, 61*(1), 83–92.

Holland, J. L. (1997). Making vocational choices: A theory of vocational personalities and work environments (3rd ed.). Psychological Assessment Resources.

Holt, L. J., Bry, B. H., & Johnson, V. L. (2008). Enhancing school engagement in at-risk, urban minority adolescents through a school-based, adult mentoring intervention. *Child & Family Behavior Therapy, 30*(4), 297–318.

Knight, J. L. (2015). Preparing elementary school counselors to promote career development: Recommendations for school counselor education programs. Journal of Career Development, 42(2), 75–85.

Levy, I. P., & Lemberger-Truelove, M. E. (2021). Educator–counselor: A nondual identity for school counselors. *Professional School Counseling, 24*(1_part_3). https://doi.org/10.1177/2156759X211007630

Lozada, M. (2001). Job shadowing--career exploration at work. *Techniques: Connecting Education and Careers, 76*(8), 30–33.

Mitchell, G. W., Skinner, L. B., & White, B. J. (2010). Essential soft skills for success in the twenty-first century workforce as perceived by business educators. *Delta Pi Epsilon Journal, 52*(1), 43–53.

National Center for O*NET Development. (2021). *O*NET OnLine.* https://www.onetonline.org/

Patton, W., & Porfeli, E. J. (2007). Career exploration for children and adolescents. In W. Patton & V. Skorikov (Eds.), *Career development in childhood and adolescence* (pp. 47–69). Brill Sense.

Schafft, K. A. (2010). Economics, community, and rural education: Rethinking the nature of accountability in the twenty-first century. In K. A. Schafft & A. Y. Jackson (Eds.), Rural education for the twenty-first century: Identity, place, and community in a globalizing world (pp. 275–290). Pennsylvania State University Press.

Succi, C., & Canovi, M. (2020). Soft skills to enhance graduate employability: Comparing students and employers' perceptions. *Studies in Higher Education*, *45*(9), 1834–1847.

Trusty, J., Niles, S. G., & Carney, J. V. (2005). Education-career planning and middle school counselors. *Professional School Counseling*, *9*(2). https://doi.org/10.1177/2156759X0500900203

Webb, K., Repetto, J., Seabrooks-Blackmore, J., Patterson, K. B., & Alderfer, K. (2014). Career development: Preparation, integration, and collaboration. *Journal of Vocational Rehabilitation*, *40*(3), 231–238.

The Career Empowerment Project

Arthur Nelson, MS

P ractical Resources are examples of work school counselors can do in applying the concepts of this textbook to their own school districts. They are also an example of assignments counselor educators could assign to their students. All practical resources were contributed by school counselors in training working toward their master's degrees.

POPULATION AND SETTING

The Career Empowerment Program (CEP) will be implemented to eighth-grade students, with the assumption that it can be adjusted for students as young as sixth grade and students as old as their final year of high school. In other settings, this program could feasibly be delivered to adults of any age. However, as it is planned, the CEP's audience is an entire class of middle-school students. Some parts of the CEP, including the speakers' presentations, are to be delivered to the entire class, estimated at 200–250 students, while the lessons will be delivered to individual classes, estimated to be 25 students each. The design of the program is aspirational, including ideal speakers and resources as examples, with an understanding that the true speakers would be constrained by local factors.

I am assuming that the population of students is diverse in terms of ethnicity, religion, sexual orientation, gender expression, ability status, political leanings, and a host of other factors, as it is in many school districts throughout the United States. That is not to say that this program would be inappropriate for a more homogenous group of students; however, the CEP is targeted not only to reflect the diversity that we find in the majority of American schools today and the increasing diversity we will experience in our future, but also to empower those students from backgrounds that are traditionally not recognized by or represented within leadership.

It is my hope that the delivery of this program will take place in an advancing American middle school, which educates a wide range of students and believes that this diversity is a supreme strength, and that its diversity will empower all of the students who participate to continue the advancement of not only their individual careers, but also their communities.

THEORETICAL UNDERPINNING

Underrepresentation and Its Consequences

Generally speaking, I am a constructivist in that I believe all humans construct their own realities and draw unique meaning from their interpretations of reality. Unfortunately, in today's 21st-century

North America, too many realities are constructed from painful experiences. This is particularly true of, but certainly not limited to, communities of color, women, transgender individuals, and those who are disabled. The ways in which our contemporary society suppresses and delegitimizes people from these populations are innumerable and complex. But, with the goal of increasing the career achievement of individuals from these populations and the groups as a whole, I will focus on the issue of underrepresentation.

In this context, underrepresentation can be defined as a dearth of participation or the exclusion of a certain group in media, the delivery of services, or positions of power, influence, and success (Shor et al., 2015). Underrepresentation is thus as multifaceted and complex as the general picture of our societal shortcomings in meeting the needs of marginalized populations. But all of these facets affect the career aspirations of our youth. As Shor et al. (2015) describe, women receive less attention in media, which disempowers young girls from believing that their society's media, and therefore their society at large, is amenable to their presence and influence.

Women and people of color are also underrepresented in certain career paths, namely business and the sciences. And, according to Jackson et al. (2016), this underrepresentation is directly correlated with a belief that certain fields are unattainable. Once minority students become aware that the rates of their group's participation in certain fields are low, they become disinclined to continue pursuit in that field, perpetuating the problem of homogenous or even culturally hostile career fields.

Students' awareness of underrepresentation in relation to careers occurs at a markedly young age. As outlined earlier, children immediately begin to recognize a lack of representation in media and within their environment. As Linda Gottfredson (1981) asserts, children as young as six begin to understand their sex and use their surrounding environment to determine what activities are "right" for them, and thus which career aspirations are achievable. Gottfredson also contends that as children get older, they start to understand their self-concept in a more holistic way that includes ethnicity and social class, but that their aspirations are nonetheless molded by what they understand is possible for people from their cultural background (Gottfredson, 1981).

The evidence of this theory manifests itself in all aspects of our White-male-driven professional culture. Of all the 2020 CEOs of Fortune 500 companies, five were African American, 37 were women, and none were women of color (Wahba, 2020). One was openly gay, and none were transgender. Only nine were Hispanic (Hinchliffe, 2020). And these are only statistics pertaining to the world of business. As discussed earlier, individuals from ethnic minority cultural groups are underrepresented in the various career fields, particularly STEM. According to the Pew Research Center, one in five workers in the STEM fields have faced barriers into and within the field based on their race or ethnicity (Funk & Parker, 2018). Over 62% say that they have faced explicit discrimination, making the field itself hostile to their progression and thus inhibiting them from pursuing such fields.

This wide body of research supports not only the existence of underrepresentation of minority groups in media, certain careers, and positions of power, but also its consequences. First and foremost, the CEP believes that students as human beings deserve to pursue the careers they feel are best for them, without preclusion due to cultural barriers. In addition, humans only perform optimally at their job if it is something they genuinely care about and feel satisfied pursuing (Karatepe, 2012). This satisfaction necessarily includes feeling safe in one's career, in order to be truly productive and happy, and is therefore something that countless people from underrepresented groups are barred from enjoying.

A world in which students of all backgrounds feel empowered to choose whatever career path best suits them, and then go on to achieve maximum innovation and productivity in those fields, is a world worth fighting for. It is for this reason that the CEP seeks to empower all students with examples of those who have broken systemic barriers to achievement, while assisting them in understanding how to select a career that is correct for them.

Career Philosophy

The CEP utilizes the work of John Holland, specifically his career code theory (Holland, 1996). I do not believe that it is a perfect measure for one's career interests or personality, but I do believe that it is a helpful starting point for students to consider how their interests and skills match with certain career fields. Thus, I use it not only to help students narrow down their career selection for their presentation assignment, but also to introduce students to career assessments.

Educational Philosophy

Because this program will be delivered in an instructional capacity, its pedagogy is as foundational to the program as the fact and consequences of underrepresentation. I subscribe to Jean Piaget's (2008) findings that educational experiences are far more meaningful when students play a role in their construction and delivery, particularly when the students are between adolescence and adulthood. This increase in meaning allows students to feel not only that they have a stake in the process, increasing self-efficacy and thus performance, but also that they have a place in contributing to the school community (Piaget, 2008). It is for this reason that students will be asked to construct a presentation and share it with their peers, an activity that has the above benefits as well as reinforcing the idea that all students, no matter their cultural background, can achieve success and contribute to their communities, a central tenet of the CEP.

An additional piece of my pedagogical philosophy is outlined by Marzano and Pickering (2007) in their holistic discussion of homework. While it can be effective, homework as it's thought of today can harm students in relation to their health and their family time, which undermines their motivation for completing it. I am not against the assignment of homework, and students are asked to complete assignments in the program, but I also give students ample class time to complete their projects. In my opinion, this increases the likelihood of the assignment's competent completion and gives students a community of their peers to work with when constructing their career presentations. The benefits of said community, outlined above, are wide-ranging and multifaceted. By working among and with peers of numerous backgrounds, students will understand that the world can be one in which all individuals contribute their expertise to improve the greater whole. In addition to the educational benefits of student-led projects, including increased self-efficacy and performance, this reinforcement of our potential as a culture is a direct parallel to what I hope to achieve with the CEP.

Another justification is needed for my intended audience. On the one hand, as Mary Ellen Flannery (2007) points out, the ability of students to select different classes in high school, including important APs and electives, means that their academic and career trajectories typically begin earlier than high school. On the other hand, some of the concepts and coursework in this program, as I've outlined it here, are outside of the developmental range of younger students. In consideration of these two factors, I've determined eighth graders to be the ideal audience for how I've formatted the program. But again, by adjusting specific activities and speakers, a counselor or other education professional can adapt this program for a variety of grades and age levels and deliver the CEP to students of all ages and backgrounds.

GOALS

The goals of the CEP are to ...

- Imbue in all students the idea that their cultural background does not preclude them from any career path.
- Inspire students by providing them with examples of individuals who have broken systemic barriers to achieve eminent success.
- Provide students with a holistic understanding of their interests, skills, and personality types as represented in the Holland Code (1996), and of the careers that may be preferable to them based on these interests and skills.
- Introduce students to career assessments and explain how they can be helpful in refining a career search.
- Inspire students to make an action plan for what courses they will take in high school, which clubs they will become involved in, and what colleges or universities they may consider.
- Help students understand that a career path is not straight and narrow, that they will encounter challenges and changes of heart along the way, and that these vicissitudes are not only acceptable but are an opportunity to learn and continue their development.
- Communicate the idea that many important factors go into a career decision, including finances, desired time off, and work culture.
- Identify resources in the world at large and in the school community that can enable students to aim toward a certain career path and achieve steps towards its realization.

Finally, the program has an indirect goal that is nonetheless a long-term goal reflecting the program's intention. This goal is to create a school culture, and thus a world, in which all students: understand what careers they may want to pursue; know of and take advantage of resources that can help them achieve their career goals; feel empowered to pursue career paths that they themselves choose; understand that barriers may try to obstruct them; and believe that they have strengths to overcome barriers and achieve their goals.

THE CAREER EMPOWERMENT PROGRAM

The following section will detail the steps and process of the CEP. Generally speaking, the program will consist of a handful of lesson plans in which a counselor introduces career assessments and what goes into them, has students find their Holland Code (1996), instructs students on what goes into a career choice, and introduces the challenges that certain career paths may present them. All of these lessons will lead to students constructing a presentation to their class (individual classes of around 25 students) about a chosen career and information regarding the career, as outlined in the rubric below. Between each of these lessons, the counselor heading the CEP will present a distinguished speaker to the entire class (250 eighth graders).

Below, for steps of the program that are speakers, I will present the speaker's relevance to the program and what I hope students will get out of listening to them. Although speakers will have the liberty of choosing the content of their speeches or presentations, it will be asked that the main theme of their talk be their careers, career progression, challenges they've faced in the professional world, how they utilized their strengths to overcome these challenges, and lessons they feel are pertinent to share with today's youth. Part of the lessons will be a counselor- or teacher-led discussion in which students comment on the speakers, their challenges, and how they overcame them. This will be introduced by a short writing activity, and will help reinforce one of the central goals of the CEP—that of inspiring students to identify challenges they may face and consider how they can utilize strengths to overcome them. These activities and discussions are outlined further in the lesson plans and the evaluation section.

Note that although I was purposefully ambitious with the specific speakers, this program can be altered to fit a local scale. For example, the first speaker I chose was Stacey Abrams, who could give students insight into how an African American woman made a career in law, politics, and advocacy. Since a school wishing to implement the CEP is unlikely to have access to a figure of national prominence like Ms. Abrams, a local African American woman who works as a lawyer, public official, or advocate may be invited. I do not mean to suggest that there are certain boxes a speaker must necessarily "check off" to be included in the program. However, as I argued earlier, representation among people of power and success, particularly representation of traditionally marginalized populations, is undeniably imperative for all of our students. It is beneficial to all students if most of the guest speakers can address how they faced and overcame systemic barriers to the realization of their career.

For steps of the program that are lessons, I have included lesson plans for analysis. Lesson plans are based on the ASCA National Model for school counseling lesson plans and are built within the ASCA-provided template. Note that these lesson plans are to be delivered weekly, meaning that each week would have one speaker followed by one lesson; however, the specific schedule can be adjusted based on when counselors usually give lessons to students. These lesson plans are consistent with the typical resources available to the average American school, but can also be adjusted for specific schools, their resources, and the grade levels they instruct.

The speakers and lesson plans for the CEP are as follows.

Steps of the Career Empowerment Program

1. Introduction to Students and Families

The CEP recognizes family participation as one of the most important aspects of a child's education. When a student goes home, their domestic environment is often the central factor in determining who they are and who they desire to become. Although almost all of the CEP will take place at the school itself, both assignments related to the program and long-term career goals will be enabled by parent and family participation. It is for this reason that counselors will pass out flyers to all eighth graders and their families, advertising the program, discussing its outcomes, and offering counselor contact information should parents have any questions.

In the same class period in which the flyers are passed out, the counselor in charge of implementing the CEP will explain to students what the next month will look like. They will pass out the rubric below and explain that students will be choosing a career and presenting to their class about certain elements of the career including why they chose it, the education required, the salary, the typical roles of the job, the challenges they may face when pursuing the job, and how they will use their strengths to overcome them. The counselor will inform students that a lot of this work will be done together with the counselor, and for now, they should just be thinking about some careers they may want to try or what careers their parents have.

Students will also be briefed on the speakers. The counselor will inform students that in between counseling classes, they will gather all of the other eighth graders and listen to presentations from some of the most successful leaders in the country, the state, or the community. The counselor will ask students to pay particular attention to the challenges these individuals faced and how they used their strengths to overcome them.

2. Speaker One: Stacey Abrams (Lawyer, Politician, and Activist)

Stacey Abrams has a plethora of experiences to share with students. In high school, Abrams demonstrated admirable self-efficacy, taking on a job as a typist for a congressional campaign. Through her hard work, she not only was promoted to the position of speech writer but also graduated from her high school as the valedictorian. In college, Abrams continued her tendency to excel in both the academic and professional worlds. She pursued her bachelor's degree in interdisciplinary studies, graduated magna cum laude, and worked for the office of Atlanta mayor Maynard Jackson. She also took part in protests aiming to remove the confederate flag from the Georgia state capitol.

Abrams went on to graduate law school and work as a tax lawyer in Atlanta, where she founded a financial services firm and a beverage company. At age 29, Abrams was appointed the deputy city attorney for the City of Atlanta. In 2018, Abrams became the first African American woman to be a major party's nominee for governor. Though she lost, she demonstrated deep resilience, immediately founding Fair Fight 2020, an organization dedicated to building voter protections in 20 states.

I believe that Abrams not only shows the traits of hard work requisite for career achievement, but also displays the happenstance nature of career development. Abrams pursued varied but related interests and had a great diversity of jobs that all centered around the theme of making the world a better place. And, as an African American woman who has excelled in the areas of law, business, politics, and advocacy, she acts as a true model for all students, particularly those who are so often marginalized. Though Abrams encountered many systemic barriers to her success, she worked tirelessly to overcome them.

3. Lesson One: Imbuing Career Considerations and Goals Into Eighth Graders

Lesson Plan

Lesson Plan for	Imbuing Career Considerations and Goals Into Eighth Graders	(lesson title)
School Counselor:	Mr. Arthur Nelson	
Target Audience:	Class of 25 eighth graders, 250 eighth graders in Total	
Mindsets & Behaviors: (limit of three)	M 4. Understand that postsecondary education and life-long learning are necessary for long-term career success B-LS 7. Identify long- and short-term academic, career, and social/emotional goals	

Lesson	1	Of	4	

Learning Objective(s)/Competencies		
Students will:	Understand the Career Empowerment Program and its ultimate goals.	
Students will:	Understand how a career assessment can provide insight into what careers they could pursue.	
Students will:	Develop a basic understanding of their Holland Code (1996) and narrow potential careers of pursuit.	
Materials:		

- Self-directed search program (20-min. program available at https://self-directed-search.com/free-self-directed-search/)
- Laptops/classroom computers
- Anchor chart displaying the Holland Code hexagon (color-coded in accordance with the above SDS code: R is red, I is orange, A is yellow, S is green, E is blue, C is purple)

Evidence Base:	
• Best Practice (x) • Action Research • Research-Informed • Evidence-Based	

Procedure: Describe How You Will ...		
Introduce	Counselor will begin by handing out Challenges and Strengths worksheet (below), giving students three minutes to jot their thoughts down, and offering students the opportunity to discuss their impressions of Stacey Abrams and her presentation. Students will be allowed to discuss openly and freely, but, if not addressed organically, counselor will ask students: • Lessons learned from the speaker • Challenges the speaker faced • How the speaker overcame these challenges Counselor will then transition to a discussion of how Ms. Abrams has had many jobs. Counselor will outline how Ms. Abrams is an example that you can have many different goals and change your career over time, but it can be helpful to know what kinds of jobs you may like the most.	
Communicate Lesson Objective	Counselor will communicate that social scientists have spent a long time creating assessments to help people find what careers may be best for them, and that these assessments are a starting point to help us think about what we might aim to do after high school. Counselor will then connect that these goals will inform what classes we take in high school, what activities we try, and what clubs we join. Counselor will inform students that we are going to take one of these short assessments today to narrow what careers and paths they might wish to pursue as they continue high school. Counselor will reveal that these codes are not a definite measure for what career the students should be pursuing, but rather a place to begin in thinking about their career and which career they'd like to select for their Career Empowerment Project (CEP, introduced in an earlier meeting).	

Teach Content	Counselor will introduce the Holland Code and explain the six categories (R,I,A,S,E,C), also providing a career example of each. R is Realistic, a personality trait that involves doing things with your hands, building things or fixing things. I is Investigative, meaning you like to think about ideas and solve problems, like a scientist. A is Artistic, which involves expressing oneself creatively. An example is a singer or artist. S is Social, meaning you like to work with or help people. E is Enterprising, a type that likes to work with people in a business-related manner. And C is Conventional, a type that likes to work with numbers and is efficient and orderly.	
	Counselor will explain that everyone is a mix of all of these personality traits. They will explain that the SDS assessment will give students their Holland Code, a three-letter combination of their traits that will put their top three traits in order. It will then give students a list of jobs that have the same three-letter code. Counselor will give an example of an individual's Holland Code, the three-letter code of a career, and explain how the code manifests itself in the job. The example used will be a secondary teacher whose code is SEC. Counselor will invite students to explain why they think the code of teachers is SEC, given their knowledge of each letter and what a teacher does. Counselor will fill in any gaps. (The S comes from the primary trait teachers have, which is working with people including students, colleagues, and families. The E comes from working with people as well in an administrative capacity. The C is due to the many tests, numbers, office work, and assessments they must do.)	
	Counselor will reiterate that this assessment is not the be-all and end-all, but a starting point to get students thinking about what careers they may want to investigate for the CEP and what types of clubs or extracurricular activities they might consider. Counselor will tell students that the career they choose for the CEP will have to have at least one letter in common with the code they receive from the SDS.	
	Counselor will pull up the self-directed search and demonstrate how to register email and answer questions (counselor will model thinking through their own preferences to select an answer for the first five questions).	
	The above portion of the lesson should take 20 minutes.	
	Students will be released to use the rest of class time (25 minutes) to complete their SDS assessments.	

Practice Content	Counselor will release students to independently complete the SDS. Counselor will walk around the room and support any students who have questions, who are struggling, or who would just like to share some information about themselves. Counselor will encourage students to use them as a resource for talking through confusion or ideas.	
Summarize	Counselor will pause when there are five minutes left in class, bring up their own SDS, and model how to look through it by speaking aloud their own quantitative measurements for each personality metric while looking at the Holland Code, then browsing recommended careers. After students complete the SDS, they will be encouraged to save the results in their email inboxes and spend the rest of the time looking into their career list. Students who have not finished can work until the end of the period. Counselor will explain that while certain careers may have their Holland Code exactly, some share the same letters but are mixed up, which means the career may still be a good fit. Counselor will describe that these codes are not a definite answer to what you should do when you grow up, but can get you thinking about what career may fit you best, and a career that you may want to select for the CEP.	
Close	Counselor will instruct students to finish the test later if they have not done so. Counselor will instruct students to think about certain careers in their code, let it sit in their minds, and even begin researching the career if they want. Counselor will also connect codes and careers to certain clubs in the school and encourage students to enroll in clubs that match their interests. Counselor will remind students that this year, they will be completing a presentation on one of the careers in their Holland Code.	

Data Collection Plan: *For multiple lessons in a unit, this section need only be completed once.*

Participation Data:

Anticipated number of students:	25 (per class, but the lesson will be delivered to all eighth graders in the school)
Planned length of lesson(s):	45 mins.

Mindsets & Behaviors Data:

- Pre-test administered before first lesson. Students will be given the brief pre-test (below) to understand the extent to which they've considered their career path and their knowledge of career paths before this lesson.
- Post-test administered after lesson (if standalone) or after last lesson of unit/ group session. This will not be administered until after student presentations on a career. Part of the assessment will be the career presentation itself, which will test student understanding of a particular career path and how they could achieve it. Students will also complete the sheet below to determine how their ideas around careers have evolved since the program and what action steps they have taken towards the realization of a career.
- Pre-/post-assessment are below.

Outcome Data: (choose one)

- Achievement (describe):
  Student results on their post-test evaluations, compared to their responses on their pre-test, will determine how successful the lesson and unit were in imbuing in students long-term career goals and providing them knowledge based around how they can refine and focus these goals. The goal is that by the end of this unit, 90% of students will feel as though they have an understanding of what is required for a certain career path (score of 6 or higher), and 90% will show an increase in their confidence in relation to their knowledge based around careers they are considering. Ideally, 90% of the students in attendance of this lesson will enroll in relevant clubs or organizations.

· Attendance (describe):	
· Discipline (describe):	

Adam Grant is an eminent thinker and pioneer in the field of organizational psychology. After graduating from Harvard University and earning a master's degree and PhD from the University of Michigan, Grant wrote two best-selling books, *Give and Take: A Revolutionary Approach to Success* and *Originals: How Non-Conformists Move the World*. Grant has since delivered a plethora of TED talks and guest lectures that discuss intra-workplace dynamics, how someone can manifest their most productive and healthy behaviors, and how the most effective and innovative people live their lives.

It is my opinion that Adam Grant would be a fantastic role model for all demographics; Adam's work habits are world-renowned, as is his ability to balance these habits with a healthy relationship with his wife and sufficient time for family. I believe that work-life balance is not only something all students should aspire to, but also something they should consider when considering a career. This is a tenet that will be covered in the next lesson plan.

Grant is a dedicated proponent of equality in the workplace, and as such, I'd expect him to explicitly outline issues pertaining to systemic barriers to entry in certain fields and in the workforce in general. I'd also hope that Grant could shed light on what makes innovative workers tick, inspiring students to apply self-efficacy and efficient working habits to their academic and professional careers. Grant's explicit analysis of these themes will be a clear and foundational benefit for students moving into high school and beyond.

Lesson Plan

Lesson Plan for	Selecting a Career	(lesson title)

School Counselor:	Mr. Arthur Nelson
Target Audience:	25 eighth graders, 250 in total

Mindsets & Behaviors: (limit of three)	M 4. Understand that postsecondary education and life-long learning are necessary for long-term career success B-LS 7. Identify long- and short-term academic, career, and social/emotional goals		
Lesson	2	Of	4

Learning Objective(s)/Competencies	
Students will:	Understand that selecting a career, both for their presentation but more importantly for their future aspirations, involves many factors.
Students will:	
Materials:	

- Computers

Anchor chart (will be visually engaging when created, but will consist of the below content)

Steps to Choosing a Career for the Career Empowerment Project

1. Look at your SDS. What code are you? What careers does the SDS recommend?

2. Go to O*NET and research a career that you may like from the SDS. Don't see anything you like? Select a letter on O*NET and see what other matches you have.

3. When selecting a career, make sure to think about …
   What people in that career do on a daily basis
   Time off and work/life balance
   Work culture
   How much school is required
   How much money you'll make
   Some challenges of the career

Evidence Base:	

1. Best Practice (x)
2. Action Research
3. Research-Informed
4. Evidence-Based

Procedure: Describe How You Will …

Introduce	Counselor will begin by passing out Challenges and Strengths worksheet, giving students three minutes to complete it, and offering students the opportunity to discuss Adam Grant's presentation. Students will be allowed to discuss openly and freely, but, if not addressed organically, counselor will ask students: • Lessons learned from the speaker • Challenges the speaker faced • How the speaker overcame these challenges	
Communicate Lesson Objective	Counselor will claim that Stacey's, Adam's, and everyone's journey does not happen in a straight line. To visualize, counselor will draw, on a whiteboard, a zig-zag line with points, emphasizing the different aspects of Adam's professional journey. Counselor will conclude by saying that thus, even though we're only choosing one career to present on, people very rarely select one career. They choose something they're interested in, and if it goes well, they stick with it, or maybe they decide to change careers. All of that changing is OK, as long as you're thinking, "What about this don't I like? What would be better?" To cement this, counselor will give students an example of a professional who is dissatisfied with his career, and students can suggest where he can go. Jeff is an accountant who loves using math at his job, but feels bored at his office. After work, he likes volunteering with kids. What advice would you give him if you were Jeff's friend?	

Teach Content	Counselor will say that when choosing the career you want to go into, there are other things you should think about. One big one is free time. Do you want to work during the day or night? Do you want to have a lot of vacation time? Do you want to work a lot or have frequent breaks? What about education? Does this require college? Do you have to do even more school, like a doctor?	
	Counselor will say that another thing to consider is money and living expenses. "Today, as we select our careers, I also want us to work out if the salary is OK for where we want to live."	
	Counselor will demonstrate how to choose a career, going on O*NET and talking out their decision-making. "My code is SAC. Let's see, I see that being a graphic designer is ASE. Remember, you can choose any career that has at least one of your letters. That has two of my letters, and I like drawing, so let's click it. OK, I see I can read the different activities that a graphic designer does. OK, it says I have to go to college. That's OK, but you know I really want a job where I can work with people more. Let's go back to my SDS. Ah, Art Therapist. That's SAI. I think I'll try that. OK, this all sounds good, but I'll have to go to college too." Counselor will google Art Therapy programs and describe how they will have to go to college and then two years of school afterward. "That's a lot of school, but I like school, so let's see that salary. This job pays $52,620 per year."	
	Counselor will then demonstrate how to divide the salary to determine monthly income. Then, counselor will model looking on apartments.com for rentals, continuing to think aloud. "Is this something I can afford? OK, if I make $4,385 per month, and I like this place in New Paltz for $1,500, that leaves me $2,885 per month. Is that enough for groceries and other things? I like to travel and buy plane tickets. Is that enough? If it is, I'll keep it. If not, I'll keep going. Remember, discussing how much education you need and how much a job makes will be a part of your career presentation."	
Practice Content	Students will be released to independently browse careers of interest, select careers, and determine if they want to go on with that career. Students will have all but the final ten minutes of class to do this and begin their presentation.	
	Counselor will put up an anchor chart to help students conceptualize the steps of choosing a career.	
	Counselor will walk around class and assist students when needed.	

Summarize	With ten minutes remaining, counselor will ask for all student attention. Counselor will ask students to share how they're doing and share some challenges they're finding. Counselor will address issues if they are fixable problems, but will also assert that it's OK not to be sure, that it's OK to change one's mind. "Remember, this is just a presentation, not choosing your career forever."	
Close	Counselor will reiterate that a lot of factors go into making a career decision. Counselor will say that students are expected to have their CEP career chosen by the next class, but if you're unsure, talk to friends, family, and the counselor! Counselor should say that their office is always open, and this is completely something they should come to the office to talk through, like they should go to their counselors in high school and college to do if they are feeling uncertain about their career track or a class.	

Data Collection Plan: *For multiple lessons in a unit, this section need only be completed once.*

Participation Data:

Anticipated number of students:	25 students per class, 250 students total	
Planned length of lesson(s):	45 mins.	

Mindsets & Behaviors Data:

- Pre-test administered before first lesson.
- Post-test administered after lesson (if standalone) or after last lesson of unit/ group session.
- Pre-/post-assessment are below.

Outcome Data: (choose one)	
• Achievement (describe): • Attendance (describe): • Discipline (describe):	

6. Speaker Three: Jay-Z (Music Artist and Entrepreneur)

Jay-Z is a model example of someone who, despite being born into astonishingly challenging circumstances, rose to become one of the most successful musical artists and business executives in American history. Jay-Z, born Shawn Carter, was raised in a housing project in Brooklyn where violence was not only rampant, but was an everyday occurrence in his childhood. However, Carter identified music as an area of intense interest and utilized the resources available to him to excel, bravely applying himself to the professional world and asking music producers to adopt him as a mentee. Eventually, Jaz-O, a musician, took on Jay-Z as a mentee, ushering in a new era of Jay's life.

In my opinion, Jay-Z satisfies a diverse group of elements that would be an extraordinary resource for students. First and foremost, Jay-Z exemplifies a strengths-based approach to overcoming adversity. His early childhood was filled with challenges and tribulations, but by focusing on music and his passion, Jay-Z was able to build a meaningful life. His message may particularly resonate with students who come from similar backgrounds, particularly those who are impoverished, live in areas that struggle with violence, or are marginalized by society.

Jay-Z also highlights key tenets of a non-traditional career path. Once Jay-Z applied his interests to progress in the music industry, he soon pursued business ventures and became an entrepreneur. He went on to establish a record label of his own, start a fashion company, and invest in sports teams. This will not only display to students the indirect nature of one's career, but also reinforce the idea that time investment in one's career does not preclude participation in another. Jay-Z has spent his life exhibiting creative ways to combine passions, interests, economics, and traditional business pursuits into a wide-ranging and successful career.

This did not come without continued work, and Jay-Z's persistence compared with his remarkable success will communicate to students that when they continue to try, they can achieve. And the fact that Jay-Z is an African American business leader will empower underrepresented students with the knowledge that the business world and CEO positions are as open to them as to anyone else.

Lesson Plan

Lesson Plan for	Beginning the Career Empowerment Project Presentation	(lesson title)

School Counselor:	Mr. Arthur Nelson			
Target Audience:	25 eighth graders (at one time, but lesson will be delivered to all 250 eighth graders in the school)			
Mindsets & Behaviors: (limit of three)	M 4. Understand that postsecondary education and life-long learning are necessary for long-term career success B-LS 7. Identify long- and short-term academic, career, and social/emotional goals			
Lesson	3	Of	4	

Learning Objective(s)/Competencies		
Students will:	Understand how to begin and build their CEP Presentation	
Students will:	Learn about and understand the expectations for their presentation	
Materials:		
Career Empowerment Project Presentation Rubric (below)		
Evidence Base:		
• Best Practice (x) • Action Research • Research-Informed • Evidence-Based		

Procedure: Describe How You Will …		
Introduce	Counselor will begin by passing out Challenges and Strengths worksheet, giving students three minutes to complete it, and offering students the opportunity to discuss Jay-Z's presentation. Students will be allowed to discuss openly and freely, but, if not addressed organically, counselor will ask students: • Lessons learned from the speaker's presentation • Challenges the speaker faced • How the speaker overcame these challenges Counselor will also use this time to ask students which presentation was their favorite and why. Though this will be an open discussion, counselor will emphasize that good career presentations have a good amount of information and that the speakers present well.	
Communicate Lesson Objective	Counselor will inform students that for today's lesson, we will be learning how to build our CEP Presentation and how to present in a way that will be engaging and powerful.	
Teach Content	Counselor will pass out the presentation rubric to all students. Counselor will share the screen of their computer and model setting up slides for each of the informational categories outlined on the rubric. "OK, so it helps me to set it up before, but you can do this as you go along too. So we need slides for the career, the code, and why I chose it. Next, I'm going to make a slide for the typical roles. Then the education and salary, and remember, that includes if I can afford to live here in our city or another area where I want to live. And, finally, challenges of the career and strengths I'll use to overcome it." Counselor will then say they have completed a presentation, and will share their presentation with the class. Counselor will then ask the students how the counselor performed, and solicit some positives about their presentation style. Counselor will reinforce that a good presentation has good information, but also is hosted by a presenter with good posture who speaks to the crowd instead of reading from the slide, makes eye contact, and uses an interested tone.	

Practice Content	Students will be released to begin their presentations. Although this class is mostly instructional, students should still have half of the remaining class time to begin their presentations. Counselor will walk around the class, assisting students with specific questions, but also noting any class-wide issues or misconceptions and pausing the class to address them.	
Summarize	With five minutes left, counselor will ask for all student attention. They will ask students to share how they're doing and share some challenges they're finding. Counselor will address issues if they are fixable problems, but will also promote students reaching out to their parents, teachers, and the counselor for help should they need it.	
Close	Counselor will state the due date for the project, but also state that there will be a full class devoted to a work period between this lesson and the due date.	

Data Collection Plan: *For multiple lessons in a unit, this section need only be completed once.*

Participation Data:

Anticipated number of students:	25 at one time, 250 in total	
Planned length of lesson(s):	45 mins.	

Mindsets & Behaviors Data:

- Pre-test administered before first lesson.
- Post-test administered after lesson (if standalone) or after last lesson of unit/ group session.
- Pre-/post-assessment are below.

Outcome Data: (choose one)	
• Achievement (describe): The primary metric of evaluating this class will be that of the presentations, which will be graded quantitatively by the counselor at the end of the next class session. Qualitative data about the students' engagement, level of understanding about the project, and how well they build their presentations will also serve as outcome data for this particular lesson. • Attendance (describe): • Discipline (describe):	

8. Speaker Four: Sharice Davids (Lawyer, Politician, and Former Professional Martial Artist)

Sharice Davids provides a shining example of a non-linear career path, and is an empowering force and role model for our society's most marginalized. A lawyer and business professional, Davids is the first openly LGBTQ Native American representative in the United States. Raised by a single mother in a country that has committed innumerable atrocities to her people, Davids had many challenges in her life and professional journey. Despite these obstacles, Davids used her academic strengths to enroll in community college, and worked her way through her bachelor's degree to eventually earn a JD from Cornell University.

Through Davids's experiences, I would hope to empower students from the underrepresented LGBTQ and Native American communities, and imbue in them the idea that through arduous work and perseverance, they could not only achieve success but also influence their societies for the better. I also believe that Davids would demonstrate to all students that these traits are the key factors in enabling someone to achieve a meaningful life.

In addition, Davids would demonstrate the naturalness of a career veering in many different directions but nonetheless being successful. Before her career as a political representative, Davids worked as a lawyer. In between these two occupations, Davids was a professional martial artist, exemplifying a non-traditional career path and the integration of a plethora of skills and interests into a successful life.

9. Lesson Four: Work Period

In this class session, students will be allowed an entire class period to work on their career presentations. Counselor will begin with a 10-minute discussion on what the students thought of Sharice Davids, her challenges, and how she overcame them. Then the work period will begin. Counselors will ensure that all students have the rubric and will walk around the room, assisting students where needed and addressing any class-wide issues. When there are five minutes left in the period, students will be reminded that the project is due next week, and that if they aren't finished, they should complete it at home before that date.

10. Student Presentations

Students will perform their presentations to their classmates as the counselor grades, using the rubric below.

Printable, Student-Facing Materials Attached Below
Each sheet is included on a separate page to give a view of what students would see.

INTRODUCTORY DISCUSSION SHEET

This sheet will be given to students at the beginning of each counseling class that follows a speaker. The sheet will function as an introductory activity to get students prepared for a brief discussion about each speaker and their strengths, but the counselor will also collect these at the end of each class to gather data on how many students are identifying challenges that speakers have faced and how they utilized strengths to overcome them.

Name: _____

Who was the last speaker that presented for us?

_____

What job or jobs did the speaker have?

_____

_____

Challenge the speaker faced:	How the speaker overcame that challenge:

PRESENTATION RUBRIC

Notes about the rubric:

- This rubric is student facing, but will be graded by the counselor who initiates the program.
- The grading process is subjective, and as such, certain counselors may grade differently than others. However, I would stress leniency and a focus on the positives of student performance rather than the negatives. There is space for comments in each section of the rubric. Grading counselors are encouraged to shine light on student strengths in an attempt to empower them to make career decisions and grant them positive feelings about their ability to perform a career search. The criteria for earning a score of 2 is specific, so as long as a student meets these minimum criteria, they should earn a perfect score. The score is also out of ten, which is intentional, lightening the weight of the assignment and enabling both counselors and students to focus more on the qualitative content and the skills that the student is exhibiting than on the quantitative grade. This latter point is why filling the comments section with student strengths is particularly important.
- With all of that being said, I am aware that classrooms rarely function in an ideal way, and as such there will surely be students who do not put in effort or dismiss the assignment. In this event, the counselor should do all they can to imbue in students the understanding of this activity's importance. Also, career searches can be fun for most students, but if a particular student is having difficulty, this program assumes that the counselor, teacher, and school staff will do all they can to discover what is holding the student back, address it, and empower them to complete the assignment with pride. Again, this cannot always happen, and in the event that a student presents a low-effort project, their grade can certainly reflect that.

Name: _____

Career Empowerment Program

Career Selection	Education and Salary	Typical Roles	Challenges and Strengths	Presentation Style
(2)- Student discusses why they chose their specific career, giving justifications including their interests (SDS) and what they want out of life and a career (work values).

Comments: | (2)- Student accurately describes the education required for their career of choice, how much this education may cost, and how much the profession makes. Student addresses if this is a sufficient salary to live in either their current hometown or the place they wish to live.

Comments: | (2)- Student provides an in-depth look into the daily activities of the profession, what kinds of skills the profession requires, and what challenges people in the profession may face.

Comments: | (2)- Student describes challenges that come with the job (e.g., low growth rate, long work hours, low pay) and how they will meet these challenges with their strengths.

Comments: | (2)- Student speaks clearly, makes eye contact, and is engaged with the content. Student is an active and respectful listener when other students are presenting.

Comments: |

(1)- Student justifies the career selection in terms of their interests or values, but not both. Comments:	(1)- Student mentions one of the above elements of the job, but not all. Comments:	(1)- Student discusses very few elements of the occupation. Comments:	(1)- Student describes challenges but does not describe how they will meet them. Comments:	(1)- Student either presents well but is not a respectful listener to others, or is a respectful listener, but could work on presentation skills. Comments:
(0)- Student does not describe why they chose the occupation. Comments:	(0)- Student does not mention education, its costs, salary, nor its implications for cost of living. Comments:	(0)- Student does not mention any functions of the role. Comments:	(0)- Student describes neither challenges nor how they will meet them. Comments:	(0)- Student's presentation skills significantly hinder understanding, and student is not an active listener. Comments:

PRE- AND POST-TEST FOR STUDENTS (STUDENT FACING)

* This test will be given before and after the implementation of the Career Empowerment Program to judge how much student attitudes and knowledge have evolved through participation in the CEP.

Name: _____

Answer the below questions to the best of your ability. You will NOT be graded for this assignment, so be honest.

1. On a scale of 1 to 10, with 1 being almost never and 10 being constantly throughout every day, how often do you think about what career you want to have when you grow up? (Circle one)

    1   2   3   4   5   6   7   8   9   10

2. On a scale of 1 to 10, with 1 being "I know nothing," and 10 being "I know everything," how much do you know about what different careers require? For example, do you know how much college, what kind of grades, what kind of classes, what kind of skills, what kind of interests, and what kind of training go into getting a certain job? (Circle one)

    1   2   3   4   5   6   7   8   9   10

3. What are some of the most important parts of considering a future career? Examples include happiness, getting to make art, making a lot of money, living somewhere exciting, etc. If you have trouble thinking of different ideas, ask your counselor! (List a few below)

    _____

    _____

    _____

    _____

    _____

4. What are some careers you are considering right now? What are some that you have considered in the past? List at least 3 for each.

    Right Now:

    _____

    _____

    _____

    _____

    _____

In the Past:

_____

_____

_____

_____

_____

5. What are some challenges that you may face in your chosen career field? How will you overcome them?

_____

_____

_____

_____

_____

6. List clubs that you have joined since completing the Career Code Activity (SDS).

_____

_____

_____

_____

_____

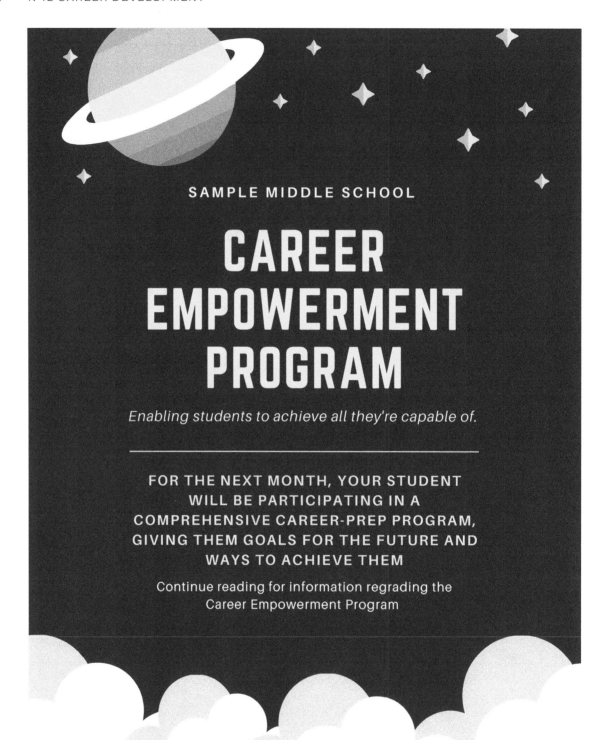

SAMPLE MIDDLE SCHOOL

CAREER EMPOWERMENT PROGRAM

Enabling students to achieve all they're capable of.

FOR THE NEXT MONTH, YOUR STUDENT WILL BE PARTICIPATING IN A COMPREHENSIVE CAREER-PREP PROGRAM, GIVING THEM GOALS FOR THE FUTURE AND WAYS TO ACHIEVE THEM

Continue reading for information regrading the Career Empowerment Program

IMG. 7.1

What is the Career Empowerment Program?

The Career Empowerment Program, or CEP, is a month-long program in which students will learn about how to determine which types of careers may be the best fit for their interests and skills. Students will also list to a host of speakers who have faced career challenges and met them head on, inspiring students to identify, face, and overcome future career challenges.

Why is my child participating?

Because of the importance and variety of AP and other advanced classes and participation in relevant clubs throughout high school, students should be thinking about career choice before they enter ninth grade. While student should have a rudimentary idea of careers from elementary school content, we are employing the CEP so that students go into high school having clarified career goals and an understanding of what they must do during high school and beyond to achieve. This early preparation will embolden your child to choose a career that he or she values, and empower him or her to work hard to achieve it.

Are are the goals and benefits of the CEP?

Specifically, students will develop a more nuanced understanding of what goes into a career choice and how their skills, interests, needs, and desires match with specific career options. After participation in the CEP, students will have a clearer direction for their future and the work they must put in to achieve their desired goals. As such, we expect to see high participation in clubs, increased academic performance, reduced behavioral issues, and increased college admissions among all students who particiapte in the CEP.

What can I do?

We recommend that you have open, encouraging conversations with you children around what career they are choosing for the CEP and express pride when they take steps to achieve that career path, such as studying for an exam or joining a club. Support your students as best as you can throughout this process, and always feel free to reach out to our school counselors should you have any questions, comments, or concerns.

IMG. 7.2

REFERENCES

Funk, C., & Parker, K. (2018, January 9). Blacks in STEM jobs are especially concerned about diversity and discrimination in the workplace. Pew Research Center. https://www.pewresearch.org/social-trends/2018/01/09/blacks-in-stem-jobs-are-especially-concerned-about-diversity-and-discrimination-in-the-workplace/

Gottfredson, L. S. (1981). Circumscription and compromise: A developmental theory of occupational aspirations. *Journal of Counseling Psychology, 28*(6), 545–579.

Hinchliffe, E. (2020, May 18). The number of female CEOs in the Fortune 500 hits an all-time record. *Fortune.* https://fortune.com/2020/05/18/women-ceos-fortune-500-2020/

Holland, J. (1996). Exploring careers with a typology: What we have learned and some new directions. *The American Psychologist, 51*(4), 397–406. https://doi.org/10.1037/0003-066X.51.4.397

Jackson, M. C., Galvez, G., Landa, I., Buonora, P., & Thoman, D. B. (2016). Science that matters: The importance of a cultural connection in underrepresented students' science pursuit. *CBE Life Sciences Education, 15*(3). https://doi.org/10.1187/cbe.16-01-0067

Karatepe, O. (2012). Perceived organizational support, career satisfaction, and performance outcomes: A study of hotel employees in Cameroon. *International Journal of Contemporary Hospitality Management, 24*(5), 735–752. https://doi.org/10.1108/09596111211237273

Marzano, R. J., & Pickering, D. J. (2007). The case for and against homework. *Educational Leadership, 64*(6), 74–79. https://eric.ed.gov/?id=EJ766368

Piaget, J. (2008). Intellectual evolution from adolescence to adulthood. *Human Development, 51*(1), 40–47. https://doi.org/10.1159/000112531

Shor, E., van de Rijt, A., Miltsov, A., Kulkarni, V., & Skiena, S. (2015). A paper ceiling: Explaining the persistent underrepresentation of women in printed news. *American Sociological Review, 80*(5), 960–984. https://doi.org/10.1177/0003122415596999

Wahba, P. (2020, June 1). The number of black CEOs in the Fortune 500 remains very low. *Fortune.* https://fortune.com/2020/06/01/black-ceos-fortune-500-2020-african-american-business-leaders/

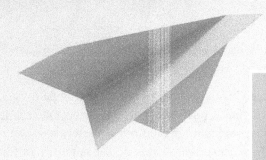

CHAPTER 8

9-12 Interventions

Take yourself back to high school. The ups, the downs, the good times, and the challenging ones. Perhaps you were dealing with finding your social circle, exploring dating life, establishing your identity, juggling academics and hobbies, or exploring your dream college or career path. Take yourself back to your emotional mindset during this time period. Did you feel confident? Did you know what you were doing? Did you have the guidance and support you needed? Where was it lacking? Who majorly guided your college and career decision-making process?

Did you meet with your school counselor during your 9–12 years? Did you have multiple meetings each year? Did you engage in individual career counseling or access schoolwide programming? What about in-class instruction? Did your school counselor or a teacher provide career exploration tools and information? In what ways was your school counselor there for you? In what ways could their efforts have been improved?

High school is a major time of self and life exploration. Given the pressures teenagers face, such as defining their identity, establishing themselves socially, exploring their romantic interests, and managing life stress, it is understandable that career development is swept by the wayside. High schoolers have extracurriculars to join, parties to attend, and TikToks to view and share—there's always more to grab their attention and always more to do. And for some, just tolerating high school and getting through it is overwhelming. What time or energy do they have to plan for more? Life moves fast for teenagers. It can be easy to slack on proactive career development planning. If a school isn't prepared to recognize this and integrate repeated career development efforts and resources into the high school learning experience, its efforts are not tailored to the practical needs of its student population.

Students' feeling that they are unprepared regarding academics and career pathways has led to an increase of first-year college seminar courses addressing these concerns (Wright et al., 2013). A nationally representative study found that approximately 30% of college students change their major within the first three years of their education (Leu, 2017). While

157

receiving extra support and changing pathways are not inherently negative aspects of the college experience, uncertainty around career path can lead to costly challenges for students. Major changes often lead to more required semesters to graduate or a necessity to switch to a different university. These aspects may cause personal, family, or financial stress, which most severely impact students who enter college at the highest level of disadvantage (Kezar et al., 2020). First-generation students, those from low socioeconomic status backgrounds, and students of color are all groups who may have their career journey put on hold or even ended by the addition of these transitional barriers on top of what they are already facing (Chen & DesJardins, 2010). While universities have increasingly offered services to students to address these concerns, these reactive measures address challenges that arise due to the school systems failing to help prepare students for their transition into the world of careers. An intentional, integrated, and streamlined approach can empower students to hit the ground running and springboard onto their path of success.

9–12 Career Interventions

Intervention Philosophy
Ideally, K–8 career education helps establish a student's sense of academic self-efficacy and aspirations. These efforts help students develop the foundational understanding of self and the world of work necessary for specific honing and action steps during the 9–12 years. Whereas K–8 interventions are broader, interventions in the 9–12 years narrow the specificity of efforts, encouraging concrete steps towards particular careers and programs of study. If adequate work has not been done in the K–8 years, this type of specific work may not suit students, who lack a background understanding of self, academics, and potential career options. All too often schools push these students along, pipelining them towards higher educational options that aren't truly a fit, causing challenges later in these students' lives. By creating systemic, regular, and integrated efforts throughout the high school experience, a district best enables students to thrive in their college and career journey.

Exploration of Interests
Many students enter high school without taking a college or career assessment. Many students walk into high school having little to no sense of how their personality, skills, or interests align with options beyond senior year. Despite this reality, some high schools lack career counseling and lessons that provide this type of opportunity for students. For the purpose of narrowing options en route to concrete choices, career and major assessments can be invaluable tools. Holland RIASEC code tests, mentioned in previous chapters, could be effectively integrated into school counseling programming and individual classroom experiences. For example, students could be tasked with finding their RIASEC code and aligning their code with potential careers and college majors. Students could be tasked with exploring potential majors based upon their results or writing essays to be graded as part of a career elective class, in the typical curriculum, or as a required document in a career portfolio.

Many students lack awareness of what types of majors exist and how they relate to or differ from typical high school subjects. There are various freely available websites, including O*NET, that allow students to explore majors as they link to potential careers. School counselors can utilize these websites to independently develop shareable worksheets, databases, and newsletters, which can promote this education for students and their families. By advertising these websites and accumulating educational information in accessible forms, the school counselor gathers resources for their work with students and empowers students and families to utilize these in their career exploration efforts.

School counselors should assist in coordinating students attending college and career fairs throughout their high school experience (Filer, 2018; Schmidt et al., 2012). The school counselor can help students access in-person or virtual career fairs as well as work to bring higher education institutions to the high school campus to ensure greater student access to these experiences. School counselors can coordinate with admissions counselors from universities to coordinate visits and informational workshops in which information is conveyed about programs of study, the cost of college, supports available at the college level, and what major options exist. These representatives can provide students an opportunity to ask questions about majors, pathways, and how these may or may not align with their interests.

Experiences also allow students to further explore and hone their career interests. School counselors can help shape and inform practical and integrated academic curricula which provide students with experiential opportunities to apply class knowledge. High schools with technical, agricultural, STEM, human service, artistic, and food-service programs empower students to functionally experience the roles of various jobs and help them sort through which career roles appeal to them more.

For example, the high school I attended had a food service program in which students took several courses related to cooking and managing within the restaurant industry. The students in these courses ran a restaurant which served faculty and students during select days of the school year. My high school also offered a comprehensive automotive program in which students performed maintenance and repairs on actual vehicles and a human services program in which students looked after children and could serve as district peer mentors to younger students. Programs like these help students jointly explore both their career interests and their skills and can help inspire them to pursue fields they had not previously imagined. These are just a few examples of how a high school's curriculum could offer core and elective courses designed to provide students actual work experience which can help them make important choices between potential fields of study.

Exploration of Skills

Students have likely experienced an academic conceptualization of how skills are utilized throughout professions by the time they reach high school. High school courses and programming can allow for practical exploration and application of these skills towards work functions. Integrated academic courses that involve hands-on application of material better allow students to assess their skills and their interest in particular fields. These integrated academic experiences include not only the practical work programs mentioned in the previous sections but also integration into standard core curriculum courses. For example, mathematics classes could integrate practical experience utilizing course concepts in the form of engineering challenges or competitions. Biology classes could involve students studying local wildlife, participating in ecological conservation efforts, and studying plant life through a school or community garden. English and computer courses could have students produce their own magazines, newsletters, and promotional videos around topics of all sorts. Practical field work applying academic principles can assist students in better determining how the skills they have mesh with the lived experience of those working in the field (Schafft, 2010).

Higher education programs often require a certain set of academic skills, which are often evaluated by standardized testing. Common tests in the United States include the Scholastic Aptitude Test (SAT) and the American College Test (ACT). Given that the language of the tests favors students who come from White middle- and upper-class backgrounds and that academic test taking is a skill separate from actual subject mastery, it is important that schools provide proactive and integrated test preparation to assist in bridging the gap for disadvantaged students (Freedle, 2003).

Schools can offer academic integration with standardized test preparation. For example, units in mathematics and English could present problems in a manner similar to the college exams. The key skills necessary to identify what the question is asking, how to extrapolate the necessary information, and how to apply academic skills to solve the problem can be facilitated in the classroom setting. The school counselor can offer standardized test preparation groups during or after school time, can assist in developing an elective course entirely dedicated to standardized test preparation, and can provide a list of study tools and preparation resources to families through newsletters. Test anxiety psychoeducational lessons or groups could further help students navigate difficult feelings related to test taking. Having these interventions available in multiple ways assures that students do not fall through the cracks, leaving these skills and needs unaddressed.

The college application process also requires a set of knowledge and skills many students and families don't have, especially if they are coming from first-generation backgrounds (Bryan et al., 2011). For students coming from families where a parent has not attended college, the application process can be confusing and intimidating. The student and their family may not know how to apply for scholarships or financial aid. These families also may not understand the different types of financial aid available and the potential debt incurred throughout the college experience. While this information can and should be covered in individual career counseling sessions with students, this level of support on its own is inadequate. A school counselor should proactively empower students to master these resources by providing this information in classroom guidance lessons and schoolwide presentations, sharing it within the school website (including posting a video of a lesson or schoolwide presentation), sending it home, and hosting college application and FAFSA nights. During these college-themed community events, families attend, learn the information for themselves, and ask the school counselors whatever important questions they have. In this way, the college application process does not rest solely upon the student and is instead reinforced by the knowledge and support of the family. Research indicates that family knowledge and support is a key predictor of college matriculation and completion (Byun et al., 2017); therefore, empowering students through family support is a key step in providing the best services we can to our school population.

Career Exploration

For students from low-income, minoritized, and first-generation college backgrounds, the pathway to college is laden with barriers (Bryan et al., 2011). Too often, schools expect students and families to know what they cannot possibly know and to make informed major life decisions without professional guidance (Grimes et al., 2019). Regular and repeated scheduling and career counseling check-ins can provide students with a place to explore their aspirations and pathway options, and to access available resources to overcome social barriers (Paolini, 2019). Traditionally, many school counselors simply focused on quickly scheduling students and providing limited information on college and career options. The transformed school counselor should take a holistic perspective into these meetings, looking to help students explore their options and access the most helpful resources to help them and their families. School counselors can be proactive in these efforts by offering monthly career and college presentations for their students and by sending important information to students and families in newsletters. School counselors should create equitable partnerships with families and community stakeholders in order to inform their interventions and approaches to serving the community (Bryan et al., 2020). The school counselor should also offer career exploration groups, held during study blocks or after school, which allow interested students to receive more direct interventions related to career development and to connect with other students who are experiencing similar concerns (Paolini, 2019).

A structural way to integrate career exploration into a school system is through the use of career exploration seminar courses, which have been shown to positively impact students' career self-efficacy and aspirations (Gaylor & Nicol, 2016). The school counselor could teach and/or help develop the curriculum for a course (required or elective) offered to high school students in which they take career assessments, engage career exploration, and explore resources to make college more affordable. Assignments could also include preparing admissions documents such as resumes and college essays and practicing college entrance interviews. This type of course should be accessible to all students and should encourage exploration of employment post high school, enrollment at community college, enrollment in technical school, and enlistment in the military. If there is room in the high school curriculum, a school counselor can help build a career exploration course progression in which students go through these processes progressively each year of high school, adding to their career portfolio each year and engaging in exploration more deeply.

Career mentoring, job shadowing, and internship programs are another structural way for the school counselor to empower students to experience the world of work and consider which options may align best with their future (Turner & Lapan, 2005). A school counselor can serve as a connection between the school and local businesses and organizations willing to collaborate in these roles. Career mentors could be local workers, professionals, and business owners willing to meet with students on a monthly basis, providing advice and guidance related to their particular career field. These mentors could also serve as role models for students from non-traditional backgrounds, helping inspire students to understand that overcoming barriers and achieving their dreams is possible.

Job-shadowing programs can be required parts of the high school experience for all students or be integrated into a career exploration course (or group) curriculum. By intentionally partnering with a diverse variety of workers and professionals in the local community, a school counselor can help expose students to a variety of jobs, work settings, and roles. Students receiving direct job-shadowing experience can determine which careers or fields they feel more connected to and wish to consider further (Choi et al., 2015). Internships can be integrated as a graduation requirement, a component of a career exploration course, or even the centerpiece of a unique internship course itself. Internships may offer students more exposure to practical work experience, which may help them determine which pathways to follow or even secure networking connections to help with the transition to college or directly to the world of work (Hutchins & Akos, 2013).

Academic Integration

School counselors should encourage or be involved with assisting in integrating concrete career development knowledge into academic courses. Such efforts could help students find the relevance of their studies to their career and life aspirations (Gaylor & Nicol, 2016; Rowan-Kenyon et al., 2011). Partnering with teachers could also allow for targeted speakers and events related to particular disciplines. Place-based educational practices such as allowing students to apply science course principles to community problems in local spaces may reinforce the relevance of academic content to everyday and professional life (Schafft, 2010).

Dual enrollment is a process in which a high school student is taking a community or four-year college course for both college and high school graduation credit. Dual enrollment allows high school students to experience the structure and rigor of college courses while exploring potential fields of study and earning meaningful high school credit (Medvide & Blustein, 2010). Dual enrollment allows students who have historically had limited to no access to the practices, norms, and cultures of college campus to begin experiencing what this world is about and learning how to prepare themselves to navigate through it (Hughes et al., 2012). Dual enrollment classes can take place at the college or university or be offered in-house at the high school, taught by a professor or even by a high school faculty member. Taking these courses not only provides students with meaningful major and skill exploration but also offers significant financial savings, since students will be able to transfer earned college credits to their institution of choice. This type of exposure can reduce financial limitations on attending institutions of higher education while also providing students the comfort, familiarity, and confidence needed to hit the ground running in a collegiate atmosphere. A school counselor can help coordinate a dual enrollment program with a local college or university, helping to ensure student access with little to no cost while promoting the affiliated institution. This type of coordination could potentially lead to more comprehensive partnerships, including mentoring programs and meaningful academic, career, or social-emotional programs facilitated by university interns.

CHAPTER SUMMARY

Comprehensive 9–12 career interventions should build upon the previous exploration efforts made throughout the K–8 years. Interventions should become more streamlined and concrete, applying exploration of knowledge, skills, and abilities towards specific career paths and postgraduate options. Proactive and integrated programming—including career development content in academic courses, career exploration courses, career development and academic skills groups, and dual enrollment—can empower students with the knowledge, skills, and resources to overcome barriers and find their desired career pathway.

TABLE OF KEY TERMS

Term	Definition
Dual enrollment	A process in which a high school student is taking a community or four-year college course for both college and high school graduation credit.
FAFSA	The Free Application for Federal Student Aid, required for students to receive federal student loans or grants and often required by universities to be eligible for financial aid.
SAT	The Scholastic Achievement Test, a standardized academic assessment often used in college admissions decisions.
ACT	The American College Test, a standardized academic assessment often used in college admissions decisions.

REFLECTION EXERCISES

Reflection exercises are designed either to be done individually within the reading or to be used as group discussion questions within the classroom setting. A series of reflection questions will be presented at the end of every chapter.

1. Consider a major academic subject offered in most high schools. How would you propose an integration of career development material into this course?
   a. How would you partner with a teacher to propose or accomplish this?
   b. Could you integrate this academic lesson with other career development programming?
2. Consider how you would help reach out to the community for a proposed college application and FAFSA night.
   a. In what ways would you get the word out to families about the event?
   b. What type of information or programming would you include at the event?
   c. How could you collect data to evaluate the effectiveness of the event or learn what information needs to be added next time?
3. Create a lesson plan regarding college major exploration to be used in a career development course.
   a. Consider the length of the lesson.
   b. Consider what information you would utilize and from what helpful resources.
   c. Select an activity for the students to complete. How would this activity help them regarding major exploration and choice?

CASE STUDY

At Long River High School, a significant number of students have one or more parents of undocumented status. These students' own situations vary; some are also undocumented, while others were born in the United States and are citizens. As the school counselor, you are aware that many students are hesitant to consider higher education due to fears that disclosing their family's finances and social security numbers as part of the FAFSA application process would put the students or their families at risk of deportation. Many of these students are unaware of what options exist to transition to higher education, what resources exist to help with the cost, and what they can do moving forward. Your counseling department is considering what types of career development resources, including events, newsletters, lessons, and connection to resources, could benefit this student population. As the school counselor, consider the following questions:

1. How would you connect with these students and their families in a positive way, given their concerns?

2. What programs or resources exist that could help your school and your students with the challenges of this situation?

3. What professional organizations could provide guidance on how to meet the needs of these students?

4. What types of events might you plan in order to assist these students and their families? Who would you need to coordinate with, and how would you execute the event?

References

Bryan, J., Moore-Thomas, C., Day-Vines, N. L., & Holcomb-McCoy, C. (2011). School counselors as social capital: The effects of high school college counseling on college application rates. *Journal of Counseling & Development, 89*(2), 190–199.

Bryan, J., Williams, J. M., & Griffin, D. (2020). Fostering educational resilience and opportunities in urban schools through equity-focused school–family–community partnerships. *Professional School Counseling, 23*(1_part_2). https://doi.org/10.1177/2156759X19899179

Byun, S. Y., Meece, J. L., & Agger, C. A. (2017). Predictors of college attendance patterns of rural youth. *Research in Higher Education, 58*(8), 817–842.

Chen, R., & DesJardins, S. L. (2010). Investigating the impact of financial aid on student dropout risks: Racial and ethnic differences. *The Journal of Higher Education, 81*(2), 179–208.

Choi, Y., Kim, J., & Kim, S. (2015). Career development and school success in adolescents: The role of career interventions. *The Career Development Quarterly, 63*(2), 171–186.

Filer, J. (2018, March 22). *Intent matters. Increasing representation of Latina women in STEM.* STEM Career. http://www.stemcareer.com/

Freedle, R. (2003). Correcting the SAT's ethnic and social-class bias: A method for reestimating SAT scores. *Harvard Educational Review, 73*(1), 1–43.

Gaylor, L., & Nicol, J. J. (2016). Experiential high school career education, self-efficacy, and motivation. *Canadian Journal of Education/Revue canadienne de l'éducation, 39*(2), 1–24.

Grimes, L. E., Arrastía-Chisholm, M. A., & Bright, S. B. (2019). How can they know what they don't know? The beliefs and experiences of rural school counselors about STEM career advising. *Theory & Practice in Rural Education, 9*(1), 74–90.

Hughes, K. L., Rodriguez, O., Edwards, L., & Belfield, C. (2012). Broadening the benefits of dual enrollment: Reaching underachieving and underrepresented students with career-focused programs. Community College Research Center. https://ccrc.tc.columbia.edu/media/k2/attachments/broadening-benefits-dual-enrollment-rp.pdf

Hutchins, B. C., & Akos, P. (2013). Rural high school youth's access to and use of school-to-work programs. *The Career Development Quarterly, 61*(3), 210–225.

Kezar, A., Hypolite, L., & Kitchen, J. A. (2020). Career self-efficacy: A mixed-methods study of an underexplored research area for first-generation, low-income, and underrepresented college students in a comprehensive college transition program. *American Behavioral Scientist, 64*(3), 298–324.

Leu, K. (2017). Beginning college students who change their majors within 3 years of enrollment. Data Point. NCES 2018-434. National Center for Education Statistics. https://nces.ed.gov/pubs2018/2018434.pdf

Medvide, M. B., & Blustein, D. L. (2010). Exploring the educational and career plans of urban minority students in a dual enrollment program. *Journal of Career Development, 37*(2), 541–558.

Paolini, A. C. (2019). School counselors promoting college and career readiness for high school students. *Journal of School Counseling, 17*(2). https://eric.ed.gov/?id=EJ1203651

Rowan-Kenyon, H. T., Perna, L. W., & Swan, A. K. (2011). Structuring opportunity: The role of school context in shaping high school students' occupational aspirations. *The Career Development Quarterly, 59*(4), 330–344.

Schafft, K. A. (2010). Economics, community, and rural education: Rethinking the nature of accountability in the twenty-first century. In K. A. Schafft & A. Y. Jackson (Eds.), *Rural education for the twenty-first century: Identity, place, and community in a globalizing world* (pp. 275–289). Penn State University Press.

Schmidt, C. D., Hardinge, G. B., & Rokutani, L. J. (2012). Expanding the school counselor repertoire through STEM-focused career development. *The Career Development Quarterly, 60*(1), 25–35.

Turner, S. L., & Lapan, R. T. (2005). Promoting career development and aspirations in school-age youth. In S. D. Brown & R. W. Lent (Eds.), *Career development and counseling: Putting theory and research to work* (pp. 417–440). John Wiley & Sons.

Wright, S. L., Jenkins-Guarnieri, M. A., & Murdock, J. L. (2013). Career development among first-year college students: College self-efficacy, student persistence, and academic success. *Journal of Career Development, 40*(4), 292–310.

Gender Non-Traditional Career Fair

Caitlin Pastore, MS

P ractical Resources are examples of work school counselors can do in applying the concepts of this textbook to their own school districts. They are also an example of assignments counselor educators could assign to their students. All practical resources were contributed by school counselors in training working toward their master's degrees.

INTRODUCTION

The intervention I have chosen to research and develop is a career fair for high school students. Unlike typical career fairs, this fair will be specifically designed to encourage gender non-traditional career exploration. This is something that is lacking in schools across the nation and it is something that I would like to implement in my school as a future school counselor. I think this intervention would be beneficial for students because it would broaden their horizons and open up doors of opportunity that they otherwise might not have been in contact with. There is much research to suggest that this intervention is one that is necessary and would be effective in application.

POPULATION AND SETTING

The target population of this intervention would be high school students in the district I work in. It would be advertised to both male and female students, including the whole student body. I would place a heavier emphasis on trying to recruit juniors and seniors to this event, but the fair would be open to anyone who was interested. I would target juniors and seniors specifically because they are at the stage where making post-graduation plans is increasingly relevant, and they have probably already begun the college search process. Freshman and sophomore students would also be encouraged to attend because they could benefit from the opportunity for career exploration that this fair would provide.

The ideal setting for this intervention would be a gymnasium or large outdoor setting like a school's sports field. The event would be structured with booths and tables for each occupation because a big, open space allows the most freedom for students to roam. They would be able to visit the tables that interested them and move at their own pace. At each table there would be one or more people, preferably volunteers from within the community, who would have informational materials to give to the students and could answer any questions they might have. The volunteers would be representing their own occupation or place of work, so they would be knowledgeable on the subject.

In searching for volunteers I would first reach out to community members. I think it's good for students to see people in their own community who are working at jobs they are interested in.

This close-to-home connection would hopefully empower the students to pursue their interests. An "if they can do it, so can I" feeling is what I would be hoping for here. It would also be a great opportunity for networking. If a student is interested in a career path and knows someone working in that field, the person can serve as a resource to the student and may even provide an advantage when the student is applying to jobs.

While community participation would be encouraged, I would not limit the volunteers at this career fair to just community members. I would want a wide array of representation and if I couldn't find someone within the community to represent a certain career path, I would search elsewhere. Additionally, having connections to people outside the community would be beneficial to students looking to broaden their horizons or move after graduation.

THEORETICAL UNDERPINNINGS AND RESEARCH SUPPORT

The theoretical foundation of this intervention involves three theories: Gottfredson's theory of circumscription and compromise (1981), Super's life-span theory (1990), and Lent and colleagues' Social Cognitive Career Theory (1994). Each of these theories plays a role in my development of this career fair, and each of them is relevant to the goals of my intervention.

At various stages of a young person's life they are affected by the developmental theory of circumscription and compromise that Gottfredson (1981) proposed. In the circumscription process, young people rule out certain professions based on a variety of social factors. In the stages of this process children become oriented to different concepts—such as size and power, sex role, and social valuation—and to an internal unique self. Sex role and prestige in particular are concepts that become very important later in their lives, when they are making career choices. The compromise piece comes in when they adjust their goals and dreams about occupations based on external reality. Vocational choices that may be found desirable are eliminated because they don't fit with the child's developing self-concept. This process of elimination sometimes ends with opting for "good enough" occupational choices rather than desired choices. In this circumscription and compromise process, children create for themselves a "zone of acceptable alternatives." This zone holds the occupations most compatible with their images of themselves.

My aim in creating this gender non-traditional career intervention is to attempt to focus on the development of sex role concept as proposed by this theory. By creating a career fair that displays people in gender non-traditional occupations, I hope to expand the zone of acceptable alternatives for my students. I don't want them compromising their hopes and dreams by not pursuing a career in something just because it's not traditionally held by people of their sex or gender. I want kids to explore all kinds of careers and choose what they want to pursue, based solely on their own passions and interests. In creating this intervention I hope to minimize the compromise piece of this process.

Though Gottfredson proposed her theory in 1981, the significance that sex role still has in relation to careers is astounding. A study titled "Gendered Perception of Professional Occupations," conducted by Couch and Sigler in 2001 exemplifies this point. In this study more than 200 students at a university were surveyed and asked to indicate whether they perceived individual occupations as either predominantly feminine or predominately masculine. The rationale behind testing these college students was that they were the youngest members of adult society to soon be entering the workforce, and would be least affected by the gendered biases about occupations that older generations held. This, however, was not the case. There were 105 professional occupations on this list, and only 30% of them were classified as gender neutral. Of the 49% of occupations classified as masculine, most of them were "power" or "control" occupations, while many of the occupations classified as feminine involved caregiving. The results of this study showed that there is certainly still a prevalence of gendered perceptions of occupations, and that there are occupations which are considered "appropriate" for individuals based on their sex (Couch & Sigler, 2001). This study shows that there is a significant need for interventions such as the one I've proposed, to encourage gender non-traditional career exploration. Without it, it seems likely that children will compromise their dreams to pursue something more socially acceptable.

The next developmental theory that influenced this intervention is Super's (1990) life-span, life-space theory. The life-span stages in particular have influenced this intervention the most. The life-span stages, as proposed by Super, encompass the process we go through in relation to career development. They include broad categories of growth, exploration, establishment, maintenance, and disengagement/decline. The proposed gender non-traditional career fair will specifically focus on the exploration stage. This stage, typically experienced between ages 15 and 24, marks a time when individuals become more aware of themselves and the world of work. They try out new things through classes, hobbies, etc. and develop tentative skills. As the stage goes on, career choices begin to narrow in as they focus on specific occupations. Oftentimes this is the point at which careers are seriously discarded because they're not seen as realistic options for the person based on their gender. This is exactly the reason I want to focus on this stage—because I want to broaden the exploration of career to include gender non-traditional options.

The third theory that influenced the proposed intervention is Social Cognitive Career Theory. There are a few major focuses of this theory, the most important of which is the concept of self-efficacy. People with high self-efficacy are more likely to set difficult goals, persist in a task even in the face of failure, and succeed in their place of work. The biggest factors that come into play when a person establishes a sense of self-efficacy are the learning experiences they go through. Vicarious experience and verbal persuasion are two learning experiences that relate to this gender non-traditional career fair. Vicarious experience includes seeing other people do things, whether it's in their personal lives or through the media. Verbal persuasion is the encouragement or discouragement we receive about something.

In my intervention, I am looking to touch on vicarious experience and verbal persuasion as they relate to pursuing gender non-traditional careers. Because these careers are labeled as gender non-traditional, children of the non-traditional gender are not seeing themselves represented in these fields. Children are also constantly being told what is socially acceptable, and this deters them from exploring half of the possible careers that exist in the world. My career fair aims to give these kids learning experiences that will encourage this exploration, not deter them from it. By providing an opportunity for them to see what gender non-traditional careers look like and to see real people who work in these gender non-traditional careers, it will hopefully provide them more support that will aid in strengthening their self-efficacy in this area. If they feel like they are not alone, or that working in this profession is not impossible, it will give them more confidence to pursue their dreams.

Davis (2014) describes the phenomenon of self-efficacy, stemming from learning experiences like vicarious experience, among women in the Science, Technology, Engineering, and Mathematics (STEM) fields. The purpose of the article is to discuss why there are so few women in STEM, and to study how human behavior influences male scientists versus female scientists. STEM has experienced explosive growth in recent years and offers great opportunities to those who enter. However, there is a significant underrepresentation of women in these fields. Despite the greater number of women getting college educations, there are far more men in STEM. One of the reasons proposed by this article is that there is a lack of female role models in the field. "Women and girls need to see female role models in the workspace that look like them over and over and over again. They need to receive the message that women can work in STEM careers and be successful and fulfilled in their work" (Davis, 2014, p. 1). This is exactly what my intervention aims to do: to show representation in gender non-traditional fields so that students will feel more empowered to pursue them.

Despite increasing social tolerance in recent years and the challenging of social norms in mainstream society, there is still significant gender segregation in occupations. According to a study by Fluhr and colleagues (2017), "as recently as 2010, approximately 80% of jobs classified by the U.S. Census Bureau were filled predominantly by one gender" (p. 1). This statistic is an alarming one. It is also important to encourage students to explore gender non-traditional career options because of the economic realities they might face. According to Cross and Bagilhole (2002), occupations traditionally held by females often offer lower salaries and earnings than occupations that are traditionally male dominated. Additionally, these female-dominated occupations can carry a social status that is presumed to be lower than that of male-dominated occupations. This gender segregation operates both horizontally and vertically. "Not only are men and women allocated qualitatively different types of jobs, the labour market is marked with women overwhelmingly concentrated at the lower levels of the occupational hierarchy in terms of wages or salary, status and authority" (Cross & Bagilhole, 2002, p.6). These assertions are also supported by another study that analyzed occupational segregation, conducted in 2004 by Huffman and Cohen. Additionally, women are less likely to hold positions of supervisory authority in the workplace than their male counterparts, even when they have the same expertise, education, and prestige (Huffman & Cohen, 2004).

I believe there is something inherently wrong with socializing young women to believe they must go into socially acceptable occupations based solely on their gender, when it is clear that they will face this kind of economic disadvantage later down the road. As previously stated, it is my goal to break this type of socialization with my intervention—or at least offer experiences that will counteract this type of socialization.

This socialization of what is considered a "man's job" versus a "woman's job" is not only problematic for women. It is also problematic for men who wish to enter the workforce in a role that is not traditionally held by men. In a study conducted by Cross and Bagilhole in 2002, 10 men who held jobs in traditionally female-dominated occupations (such as nurse, social worker, midwife, cleaner, etc.) were interviewed and followed for a period of time. The study aimed to explore the experiences of these men and see if the gendered work settings had any effect on how they defined their own gender identity and masculinity. The findings of this study were interesting; about half of the men distanced themselves from the women in their place of work and tried to maintain traditional masculinity, while the other half tried to reconstruct masculinity to some extent to include more typically female traits. Many of these men hid the fact that they worked in caretaking fields from people in their life, out of fear that they would be harassed and have their manhood called into question (Cross & Bagilhole, 2002). Many of these results can be tied back to that socialization process wherein young boys are taught what is and is not acceptable to do based on gender roles. "Such indirect pressure to enter a workspace saturated with traditional masculine values means that men who pursue caring work risk being seen as different from 'real men,' who not only confirm their masculine identity, but also their heterosexuality, through doing 'men's work'" (Cross & Bagilhole, 2002, p.9).

GOALS

I have set several goals for the intervention. Broadly stated, they all revolve around fostering the exploration of gender non-traditional occupations for my students. My female students will get a sense of what it would be like to work in typically male-dominated areas, and my male students would get a sense of what it would be like to work in typically female-dominated areas. But there are also certain benchmarks that I'm aiming for throughout this process. These benchmarks have to do with counteracting the socialization process that students go through as it pertains to gender identity and the workplace.

One specific goal is to provide learning experiences such as vicarious learning and verbal persuasion, in order to increase students' self-efficacy in gender non-traditional settings. If these students are able to interact with adults who are successful in their field and have succeeded where others have not, they can serve as role models. As parts of my literature review described, people need to see themselves represented in fields they want to enter in order to increase their drive to enter the fields themselves. This is especially true in settings where gender non-traditional careers are involved. For example, if young female students can talk to successful women in STEM, and young male students can talk to successful men in caretaking fields, they will be more likely to envision themselves in those roles. If they never see this kind of representation, they will likely not have the ability to envision themselves in that kind of role. The same process is true when it comes to verbal persuasion. When these young students interact with the professionals at this career fair, they will be able to communicate with people who are prepared to give them accurate information without any gender biases. Nobody at this fair will be told, "No, you can't do this job because you're not a [man/woman]." Their curiosity and interest will be met with encouragement and empowerment rather than dismissal and ridicule.

Another goal of my intervention is to counteract the gender socialization process students go through during the formative years they are in school. If more men and women were proudly visible in gender non-traditional fields, it would show the kids that it's okay, and even encouraged, for them to explore these options. They shouldn't have to face any fear of harassment; my career fair would be a safe space for them to engage in this exploration. And while this intervention might not be a definite fix for the systems currently in place, it certainly would serve as a first step towards making change. If my career fair could help even a handful of kids by giving them an opportunity to explore something they're interested in and boosting their confidence to pursue it, then it would be worth the effort. My hope is that counteracting this socialization process will broaden their zones of acceptable alternatives. At the very least, it should broaden the cut-off lines on the masculine/feminine axis in my students' zones of acceptable alternatives.

INTERVENTION

The first step in planning this career intervention is to make a list of careers to have present at this fair. Think wide when brainstorming these careers. Be sure to include careers that are typically dominated by one sex over the other, but don't limit the options to just those that are the most occupationally segregated; have a broad selection. When in this process, communicate with the students in your district. Let them know explicitly that gender non-traditional career exploration is being encouraged, and send out a survey asking them what careers they are interested in learning more about.

The next step is reaching out to businesses and employers to see if they would be willing to participate in the career fair. In this step you should take into account the occupations listed in the student interest survey. When looking for business to contact, work locally if you can. Having community members at this fair can make some students feel more comfortable and can make the volunteers seem more relatable to the students. Send out invitations to these businesses or call them on the phone. Be sure to explain to them that this is specifically a gender non-traditional career fair. If they are willing and interested in participating, make sure you are clear that you want representatives at the fair who are of the gender that is not traditional in that occupation. For instance, if you want a table at the fair dedicated to the nursing profession, be sure that they send a male nurse instead of a female one. If you want a table dedicated to STEM, be sure they send a woman.

After you have contacted everyone who is willing to participate in the career fair, the next step is arranging to set up the location of the fair. Figure out how many tables and chairs you will need, and make sure you are cleared to use the location you decide on (the gymnasium, the auditorium, an outdoor field, etc.). After you have done this, see if you can recruit some volunteers to help you staff the event and a welcome table.

After you have confirmed the date, time, and location of the event and coordinated with every outside contact coming to volunteer, advertise the event! Post flyers all around the school building, make announcements on the morning loudspeaker, and have students spread the word about the event. It's important that you advertise well enough in advance that students can prepare for it.

Next, send out another student interest survey. On this survey should be a list of all outside contacts coming in, with the occupation or business they are representing. Have students identify three of these contacts who they would like to speak with at the fair. Once you collect the results, you can use this information to determine which students will start the event at which table. This can be beneficial in many ways. First, it can help students who may be too shy to approach certain tables on their own. By having a predetermined list of which students will begin at each table, students can also prepare questions they may have ahead of time. Another benefit of this process is that volunteers will be able to get an idea of how many students will want to talk to them.

The last step of this process is taking care of what needs to be done on the actual day of the event. After the setup is complete, be sure to attend the event yourself. Float around and talk to students who may seem shy or lost. If anyone needs help, offer it. And, at the end of the event, give students an evaluation form to fill out and hand back before leaving the event (more on this form later).

EVALUATION

My method of evaluation would be in the form of a post-test survey. An example of this survey is attached at the end of this section. The purpose of this survey is to evaluate the effect that this gender non-traditional career fair had on students. The survey aims to assess whether students: found the career fair helpful, explored a career they otherwise would not have, are more knowledgeable about gender non-traditional fields than they were before, feel empowered after seeing people who look like them succeeding in a field dominated by the opposite sex, are more likely to explore one of the fields they learned about today than they were before, and feel like their career options have been expanded. The survey also allows space for comments on what the student most enjoyed about the fair, and what they would change to improve it. In using a survey like this, you can get direct results and feedback from the population you created it for—the students. If they fill it out at the end of the fair, their thoughts are fresh in mind, and you can get accurate and honest feedback.

GENDER NON-TRADITIONAL CAREER FAIR: POST-EVALUATION

Student Name: _____

1. I found this career fair to be: (circle one)

    _____

    Very Helpful   Somewhat Helpful   Not at All Helpful

2. I feel like I explored a career that I wouldn't have otherwise: (circle one)

    _____

    Strongly Agree   Somewhat Agree   Do Not Agree

3. I know more about a gender non-traditional field now than I did before: (circle one)

    _____

    Strongly Agree   Somewhat Agree   Do Not Agree

4. I feel empowered after seeing someone like me succeed in a field dominated by the other sex: (circle one)

_____

       Strongly Agree   Somewhat Agree   Do Not Agree

5. I feel more likely to pursue a career in one of the fields I explored today: (circle one)

_____

       Strongly Agree   Somewhat Agree   Do Not Agree

6. I feel like my career options have been expanded after attending this fair: (circle one)

_____

       Strongly Agree   Somewhat Agree   Do Not Agree

7. Something I especially enjoyed about this fair was:

_____

_____

8. I think the following could have made this fair better for me:

_____

_____

9. Overall, I would rate this career fair: (Circle one)

  1   2   3   4   5   6   7   8   9   10

  AWFUL   EXCELLENT

  Additional Comments:

_____

_____

REFERENCES

Couch, J. V., & Sigler, J. N. (2001). Gender perception of professional occupations. Psychological Reports, 88(3), 693–698. https://doi.org/10.2466/PR0.88.3.693-698

Cross, S., & Bagilhole, B. (2002). Girls' jobs for the boys? Men, masculinity and non-traditional occupations. Gender, Work and Organization, 9(2), 204–226.

Davis, R. (2014). Women in STEM and human information behavior: Implications for LIS educators. Journal of Education for Library and Information Science, 55(3), 255–258. http://www.jstor.org/stable/43686988

Fluhr, S., Choi, N., Herd, A., Woo, H., & Alagaraja, M. (2017). Gender, Career and Technical Education (CTE) nontraditional coursetaking, and wage gap. The High School Journal, 100(3), 166–182. https://www.jstor.org/stable/90024210

Gottfredson, L. S. (1981). Circumscription and compromise: A developmental theory of occupational aspirations. *Journal of Counseling Psychology, 28*(6), 545–579.

Huffman, M., & Cohen, P. (2004). Occupational segregation and the gender gap in workplace authority: National versus local labor markets. Sociological Forum, 19(1), 121–147. http://www.jstor.org/stable/4148809

Lent, R. W., Brown, S. D., & Hackett, G. (1994). Toward a unifying social cognitive theory of career and academic interest, choice, and performance. Journal of Vocational Behavior, 45(1), 79–122.

Super, D. E. (1990). A life-span, life-space approach to career development. In D. Brown & L. Brooks (Eds.), Career choice and development: Applying contemporary theories to practice (pp. 197–261). Jossey-Bass.

PART III

Advanced Considerations

CHAPTER 9

Critical Cultural Considerations

The school counselor must always consider the sociocultural identity of the population whom they serve as well as their own identity construction and biases. This process is not simply an academic exercise, however. All too often, school counselors learn to "talk the talk" and reflect upon these processes without "walking the walk" and engaging in tangible practices that bridge opportunity gaps and address issues of racism. Culture is inherently part of every individual and system we encounter, and to not acknowledge these realities as a core principle of every assessment and intervention within a school would be a mistake. A school counselor must have a mind towards integrative social justice and anti-racist advocacy if they are to transform school systems and empower all students to succeed.

Think about your strengths in these areas and your need for growth. What personal biases are you aware of? What is your sense of opportunity gaps in society and within particular communities? How do you think you'd address such gaps within a school system? Do any types of interventions come to mind? How do we inform the intervention and assess its effectiveness in a culturally competent way? Keep these questions in mind as we explore culturally informed school counseling.

Social Justice and Community Partnerships

While school counselors serve as social justice advocates for their entire student population (Ratts & Greenleaf, 2017), research indicates that the benefit of the school counselor may depend upon school context and sociocultural variables (Bryan et al., 2011). Bryan and colleagues (2011) found that the school counselor serves as an important social capital resource for students in school settings. Social capital is defined as the resources that flow through relationship and networking ties, namely the constellation of relationships that imbue an individual with the knowledge and skills necessary to succeed and access opportunity within social systems (Coleman, 1988). Families who have college-educated parents, professional jobs, and networking connections have higher levels of social capital to bestow on their children to use in the college and career development process (Byun et al., 2017). Given that this capital has historically been held by White upper-class individuals, students with low socioeconomic status and students of color often lack the capital required to make the most out of college and career development decisions (Bryan et al., 2011). Family social capital has consistently predicted student college and career aspirations (Byun et al., 2017). The school counselor, however, can serve as a source of school social capital for students who lack family social capital, linking them to the knowledge, skills, and processes required for a successful transition to college and the world of work (Bryan et al., 2017).

Students of color and students from low-income and/or traumatic backgrounds may have parents who become limited in their capability to provide assistance in career development due to external life pressures (Bryan et al., 2011). A proactive and systemic K–12 career development program, along with a strong and caring relationship with the school counselor, can assist in providing these students and families the holistic career development required for ultimate success (Bryan et al., 2017). Whereas some research indicates that school counselors are beneficial to the college applications of students of color (Bryan et al., 2009), other research suggests that school counselor contact may actually have a negative impact on the willingness of Black students to apply to colleges (Bryan et al., 2011), potentially suggesting that a lack of culturally competent school counseling services can cause damage instead of benefit to student populations.

Bryan and colleagues (2011) suggest that school counselors should have prepared and reached out to students and their families regarding college and career development before sophomore year, in an attempt to solidify a college-going culture and inspire students from all backgrounds to believe they are capable of transitioning to higher education. These efforts are particularly important for communities of color and for students from familial/cultural backgrounds where there is limited college-going social capital and knowledge (Bryan et al., 2011). The authors highlight the particular important of positive, strengths-based parental involvement and community engagement, which should begin as early as elementary school (Bryan et al., 2011; Trusty et al., 2008). The school counselor can serve as an agent of change by providing these families with the knowledge and social capital necessary to make intentional and informed decisions regarding college and career.

It is further critical to consider that efforts to involve parents who come from minority and underserved communities may look different from traditional parental involvement efforts (Bryan et al., 2011). Members of these communities may have had negative experiences with school and/or may not have been welcomed to or become familiar with standard events such as parent-teacher association meetings (Bryan et al., 2011). The school counselor should therefore facilitate school-to-community integration including connection with local churches, community social service agencies, and collegiate programs such as Upward Bound where students from non-traditional college backgrounds receive informative and interactive college programming and experiences (Bryan et al., 2009, 2011). Bryan and colleagues (2020) present the following table, adapted from the work of Bryan and Henry (2012), to guide school counselors in creating and maintaining school and community partnerships.

TABLE 9.1. School–Family–Community Partnerships Process Model ✳

Process stage	1. Preparing to Partner	2. Assessing Needs and Strengths	3. Coming Together	4. Creating Shared Vision and Plan	5. Taking Action	6. Evaluating and Celebrating Progress	7. Maintaining Momentum
Guiding question	Where do we begin?	How do we identify the goals of the partnership?	How do we bring partners together?	How do we get all partners on board and on the same page?	What will we do and how?	How will I measure our success?	How will we sustain this partnership?
Main tasks	• Become familiar with school's cultural groups • Challenge beliefs and stereotypes about diverse families and students • Align partnerships with school's vision • Examine inequities in student outcomes • Get principal and teacher buy-in using rationale based on research about partnership benefits and school data on student outcome	• Conduct needs and strengths assessment (interviews, surveys, focus groups) • Meet cultural brokers/persons of influence • Identify existing partnerships • Identify potential partners in school and community • Create community assets map (people, services, resources, organizations, spaces)	• Create a partnership leadership team (PLT) • Extend outreach and invitations to potential partners, cultural brokers, and persons of influence • Share data and identified needs and strengths to get partners' buy-in • Solicit feedback from PLT • Discuss partner commitments and contributions • Determine roles of each partner on PLT	• Create consensus and shared partnership plan • Build on existing partnerships or start new partnership • Brainstorm nontraditional ways to partner with diverse families • Create goals and outcomes • Develop logic model to help with planning (inputs, outputs, short-term, intermediate, and long-term goals) • Create timeline • Determine how each partnership will be evaluated • Identify instruments, surveys for measuring outcomes • Share plans with stakeholders (school staff, families, community members)	• Delegate leadership and responsibilities for each event • Delegate based on each team member's strengths (skills, resources) • Start small • Plan for barriers and challenges; implement anyway • Implement activities according to timeline	• Conduct evaluation (before and after events, at identified points in school year) • Analyze outcome data and create user-friendly presentation of data • Share outcomes and accomplishments with all stakeholders (administration, teachers, other staff, students, families, and community) • Celebrate all partners and partnership accomplishments	• Discuss evaluation results • Improve and make revisions to the plan • Share new plan • Contact partners prior to and early in the school year (retreat) • Consider extensions of existing partnerships • Identify possible new PLT members and partners • Repeat steps in partnership building process

Julia Bryan, Joseph M. Williams and Dana Griffin, School–Family–Community Partnerships Process Model from "Fostering Educational Resilience and Opportunities in Urban Schools Through Equity-Focused School–Family–Community Partnerships," Professional School Counseling, vol. 23, no.1. Copyright © 2020 by SAGE Publications. Reproduced with permission.

Critical considerations go beyond creating an open and welcoming school environment and community partnerships, however. Social-justice-driven career counseling requires a critical examination of a counselor's beliefs, biases, assumptions, power, and privilege within the counseling room (Ratts & Greenleaf, 2017). While students from similar ethnic and cultural backgrounds may experience similar barriers, every student is a unique culture of one and must be considered within their own context when the counselor is conceptualizing and meeting their career development needs (Vela et al., 2015). The school counselor cannot assume that the same information or counseling approaches will be received in the same manner across all students overall or all students from a specific cultural background. A critically conscious school counselor should consistently evaluate what is necessary to honor the unique identity and culture of every single student and strive to personalize their approach to best support each individual student's holistic growth and well-being. This support should include concrete information, steps, and action plans that have been shown to significantly increase the likelihood of students applying for colleges versus simply talking about these concepts (Bryan et al., 2017). This type of concrete action planning often occurs in high schools during senior year but should be integrated much earlier in a student's education, to provide them the knowledge and experience necessary to be able to make an informed decision and follow through with it (Bryan et al., 2017).

Systemic thinking is required to insure the conditions necessary to provide such attention to every student. For example, a school counselor must advocate for their job consisting of only appropriate roles and that their school adhere to the American School Counseling Association (ASCA)-recommended ratio of one counselor per every 250 students (Bryan et al., 2011). These efforts are not secondary to the school counselor's work with students but instead are integral as they lay the foundation for a comprehensive school counseling program to be built, maintained, altered, and improved. Advocacy for underserved student populations is done not only in direct work but also in systemic and societal change, including involvement with professional organizations which can influence state laws to require adherence to school counseling ratios, budgets, and programming.

Advanced Advocacy

School counselors should advocate not solely for their individual students but for all student populations through societal and systemic advocacy (Dahir & Stone, 2009). School counselors can influence and reduce barriers facing student populations (in the present and future) through involvement with professional organizations such as the ASCA and their local state school counseling association. A clear example is advocacy work done in the state of Virginia, where through lobbying by the ASCA, the state mandated the ASCA-recommended school counseling ratio of one counselor per every 250 students. New York has also benefited from advocacy put forth by the New York State School Counseling Association, which lobbied to help craft legislation requiring all students to have access to a school counselor. By bringing professionals in the field together, compiling both human and financial resources, professional organizations can inspire initiatives and legislation that help student populations for years to come.

If school counselors are involved with these professional organizations, they can share their wisdom, expertise, and particular experience with their student and community populations (Stone & Dahir,

2015). For underserved student populations, it can be critical to be represented in major professional initiatives such as education (conference presentations, webinars, and special journal issues), research (partnerships between stakeholders and new explorations of complex problems), and funding (access to grant opportunities, school consortiums, and free professional training). Professional organizations are often the origin point of meaningful work done to address gaps facing underserved student populations. When caring professionals come together to present and collaborate on research or advocacy work, it is more likely that awareness toward specific barriers and needs will be raised. Professional organizations also have the resources and lobbyist connections necessary to influence major legislation, which can create new career development programs, funding, educational resources, and grants linked towards promoting equity for all students. Being connected to and involved with these professional organizations empowers the individual school counselor to learn and grow in their pursuit of serving their entire student population while linking them to valuable resources. Further, a school counselor's involvement contributes to increasing awareness of student population needs, helping to inform current and future generations of school counselors in their pursuit of culturally competent practice.

ASCA has free resources on working with students from different cultural backgrounds and students with a variety of specialized presenting concerns. ASCA also offers professional development, newsletters, and access to research articles for its members. ASCA provides templates and even direct guidance lessons linked to career development, academic, and social-emotional concerns. These resources empower the individual school counselor's interventions to be based in ethical, research-based best practices and to be informed by the experience of school counselors across the nation. Going to the ASCA national or state (county/regional) meetings can help the school counselor network with other collaborators who are ready to share resources, ideas, and support, and to create new initiatives benefiting specific student populations. A wonderful thing about school counselors is that they care about students and are helpful collaborators—be sure to take advantage of this as a professional, to be best empowered to meet the unique needs of your students!

Anti-Racism and the School Counselor

The murder of George Floyd, a Black man, at the hands of police officers in Minneapolis in 2020 ignited a series of protests related to systemic racism in policing, and in society in general, in the United States. This event, along with the proliferation of racial profiling and racial violence in the United States, continues to illustrate the need for anti-racist and advocacy practices throughout the nation. School counselors can be advocates in directly combating structural racism within school systems (Ieva et al., 2021). The traditional nature of schooling in the United States is normed from a colonizing framework, meaning that White upper-class cultural norms have shaped what is expected in education, who is supported in educational systems, and who has a voice in educational systems (Ieva et al., 2021). These discrepancies result in inequitable resource allocation, inadequate prioritization of the needs of students of color, racially disproportionate disciplinary practices, and harmful power dynamics in which educators act as oppressors instead of advocates. A simple example is that some school systems have prohibitions around certain hairstyles, such as dreadlocks, which are more common in Black communities. This exclusionary practice criminalizes the culture of a community. Other examples include the tendency of schools to refer Black males to special education at higher rates than their White peers and to send them to discipline more often for lesser infractions (Ieva et al., 2021; McCardle, 2020; Okonofua et al., 2016). The criminalization of African American cultural characteristics and behavior has created the school-to-prison pipeline, in which Black students are labeled as problematic, defiant, and at deficits, resulting in students exiting the school system and transitioning into the criminal justice system (American Psychological Association, 2012; Ieva et al., 2021).

School faculty are often unaware of the disproportionate impact of their rules, practices, and behaviors due to these things going unexamined, with most preferring to simply adhere to the culture and practice of how things have always operated (Andrews et al., 2019; Harris et al., 2021; Ieva et. al., 2021). Anti-racist school counseling, therefore, includes not only the school counselor's individual work with students and the community but also efforts geared at educating faculty and transforming systemic practices that harm students of color. Put simply, the school counselor should not be an agent of a colonizing system, reinforcing its implicit and explicit racism, but rather a proactive advocate of change promoting equity for all students (Harris et al., 2021). Anti-racist school counseling requires a critical examination of one's personal cultural viewpoint and biases, an analysis of the impact of the school system on students and the community, and nuanced counseling skills to address complex situations (Harris et al., 2021). The following table, created by Ieva and colleagues (2021), lists the required knowledge, skills, and competencies required to engage in anti-racist school counseling practices.

TABLE 9.2. Required Competencies for Anti-Racist Healing-Centered Engagement Delivery in Group Practice and Supervision for School Counselors

Knowledge	Skills/Dispositions	Strategies for Competency Development
History of the United States and connection to racism	Validate and affirm racial injustice Compelled to decolonize and disrupt racism (practices and policies) in school	Literature review/podcasts Book clubs Diversify electives
Anti-Blackness	Recognize how anti-Blackness presents in systems, policies, and individuals	Infuse in each course Decolonize syllabi and curricula Ongoing professional development Include student voice Department action plan addressing anti-Blackness with accountability

(Continued)

TABLE 9.2. (*Continued*)

Culturally sustaining counseling theories and techniques (e.g., critical race theory and relational cultural theory)	Refrain from dismissal of others based on unconscious awareness of privilege	Audit and decolonize syllabus Remove antiquated theories and techniques Infuse Western forms of counseling
Ecological systems framework	Connect systems inequities across multiple systems and educate adults and students Identify and remove barriers across systems levels	Work to identify and remove barriers across systematic levels, model for students at higher ed level Ongoing professional development and supervision Train all counseling specializations in EST from a school and connect systems lens Involve community systems in coursework
Critical consciousness (e.g., power, privilege, oppression, and intersectionality of self and others)	Self-awareness including one's own conditioning through the years Facilitate awareness and connection in others Challenge policies of ideologies	Continuous reflection and supervision in relation to current and historical events Utilize an anti-racist supervision model, such as the Anti-Racist Inclusive Model of Systems Supervision (AIMSS; Ieva et al., 2021) Peer consultation/intentionality
Conflict resolution (centered in race)	Conflict mediation while maintaining group cohesion Comfortable with conflict Emotional stability	Infuse in techniques, theories, and group coursework Concrete and practical case studies role-play Field experience requirement: Observe Mediate/Practice/Reflect

TABLE 9.2. (*Continued*)

Racial identity models and strengths-based (asset-based approaches)	Decolonize identities Discuss varying worldviews while building cohesion Explore others' racial identity Promote healthy racial identities	Continuous reflection, professional development, and on-going supervision Infuse across curricula Practical case studies/self-analyses
Difficult Dialogue, Courageous Conversations, and Braver Space models	Utilize and implement in the right context Connect tier 2 data to delivery method	Continuous reflection, professional development, practice, and on-going supervision Central to programming and teaching, specifically in group context
Group counseling through an anti-racist lens	Ability to broach race in group settings Recognize and challenge implicit bias and microaggressions while maintaining emotional safety Understand the appropriate use of self-disclosure and here-now when confronted with racist remarks or discussions on racism and oppressions	Continually reflect on one's implicit bias, acknowledge racial battle fatigue, and directly address microaggressions Willingness to foster discussions on racism and oppression, open to confronting racist and violent remarks
Advocacy (in public schools, community, and political realms)	Engage in discovering inequities with students and communities Plan activities that align with salient and current issues Act with intention and join other stakeholders in action-oriented activities (e.g., protest, communicating with legislators, school board and parent–teacher meeting attendance)	Collective reflection, challenging longstanding policies and practices, assignments that support advocacy work in schools and across systems, seeking counseling as needed, engaging in self-care, and utilizing peer and group supervision

(*Continued*)

TABLE 9.2. *(Continued)*

Culturally inclusive program evaluation and outcome frameworks	Flexible qualitative strategies, mixed methods (e.g., focus groups, journal prompts/entries), critical incidents reflection and discourses; artifacts as evidence include artwork, music (e.g., mixtapes), pictures, videos, and PowerPoints	Acknowledge that students and families are agents of change, use an anti-racist framework in examining data, introduce critical methodologies and frameworks, regularly reflect on one's own positions of power, privilege, and oppression, explore one's personal impact on the outcomes sought and desired, and be willing to adjust to the needs of students/clients

Kara P. Ieva, Jordon Beasley, and Sam Steen, Required Competencies for Anti-Racist Healing-Centered Engagement Delivery in Group Practice and Supervision for School Counselors from "Equipping School Counselors for Antiracist Healing Centered Groups: A Critical Examination of Preparation, Connected Curricula, Professional Practice and Oversight," Teaching and Supervision in Counseling, *vol. 3, no. 2, pp. 72–73. Copyright © 2021 by Kara P. Ieva, Jordon Beasley and Sam Steen. Reprinted with permission.*

COVID-19, Trauma, and Inequity

The COVID-19 pandemic caused unprecedented historical and societal upheaval, governmental lockdowns, the loss of jobs, school closures, and a switch to distance learning at many institutions of learning. These major shifts and stressors created new social-emotional stressors for students and exacerbated issues for those already facing challenging life situations and social barriers (Yip, 2020). Many of us reading this text are well aware of the increased anxiety, depression, and stress COVID brought into our lives. Now let's imagine we are a young child, completely without control of our own life situation, dependent upon structure to understand ourselves and the world, with our main outlet of socialization and understanding being school. And then, so suddenly, all of it is taken away. Think back to yourself as a child: What stressful situations were you enduring? What painful feelings did you have to sit with? Now imagine sitting with them alone in a room, your only connection to friends being through a virtual classroom, if you even have access to internet at all. We can all see how this would lead to increasing levels of anxiety, depression, social difficulties, and academic struggles, which have permeated youth since the onset of the pandemic (Yip, 2020).

Students who were already at risk for school difficulties were those most severely impacted by the educational disruption. As is often the case in times of societal trauma, those already facing barriers had their challenges compounded. Educational disruption is yet another heavy weight added on top of those placed by systemic racism, generational poverty, parental employment instability, grief and loss, limited access to physical and mental health resources, and national political instability (Ieva, 2020; Yip, 2020). The result of this additional strain has been students missing school at higher rates than ever, and students struggling to complete academic assignments and failing courses. Schools have become overwhelmed by the mental and physical health needs of students, families, and faculty members. Students of color, who were already at risk of experiencing systemic barriers toward their success, find themselves disproportionately impacted by this societal trauma, without schools providing adequate levels of support to combat it (Yip, 2020).

While the COVID-19 pandemic has changed the world permanently, it has drawn attention to systemic inequities that have always been present. As a social justice advocate, the school counselor has a responsibility to continually assess what structures and practices disproportionately disenfranchise which student populations and what changes are necessary to best support their needs. The isolation that results from lockdowns and virtual learning may require more targeted and persistent outreach from school counselors to identify which students are struggling and how to best meet their needs. More integrated social-emotional learning and mental health resources are required to help empower students and families to understand what is happening and how to access appropriate types of support. The school counselor can be integral in transforming school practices so that contact from the school is not othering or punitive, as is the case when schools reach out regarding truancy and academic deficiency, but instead is welcomed as a helping hand. If the school provides access to support such as additional programs, mental health resources, and service coordination, it can be viewed as an ally bringing the community together during difficult times, rather than yet another institution presenting barriers to children and parents.

Trauma-Informed Career Development

The COVID-19 pandemic has illuminated the fact that many students who struggle in school have experienced or currently are experiencing some form of trauma. Trauma can result from experiencing a single abusive or violent event, witnessing such an event, going through several of such events, living in an unsafe situation, and/or experiencing poverty, food insecurity, or a serious medical situation, as well as many more causes (Yip, 2020). Students who experience trauma may face difficulties in school due to their mind and emotions being in other places (how natural it is to worry about an unsafe home instead of your math assignment), increased rates of anxiety, depression, and other mental health concerns, and social-emotional challenges with peers and staff. For example, imagine you were raised in a situation where an adult being dissatisfied was the precursor to emotional abuse or physical violence. Would it make sense that if a teacher corrected you in class, you may have a strong emotional reaction linked to your trauma and your desire for safety?

School behavioral management and discipline practices often are not normed from a trauma-informed framework, resulting in students who have experienced trauma facing additional barriers to their emotional well-being and academic success (Thomas et al., 2019). Trauma may understandably be the number one concern and issue within a student's life, making them unable to access academics or positive social interactions due to the ongoing symptoms of their struggles. Unfortunately, many schools stigmatize these students as the problem children, putting the onus of blame solely upon their efforts without doing the work to ensure that the school environment is safe and supportive for all, and that children and families have increased access to supportive mental health resources. Trauma can influence a student's ability to progress in academics and consider long-term career paths.

It is important to realize that career development work in schools is not divorced from the social-emotional and academic domains (Levy & Lemberger-Truelove, 2021). For a student to access academics and career development, their social-emotional needs must be met. Thus, the work of the school counselor in career development is tending not only to one area of need or one aspect of students, but rather to the holistic constellation of their needs and to who they are as a person. Integrated and trauma-informed career development work therefore needs a recognition of the whole student self, and must be supported by robust programs assisting with the full range of student needs in order to be the most effective. Interventions supporting social-emotional and academic needs should be designed with career development in mind and vice versa, allowing for intentional cross-beneficial programming assisting all students and the community. The most effective career development programming for students experiencing trauma therefore comes from a school rooted in trauma-informed behavioral management and disciplinary practices that provides access to detailed social-emotional guidance lessons, programming, and resource referrals. It is critical that the professional school counselor demonstrate an awareness that the three domains of school counseling work are not separate entities but are all part of the same intentional and informed process (Levy & Lemberger-Truelove, 2021).

CHAPTER SUMMARY

Social inequities fuel the educational opportunity disparities present in American society. A school counselor must mindfully keep these processes in the forefront of their social justice advocacy if they are to serve all student populations. Community acclimation and outreach are essential in building the bridges and partnerships required for school to benefit the students it serves. A school counselor must be a social justice and anti-racism advocate if they are to reform the oppressive cultural framework constructing school and societal systems to this day. Advocacy can go beyond the district level through intentional involvement in professional counseling organizations. Societal, racial, and other forms of trauma are important to consider in a comprehensive school counseling approach, and it is imperative for a school counselor to recognize that trauma often disproportionately impacts students who are already at the highest risk of academic, personal-social, and career concerns.

TABLE OF KEY TERMS

Term	Definition
Trauma-informed	A term describing a series of educational, psychoeducational, and counseling practices informed by the science and impacts of trauma meant to provide equitable access to wellness and success in populations who have experienced trauma.
Anti-racist school counseling	School counseling identity and practices aimed at decolonization of educational systems in order to remove barriers and promote equity for all students (Harris et al., 2021).
Social capital	Social capital is defined as the resources that flow through relationship and networking ties, namely the constellation of relationships that imbue an individual with the knowledge and skills necessary to succeed and access opportunity within social systems (Coleman, 1988).

REFLECTION EXERCISES

Reflection exercises are designed either to be done individually within the reading or to be used as group discussion questions within the classroom setting. A series of reflection questions will be presented at the end of every chapter.

1. In what ways have school systems you've been a part of engaged in colonized forms of education?

    a. How were school norms and cultural values shaped from this perspective?

    b. What school counseling practices would have been helpful in dismantling these practices to promote equity for all students?

2. Consider Ieva and colleagues' (2021) model, Competencies for Anti-Racist Healing.

    a. What knowledge do you have that will help your anti-racist school counseling practice? In what knowledge areas do you need growth?

    b. What skills and dispositions do you have that will help your anti-racist school counseling practice? In which of these areas do you need growth?

    c. What strategies for competency development have you enacted in your life? What strategies would be helpful to increase your anti-racist school counseling practice?

3. Consider Bryan and Henry's School–Family Partnership Process Model.

    a. Evaluate a local school district and its local community through each of the seven process steps.

    b. Break down what information and action steps are needed at each step to fully progress through this model.

    c. What do you believe the benefits would be of utilizing this model for your chosen school and community?

4. In what ways have racism and/or trauma impacted your life? .

    a. How did the educational systems you went through assist these challenges or contribute to them?

    b. How does your knowledge and experience empower you to be an advocate as a school counselor?

    c. What groups, organizations, or initiatives could you partake in for broader systemic advocacy around these issues?

CASE STUDY

Crescent Heights High School is a charter school in a low-income inner-city neighborhood that primarily serves Black and Latinx students. Crescent Heights's school mission is to "empower every graduate to learn, grow, and obtain a college education." The major focus of educational efforts at Crescent Heights is improving standardized testing scores and coaching students through college application and admission processes. While the faculty in Crescent Heights are from Black, Latinx, and White backgrounds, the administration and major policy makers are entirely White. Crescent Heights has been having an influx of concerns around its professional language and dress codes, which strictly emphasize "proper" manners of speech and dress, creating a tension between staff members and students who do not conform. Crescent Heights's policy includes strict definitions of acceptable and unacceptable types of shirts and pants, length of clothes, and accepted hairstyles and colors. Students at Crescent Heights receive monthly professionalism workshops in which the value of these rules and their intention is clearly reinforced. The school counselors at Crescent Heights are tasked with designing and keeping up these workshops. The main responsibility of the school counselors at Crescent Heights is college and career prep, including having individual meetings with students centered around the college search and hitting a set quota in which each student applies to at least eight colleges. Any guidance lessons are focused on the college search, essay writing, financial aid, and standardized prep processes. As a new school counselor, however, you recognize the growing discontent and the challenges facing students related to the curriculum, professional codes, and the lack of connection from school to community. In fact, a growing contingency of students is disconnecting from school and failing their courses, and it is your assumption that these processes may be linked.

1. How would you apply an anti-racist school counseling framework to the situation at Crescent Heights?
2. How can the Competencies for Anti-Racist Healing and the School Family Partnership Process Model be applied to this situation?
3. What systemic change and advocacy is necessary to benefit the students at Crescent Heights High School? How would you enact these changes or interventions?
4. What type of data would you collect, or existing research would you present, to help make changes at the administrative level?

References

American Psychological Association, Presidential Task Force on Educational Disparities. (2012). *Ethnic and racial disparities in education: Psychology's contributions to understanding and reducing disparities.* https://www.apa.org/ed/resources/racialdisparities.pdf

Andrews, D. J. C., Brown, T., Castillo, B. M., Jackson, D., & Vellanki, V. (2019). Beyond damage-centered teacher education: Humanizing pedagogy for teacher educators and preservice teachers. Teachers College Record, 121(6), 1–28.

Bryan, J., Farmer-Hinton, R., Rawls, A., & Woods, C. S. (2017). Social capital and college-going culture in high schools: The effects of college expectations and college talk on students' postsecondary attendance. *Professional School Counseling, 21*(1), 95–107.

Bryan, J., & Henry, L. M. (2012). A model for building school–family–community partnerships: Principles and process. *Journal of Counseling & Development, 90*(4), 408–420.

Bryan, J., Holcomb-McCoy, C., Moore-Thomas, C., & Day-Vines, N. L. (2009). Who sees the school counselor for college information? A national study. *Professional School Counseling, 12*(4). https://doi.org/10.1177/2156759X0901200401

Bryan, J., Moore-Thomas, C., Day-Vines, N. L., & Holcomb-McCoy, C. (2011). School counselors as social capital: The effects of high school college counseling on college application rates. *Journal of Counseling & Development, 89*(2), 190–199.

Bryan, J., Williams, J. M., & Griffin, D. (2020). Fostering educational resilience and opportunities in urban schools through equity-focused school–family–community partnerships. Professional School Counseling, 23(1_part_2). https://doi.org/10.1177/2156759X19899179

Byun, S. Y., Meece, J. L., & Agger, C. A. (2017). Predictors of college attendance patterns of rural youth. *Research in Higher Education, 58*(8), 817–842.

Coleman, J. S. (1988). Social capital in the creation of human capital. *American Journal of Sociology, 94,* S95–S120.

Dahir, C. A., & Stone, C. B. (2009). School counselor accountability: The path to social justice and systemic change. *Journal of Counseling & Development, 87*(1), 12–20.

Harris, P. C., Hines, E., & Mayes, R. D. (2021). Introduction to the special issue: Anti-racist counselor education. *Teaching and Supervision in Counseling*, 3(2), 1.

Ieva, K. P. (2020, September). Filling the emotional cup: Grow your own network. School Counselor News. American School Counselor Association. https://asca-prod.azurewebsites.net/newsletters/september-2020/filling-the-emotional-cupgrowingyour-own-suppor?st=N

Ieva, K. P., Beasley, J., & Steen, S. (2021). Equipping school counselors for antiracist healing centered groups: A critical examination of preparation, connected curricula, professional practice and oversight. *Teaching and Supervision in Counseling*, 3(2), 7.

Levy, I. P., & Lemberger-Truelove, M. E. (2021). Educator–counselor: A nondual identity for school counselors. Professional School Counseling, 24(1_part_3). https://doi.org/10.1177/2156759X211007630

McCardle, T. (2020) A critical historical examination of tracking as a method for maintaining racial segregation. Educational Considerations, 45(2), 1–14. https://doi.org/10.4148/0146- 9282.2186

Okonofua, J. A., Walton, G. M., & Eberhardt, J. L. (2016). A vicious cycle: A social psychological account of extreme racial disparities in school discipline. Perspectives on Psychological Science, 11(3), 381–398.

Ratts, M. J., & Greenleaf, A. T. (2017). Multicultural and social justice counseling competencies: A leadership framework for professional school counselors. *Professional School Counseling*, 21(1b). https://doi.org/10.1177/2156759X18773582

Stone, C., & Dahir, C. A. (2015). *The transformed school counselor* (3rd ed.). Cengage Learning.

Thomas, M. S., Crosby, S., & Vanderhaar, J. (2019). Trauma-informed practices in schools across two decades: An interdisciplinary review of research. *Review of Research in Education*, 43(1), 422–452.

Trusty, J., Mellin, E. A., & Herbert, J. T. (2008). Closing achievement gaps: Roles and tasks of elementary school counselors. *The Elementary School Journal*, 108(5), 407–421.

Vela, J. C., Flamez, B., & Clark, A. (2015). High school counselors' support and Latina/o students' career development. *Journal of School Counseling*, 13(11), n11.

Yip, T. (Ed.) (2020). Addressing inequities in education during the COVID-19 pandemic: How education policy and schools can support historically and currently marginalized children and youth. Society for Research in Child Development, Statement of the Evidence. https://www.srcd.org/sites/default/files/resources/FINAL_AddressingInequalitiesVolume-092020.pdf

CHAPTER 10

Systemic Data and Accountability

T hink about the word data. What images or emotions come to mind? Do you feel happy? Excited? Enthralled? Captivated? Encouraged? Some of us certainly may, but for many, the words *data* and *analysis* come with negative connotations. Whether it be intimidation, confusion, uncertainty, or even feelings of boredom, many school counselors find the world of data analysis unappealing. And how natural this is for many school counselors—what draws so many to the field are warm and human interactions. Crunching numbers on a computer may appear to be the exact opposite of that!

Data analysis, however, is a much more dynamic and alive process than we might think. It is not separate from the creative and impactful interventions we deliver, but rather a core component of them. Data allows our initiatives to get off the ground and moving, informs our adaptations and changes, and allows us to see which students we can further serve and how. Data provides directionality and intentionality to our warmth, engagement, and advocacy. Data is also not simply numbers in a spreadsheet—it is observations, feedback, paragraphs, ideas, reactions, and circled smiley faces on sheets of paper. We normally think of data as numerals, when truly there are many dynamic and creative ways to source meaningful data and to use this information for the upkeep and renovation of our career development programming. So much of data and analysis is not pure crunching of numbers but designing interventions and programs to include feedback from participants and other stakeholders. If seeking feedback is built into programs and interventions, the data and analysis will come from there.

Stakeholder Needs Assessments

When you are beginning career development (or any) school counseling programming, a needs assessment across multiple groups of stakeholders can help shed light on the needs of your student community as well as what perspectives are shared, which differ, and which need further analysis (Young & Kaffenberger, 2018). If a school counselor were looking to develop career development programing for the first time at a school, for example, it would be incredibly beneficial to seek feedback from stakeholders about the needs of that school. A faculty needs assessment could include questions on a 1–5 Likert scale on their perception of student awareness of careers (general or specific) and student readiness for college/careers (one section exploring academic readiness, another exploring college/career awareness, and another exploring emotional readiness). The survey could also include open-ended responses in which faculty could elaborate on what they perceive are the biggest needs and what would best help support the school in addressing these needs. This same assessment (with the same domains of questions modified slightly for each audience) could be given to the students and parents in the school community. In this way, we can analyze the perceptions of all stakeholders. Do they agree on the needs? Disagree? Do the differing perspectives show a disconnect or simply suggest different avenues of exploration?

The data analysis in this case can be multitiered. Means, medians, and modes from the Likert scales can be compiled across each individual question and each cluster or domain. These means, medians, and modes can be compared between groups (for example, showing differences in faculty, student, and community perceptions) or within group (for example, disaggregating differences based upon gender or race of students, faculty role/subject taught, parent gender or race, etc.). By having sociodemographic questions at the beginning of a survey, we can compare the differing views of different groups of stakeholders, which may provide a deeper insight into who is accessing or influencing career development and why. Means, medians, and modes are simple statistics that can be compiled easily within programs such as Microsoft Excel, which even allows for chart depictions of results. These depictions can be key in presenting the results of data to stakeholders to win support for new interventions.

EZAnalyze, an Excel add-on, is a free and handy tool that more easily allows for the charting of school counseling data (EZAnalyze, 2021). EZAnalyze allows for simple computations such as mean, median, and mode but also allows for more advanced operations such as correlations and disaggregation by multiple variables. For example, a school counselor could find the mean interest in college among students who are in sixth grade. EZAnalyze also would allow the school counselor to see the mean interest in college among students who are in the sixth grade and who also identify as female. This second level of disaggregation analysis can be quite helpful for a school counselor to get a deeper picture of the sociocultural dynamics at a school, and thanks to EZAnalyze, this can happen with a few clicks of a mouse instead of requiring manual computation. In addition to EZAnalyze, there are several survey programs that allow for instant analysis of survey results. Qualtrics is an example of a survey tool that some districts utilize for data collection and disaggregation purposes. A survey could be set up in Qualtrics to allow for data to be compiled and results to be analyzed and displayed in graphical format. There are other free-to-use options, such as Survey Monkey and other tools, that allow for representation of basic results, with less access to more complex calculations.

The qualitative data collected in these surveys can be comparatively analyzed in several ways. While quantitative data tends to represent trends and outliers numerically, well describing what is happening, qualitative data imbues theory or meaning into the results. In short, quantitative data provides the "what" while qualitative data provides the "why" (Creswell & Creswell, 2017). Qualitative data can be incredibly helpful in humanizing the data and allowing us to make sense of why the results are as they are, since we have direct testimony from the participants who responded. In a career development survey focusing on student emotions related to the college/career transition process, for example, quantitative results may indicate a certain demographic of students as having higher levels of fears or uncertainties, while the qualitative results may give insight into what these specific fears or uncertainties are and why they exist. Qualitative data analysis could be done through thematic coding, a process by which the school counselor reads through the results and searches for commonly expressed ideas or meanings (Creswell & Creswell, 2017). For example, there may be a multitude of responses indicating that students of color are uncertain about career paths due to feeling they are unaware of role models from their background participating in certain fields. A school counselor may highlight examples of these responses and present the data as indicating a theme of "representation" as a major area to address within the school's career development efforts. Several themes could potentially be created through this type of coding, with individual quotes utilizes as examples of how the themes are presenting in the school. Further, responses could be compiled to form a word cloud (available for free through various applications and websites) to artistically portray the mix of words and feelings expressed by stakeholders.

The quantitative results of a needs assessment may help depict the awareness, thoughts, ideas, and feelings of several groups of stakeholders, while qualitative results may provide meaning and reasoning behind it all. With this information from various perspectives, a school counselor can more readily develop outreach and programming to address the career development needs as they exist and potentially tailor approaches to different stakeholder groups and student subpopulations. It is important to have an adequate sampling of each of these groups in order to develop concrete conclusions. For example, we would not want to derive our conclusions regarding faculty perspectives from a survey of only one teacher. Rather, we should aim at surveying all teachers and have a representative sample across grade levels and subjects taught. Similarly, we should seek data from our students, and from a community that is representative of the breakdown of each of these groups. It would be folly to norm our career development interventions from results only representing certain groups of students, with others still not having their voices heard.

There are times, however, where it may be difficult or even impossible for a school counselor to access a high quantity of responses from students, faculty, or community members. In these cases, focus groups can be incredibly helpful. A focus group is a representative group of individuals (students, faculty, or stakeholders) whose composition mostly mirrors that of the larger group they are a part of (Creswell & Creswell, 2017). Focus groups usually provide interviews and feedback around specific issues and their perspective upon what is needed. For example, a school counselor may wish to create a focus group of students to understand more deeply the barriers facing students in career development. If a school counselor is exploring this issue particularly for students of color, they may select certain students from across every grade level who represent the racial breakdown of students of color. These students and their perspectives could provide meaningful directionality to future interventions.

Data and the ASCA National Model

The ASCA National Model has four quadrants: Assess, Manage, Define, and Deliver (American School Counselor Association, 2016). The Assess quadrant highlights the need for data-driven assessments to guide school counseling practice and interventions. The Manage quadrant speaks to the need for ongoing management of programs through the use of resources and partnerships with stakeholders. The Deliver quadrant focuses on the actual delivery of services, including individual and group counseling, classroom lessons, and school counseling programs. These three quadrants in particular have data ingrained into their function. The Assess quadrant focuses highly on seeking and analyzing data to give directionality to a program. Effective upkeep and management cannot occur without feedback from students, stakeholders, and program partners, making it an integral aspect of this quadrant as well. Appropriate and effective delivery is often informed and guided by the data assessment has provided, meaning that school counseling approaches truly are steeped in data, feedback, and the ongoing analysis of these dynamics. A transformed and professional school counselor, therefore, integrates data throughout their career development and holistic school counseling work (Stone & Dahir, 2015).

Data Collection for Program Maintenance and Evaluation

Initial assessments are effective for evaluating what types of career development programming can be created. Once created, however, a program should be maintained through compilation and analysis of feedback data (Young & Kaffenberger, 2018). Pre/post evaluations are critical for school counselors to evaluate the effectiveness of groups, lessons, and programs (Young & Kaffenberger, 2018). Pre/post assessments include an assessment before the intervention begins and after it is delivered. For example, a school counselor conducting a series of guidance lessons on careers in Science, Technology, Engineering, and Mathematics (STEM) could evaluate students' awareness of and interest in STEM careers before delivering the lessons. Afterwards, they could deliver the same assessment and evaluate how much the lessons impacted students' awareness and interests. These results, along with any qualitative feedback provided, allow the school counselor to modify the lessons to improve them for their next delivery. The same type of data collection and analysis should exist for large-scale programs such as field trips, career days, career speakers, and school-to-work internship programs.

Data should also be collected and analyzed while interventions are in progress. A career exploration group, for example, could end each session with a formal or informal evaluation of how the individual group session went and how the group is going overall, as well as what could be changed. The data between sessions can influence the directionality of future content and processing, while data collected at the end of the intervention can inform direct changes to be made for the next iteration of the group. This type of data and analysis can be quite similar to previously mentioned methods. Means, medians, and modes based upon Likert-scale response items can provide insight into thoughts, feelings, beliefs, and knowledge. It is important for the school counselor to analyze what domains are important to evaluate as part of the group intervention and provide an adequate number of questions per section. Correlation, disaggregation, and qualitative thematic coding can provide deeper insight into the data compiled.

Data is also readily accessible within schools, without the use of newly created assessments. Schools often track GPAs, attendance, grades between semesters, the number of student college applications, and the number of students who transition to college. These already-available data points can be analyzed by student demographic characteristics to understand the reality of career development for students in the school. Individual course grade and GPA tracking can be used to evaluate the effectiveness of academic and career programs which certain students participate in, providing outcome data on the effectiveness of interventions.

Depending upon the age group of the participants, there may be more or less questions (high schoolers versus elementary age students), and the manner in which questions are asked may also be different. For example, when collecting data from K–2 students, it may be appropriate to utilize a three-point Likert scale represented by a frowning face, a neutral face, and a smiling face. Students could have the questions read to them and circle the face that corresponds to how they feel about the item (e.g., "I enjoyed learning about new jobs"). A school counselor should be aware of the purpose of the data collection (what is being informed/examined) and the ideal delivery method (paper survey, online survey, length of questions/method of indicating response). Certain schools may have easy access to computers for every student, allowing results to be collected quickly and efficiently. Other schools may not have such computer access, meaning the school counselor would need paper versions of surveys for students. Younger students may need more guidance and assistance in responding to surveys, while older students may be able to respond more easily.

While data is critical to the upkeep and evaluation of school counseling programs, schools may have unique rules and policies related to surveying students, especially in regard to confidentiality. It is therefore critical to have all data collection efforts approved by administration and to follow through with all established school procedures for collecting, storing, and analyzing data. An ethical school counselor must keep the principles of informed consent in mind when administering surveys to students, faculty, and staff, and inform all parties as to whether identifiers will be used, what the data will be used for, and how it will be represented. Understanding the protocols, procedures, and methods of delivering surveys in a district allows a school counselor to be professional, ethical, and prepared.

Presenting Data to Stakeholders

Data not only is essential for the continued maintenance of school counseling programs, but also assists in developing partnerships and ongoing support for important initiatives (Young & Kaffenberger, 2018). School counseling needs assessment data, for example, could be visually depicted and presented to an administrator to underlie the deep need for more integrated career development programming within a school. The impact of career development lessons and programs on college-going rates and increased academic performance can be charted to demonstrate the continued need for a school to invest in career development efforts. Presenting data to administrators and at faculty in-service days helps convey the importance of school counseling initiatives while also winning over key allies who could assist in the implementation and maintenance of programs. A clear depiction of needs and results in trend lines, bar graphs, and pie charts helps make data accessible to other stakeholders, who may then be inspired to contribute to school counseling program practices. These same data depictions should be provided to parents in the form of presentations or newsletters home, inviting them to understand the school's needs and programmatic effectiveness. These newsletters may also invite parents to contribute to the success of a career development program through feedback or partnerships. These types of partnerships should also exist at the district level. School counselors can work with counselors in the district to streamline data collection from district-wide programs. For example, school counselors in a middle and high school can collaborate to analyze data related to programming addressing the transition to high school. Data can be collected during the middle school and high school years to show the benefits or drawbacks of the program and show what students perceive they need/needed during each grade level. More advanced career development programming, such as district-wide mentoring programs or internship programs, can also benefit from streamlined data collection and representation processes between school buildings.

Interns and Data Collection

Accepting interns is a professional responsibility of the school counselor, in order to keep up the training and success of the profession (Stone & Dahir, 2015). School counselors may find themselves inundated with responsibilities, making assessment creation and data analysis difficult. Interns are an incredible resource for data-driven analysis and decision making. Many interns are trained in the latest trends in data and analysis, and they are often comfortable utilizing computers and software to disaggregate data. Interns could take the lead on assessment and analysis projects, contributing positively to the intentional function of the school while earning incredibly valuable school counseling experience. In addition to partnering with other community collaborators and stakeholders, it is important for the professional school counselor to utilize resources within the school counseling and counselor education community, to maintain adherence to these critical professional practices and standards.

CHAPTER SUMMARY

Data collection and analysis processes may appear intimidating, but there are a multitude of software resources designed to make disaggregation simpler for school counselors. Intentionally collecting and analyzing data is integral to the creation, operation, and upkeep of school counseling programs and initiatives. While certain types of data collection may require the creation of new assessments, schools often collect student process and outcome data, which can be analyzed to identify areas of need and programmatic progress. It is important to consider not only how to collect and use data but also how to present data to relevant stakeholders to maintain and bolster buy-in and partnerships. School counseling interns are a valuable resource in assessment creation, data collection, and intentional data analysis.

TABLE OF KEY TERMS

Term	Definition
Quantitative data	Data that can be represented and analyzed numerically to derive means, medians, modes, correlations, and trends.
Qualitative data	Data that can be transcribed and analyzed for themes, including interviews and written feedback.
Pre/post assessment	An assessment given before and after an intervention to analyze the influence/effectiveness of an intervention after it is delivered.

REFLECTION EXERCISES

Reflection exercises are designed either to be done individually within the reading or to be used as group discussion questions within the classroom setting. A series of reflection questions will be presented at the end of every chapter.

1. What are your reactions to the concepts of data collection and analysis?
   a. What is your comfort level with engaging in these practices?
   b. What strengths do you bring to the table?
   c. In what areas are you least comfortable and why?
2. Consider quantitative and qualitative data analysis.
   a. Which are you most comfortable with and why?
   b. How do you see yourself using both as a future school counselor?
3. Consider collaboration in data management and analysis.
   a. Which district and community partners do you view yourself collaborating with regarding data collection and analysis?
   b. How comfortable are you presenting data results to these stakeholders and why?
4. Consider how you would utilize an intern to assist in data collection/analysis for a particular school counseling program.
   a. What roles would you assign them to within this process?
   b. How would these assignments positively influence the data analysis and program overall?

CASE STUDY

Twin Lakes Middle School is a public middle school in a rural location. Twin Lakes students attend the same small school (average of 40 students per grade level) from grades K–8. After grade 8, students transition to a large high school outside of the local community, which accepts students from approximately 10 different communities. A school counselor from the high school notes that Twin Lakes students seem to struggle with the high school transition, with their behavior and grades suffering as a result. This has impacted their willingness to engage in academics and to look forward to career development beyond. While the school counselor has reported this, it has simply come from her impressions of seeing and working with Twin Lakes students throughout her last few years as a school counselor. There is no data collected from students, from school counselors, from teachers, or from community members regarding this. The district does run a high school transition program in which students from Twin Lakes visit the high school, along with students from each of the other schools that feed into the high school. The day is set up as a series of tours of school facilities and services, along with ice-breaking activities to get students used to one another. Faculty believe the program is valuable and successful, but no data is collected or analyzed. Consider the following questions as the school counselor:

1. What type of data would you collect regarding the potential transition challenge, and from what sources? What data collection instruments would you use?
2. How would you present the results of this data analysis and to whom?
3. What type of data would you collect regarding the high school transition program and from whom?
4. What initial ideas do you have for changes to benefit the academic and career success of Twin Lakes students, as it relates to the high school transition process?

References

American School Counselor Association. (2019). *ASCA National Model: A framework for school counseling programs* (4th ed.). American School Counselor Association.

Creswell, J. W., & Creswell, J. D. (2017). *Research design: Qualitative, quantitative, and mixed methods approaches.* Sage.

EZAnalyze. (2021). *Excel-based tools for educators.* http://www.ezanalyze.com/index.htm

Stone, C., & Dahir, C. A. (2015). *The transformed school counselor* (3rd ed.). Cengage Learning.

Young, A., & Kaffenberger, C. (2018). *Making data work* (4th ed.) The American School Counseling Association.

INDEX

A

ableism, 2
Abrams, Stacey, 131–132
academic integration, 94–95, 162
accountability, 51
advanced advocacy, 179–180
African American cultural characteristics, criminalization of, 181
after-school peer mentor program, 64
American College Test (ACT), 160
American School Counselor Association (ASCA), 7–8
American School Counselor Association (ASCA), 16
  career development guidelines, 16–17
  National Model, 194
  recommended ratio of counselor per student, 179
  student standards, 99
anti-racist school counseling, 180–184
asset mapping, 51–52

B

Backpack program, 66–67
  delivery of services, 66–67
  intended outcomes, 67
  method of measuring effectiveness, 67
  resources/stakeholders/partnerships, 67

C

Career Cruising Spark, 93
career cut-outs, 104
career day, 100, 103–105
  presentations, 110–111
career development, 3, 87
  ASCA guidelines, 16–17
  barriers to, 19–20
  choice in, 5
  education and, 5
  evaluation of programs, 194–195
  historical perspective, 4–6
  partnering with local businesses, 18
  personal skills, 116–118
  school counselor and, 17–18
  sociocultural influences, 21
  stages, 29

statewide responses, 17
success and, 6
targeted career exploration, 18
Career Empowerment Program (CEP)
  career philosophy, 128
  career selection, 137–142
  Davids's experiences, 146–147
  discussion sheet, 148–149
  goals, 129
  Grant's experiences, 137
  imbuing career considerations and goals into eighth graders, 132–137
  Jay-Z's experiences, 142–143
  pedagogical philosophy, 128–129
  population and setting, 126
  pre- and post-test for students (student facing), 152–155
  presentation rubric, 149–151
  steps and process, 130–147
  student presentations, 143–147
  underrepresentation and its consequences, 126–128
  work period, 147
3–5 career interventions
  abilities exploration, 90–92
  academic integration, 94–95
  careers exploration, 92–94
  interests exploration, 88–90
  philosophy, 88
  social sorting, 88
6–8 career interventions
  interests exploration, 114–116
  philosophy, 114
  skills exploration, 116–118
9–12 career interventions
  academic integration, 162
  career exploration, 160–162
  interests exploration, 158–159
  philosophy, 158
  skills exploration, 159–160
career goals lesson plan
  data collection plan, 85–86
  learning objective(s)/competencies, 84
  materials, 84
  procedure, 85
career mentoring, 161
career vocabulary words, 106–107
classism, 2

classroom lessons, 10
class status, 5
college-educated professional roles, 93
community challenges in career development
  rural communities, barriers in, 45–46
  understanding of self, 45
  urban communities, barriers in, 46–47
community outreach, 48–54
  asset mapping and partnerships, 51–52
  data-driven advocacy, 51
  multitiered systems of support (MTSS), 53–54
  with community, 50–51
  with faculty, 49–50
  with students, 49
contextual influences, 37
counselor conceptualization, 9
COVID-19 pandemic, 32, 70
  shifts and stressors associated with, 184–185

D

data analysis
  ASCA National Model, 194
  for program maintenance and evaluation, 194–195
  interns and, 196
  presentation of data, 195–196
  stakeholder needs assessments, 191–193
data-driven advocacy, 51
Davids, Sharice, 146–147
"day in the life" journal entry, 111
discrimination, 4
dual enrollment program, 162

E

experience-based workshops, 117
explorations
  career, 78–79, 92–94, 160–162
  of abilities, 77–78, 90–92
  of interests, 74–76, 88–90, 114–116, 158–159
  of skills, 116–118, 159–160
EZAnalyze, 192